UNIONISTS

IN VIRGINIA

UNIONISTS
IN VIRGINIA

POLITICS, SECESSION AND
THEIR PLAN TO PREVENT CIVIL WAR

Lawrence M. Denton

THE
History
PRESS

Published by The History Press
Charleston, SC 29403
www.historypress.net

First published 2014

Manufactured in the United States

ISBN 978.1.62619.745.9

Library of Congress CIP data applied for.

For David M. Potter (1910–1971), Pulitzer Prize–winning historian of the South whose work changed the way students of the war view the secession crisis.

CONTENTS

PREFACE

During the thirty-plus years that I have been writing and lecturing about the secession crisis, two fundamental themes have emerged that make studying the antebellum era so complex for the modern researcher.

First is the primitive nature of the social and behavioral sciences during that period of time, which led to society being downright primitive as well. Medicine was in its very early stage of modernization; head or abdominal wounds were considered fatal because physicians simply did not know how to treat them. Pasteur was just publishing his research on the "germ theory," but it was not widely known and certainly not practiced. Psychology was in its infancy. Mary Todd Lincoln was put in an asylum for her bipolar disorder in May 1875, but nobody knew quite what to do with her other than isolation.[1] Sociology was in its infancy, too. It was thought that to educate a woman would do her physical harm. Slavery, yet another cruel beast of the era, was still practiced throughout the world. The social mores of the antebellum were downright crude.

A rather strict social "pecking order" was still in vogue. The vast majority of Americans, from both the North and South, were treated with near-contempt by the "upper crust." Punishment for crimes, some quite trivial, was often cruel and even inhumane (whipping was still practiced). Basic cleanliness and simple clothing necessities were often neglected. Folks usually bathed once a week, if that. Bruce Catton described the young recruits from what was then called the Northwest (today's Midwest) being handed underwear and, never seeing it before, laughing and placing it on their heads.[2] Malnutrition was widespread, and common diseases of today often proved fatal. Infant mortality, especially among poor whites and free blacks, was exceedingly high. Dirty water was everywhere; it was claimed that Lincoln's son, Willie, died from drinking polluted water in the White House. Mid-nineteenth-century America was, indeed, very primitive. For the twenty-first-century researcher, this crude nature of society must constantly be kept in mind; otherwise, very little makes much sense.

Second is the issue of the "slows," the phrase Lincoln used to describe General McClellan after the Battle of Antietam. News traveled slowly. In the big cities, most papers were printed weekly, as only a handful of daily papers existed. While scientific work was in play, no radio, no telephone and certainly no television existed. Mail moved so slowly that often it took weeks for letters and newspapers to reach folks in rural areas. While the telegraph, the revolutionary new means of communication, was available, it only reached cities and towns serviced by railroads (as the lines ran alongside railroad tracks). It was often unreliable and never secure. And railroads, the other revolutionary nineteenth-century invention, were considered rapid for running fifteen to twenty miles per hour. Most folks, in fact, walked or rode horses or wagons from place to place. Thus, the "slows" made it unbelievably difficult to control or influence rapidly changing events, much less keep track of them. Again, the modern researcher must keep the "slows" in mind when trying to understand the movement of events and the oftentimes haphazard way they transpired.

The primitive nature of antebellum society would produce scenes of a truly barbaric nature, as events in the upcoming war would so aptly demonstrate. Young boys would stand a few yards apart and shoot at one another from point-blank range. The "slows" would produce scenes from a tragic-comic opera. The right hand so often did not know what the left hand was doing that events often controlled the leaders, as Lincoln so poignantly observed late in the war. These two fundamental themes of antebellum America added an enormous complexity to an already complex setting.

With regard to the enormous complexity of the secession crisis, this work has not attempted to cite a plethora of primary sources—sources that have been, for the most part, researched and cited hundreds of times. Rather than cite mostly primary sources, the focus here is to present the best of the secondary sources—works from authors who have spent years thinking about the events in an effort to inform the reader of the points of view of leading authorities. Primary sources are presented when they are particularly germane to a given discussion or when they address a new interpretation of an event. To categorize the Unionists of Virginia and the dilemma they dealt with is exceedingly difficult; it is hoped the reader will appreciate a somewhat different approach.

ACKNOWLEDGEMENTS

When researching and writing any work of this sort, many people are involved. They need to be acknowledged.

During the research phase, librarians from Washington College, West Virginia University, the University of Virginia and the Library of Virginia were very helpful. L. Paige Newman at the Virginia Historical Society devoted hours researching items of interest. Scott Nesbit at the University of Richmond guided me through several pertinent websites. Librarians deserving special mention are: Kevin Fredette, West Virginia University Library, who spent time with me in the early research phase; Kelly Sizemore and Dale Neighbors at the Library of Virginia offered sound guidance; Dana Puga at the Library of Virginia was especially helpful during my search for photographs in the collection; Gary Treadway at the University of Virginia offered research advice; and Ruth Shoge, director of the Miller Library at Washington College, was helpful throughout the project. Ruth introduced me to Jennifer Potts, a junior history major at Washington College, who became my indispensable research assistant for nearly four years. Jen saved me countless hours during the research phase, and I remain deeply indebted to her.

During the writing phase, first-draft reviewers included writers and Civil War buffs who endured the "ugliness" of a first draft. Paul D. Denton, Captain William Dial (USN-Ret), Robert A. Lonergan and William S. Myers deserve special credit. They offered many helpful comments and suggestions, most of which were included in the second draft. The second draft was reviewed by three historians with backgrounds in the subject matter: Daniel W. Crofts, the College of New Jersey; Nelson D. Lankford, the Virginia Historical Society; and Brent Tarter, Library of Virginia. I am, indeed, grateful for their expertise. Brent spent many hours with me and offered many comments that clarified my views on Virginia Unionism. Nelson offered sage advice that found its way into the pages. Dan counseled me over many years regarding the nuances of Southern Unionism. Most of their suggestions were included in the third draft.

The third draft was reviewed by Paul Denton and Bob Lonergan, both of whom noted improvement and again offered comments of substance. Henry Stansbury offered a fresh perspective during several interesting conversations and added much to the final product. To all of these gentlemen, I owe a deep sense of gratitude. They were a constant source of inspiration. However, I take full responsibility for all that is presented here, including the errors that inevitably creep into every manuscript.

Special mention must be made regarding two historians who have inspired me for decades. This work is dedicated to David M. Potter, whose landmark book, *Lincoln and His Party in the Secession Crisis*, challenged me to explore the secession crisis from a different perspective. Daniel W. Crofts published *Reluctant Confederates* in 1989, and it has been my constant guide for the past twenty-five years. Yet another historian who deserves special mention is John R. Hildebrand, author of *The Life and Times of John Brown Baldwin*. John lent me hundreds of pages from his research notes that proved enormously helpful.

I want to acknowledge the many friends and family members who encouraged me over the course of several years. Sometimes just a "how's the book going?" would make my day, and often the individuals inquiring would not realize the impact their subtle remark would have on my well-being. Several organizations deserve mention as well. The Talbot Investors Group; the Free & Eazy Band (in which I play mandolin); the Oxford Men's Breakfast, led by Ray Stevens; and the Talbot Historical Society all provided solace, and many members offered support as well. Mark D. Garrett helped me through some computer glitches, Paul Denton provided some research regarding the railroads of interest to this work, Tom Reynolds provided a valuable letter from his family's archive and Richard and Laura Price assisted with photographs and copying. A special thanks is due Dick and Kate Carraher for giving me access to Windrush Farm—it has been the perfect place to write. Finally, my wife, Susan, deserves credit for her quiet tolerance. All of these fine folks were truly relieved when I announced, "It is done."

LAWRENCE M. DENTON
Oxford, Maryland
Spring 2014

CHAPTER 1

WAIT FOR VIRGINIA

Wait for Virginia. See what she does.
—*William Wilkens Glenn, editor,* Baltimore Daily Exchange, *April 1861*

Virginia was the most populous and wealthiest state in the South during the antebellum years. Geographically, it bordered two lower Northern states, Pennsylvania and Ohio, and two Southern border states, Maryland and Kentucky. From its shore across the Potomac, one could see the White House. But Virginia was much more than statistics and geographic happenstance. The state had a special aura about it—it was the cradle of the nation's first settlements, the birthplace of the "father of the country" and the incubator of the American form of republican government. Washington, Jefferson, Madison and Monroe added a luster that was unmatched by any other state. Virginia truly occupied a unique position at this crucial moment in the nation's history.

In light of continuing scholarship regarding the secession crisis, is it fair to ask again: Could Virginians, with their rising Unionism, and with their rising anti–Slave Power sentiment, have led the nation from the brink of civil war during the winter and spring of 1861?[3] William Henry Seward, "Mr. Republican" and secretary of state-designate during the Secession Winter, clearly saw the possibility and worked tirelessly to encourage the Unionists of Virginia to defeat the secessionists of the state. Abraham Lincoln, because of his lack of experience and unfamiliarity with the key players at the national level, was more reluctant than Seward to reach out to the Unionists. When

Richmond, Virginia, as seen from the south bank of the James River. Richmond was the most magnificent city in the South in 1861. *Courtesy of the Library of Virginia.*

he arrived in Washington, exhausted from his arduous trip from Springfield, he was badgered by men from all sides of the political spectrum, and he had virtually no close friends to lean on for advice. In the chapters that follow, the efforts of Virginia Unionists to defeat secession will be reviewed—and how close they came to being true heroes by preventing Virginia from seceding will be documented.

First, Unionism and anti–Slave Power (and the antislavery element within this sentiment) must be defined for Virginia in particular and for the Upper South in general.

Simply, Unionism can be described as those who favored staying in the Union and thereby opposed secession during the Secession Winter of 1860–61. Several forms of Unionism existed, ranging from unconditional Unionism, such as espoused by Tennessee governor William B. Campbell ("Our only safety is in the Union and we must stand by it to the end") and several types of conditional Unionism, such as the anticoercionists (those opposed to the Federal government using armed force to coerce a state—or states—to remain in the Union) to the ultimatumists (those who would stay in the Union until all compromise efforts had been exhausted) and various combinations of the above.[4] Although conditional Unionism has produced a somewhat cynical response from many modern historians, secession crisis expert Daniel Crofts observed, "By far the larger number of conditional Unionists preferred that the states of the Upper South remain in the Union and try to rebuild it."[5] Indeed, just after Lincoln's election, the vast majority of Southerners (Lower South, Upper South, Border South) did not favor secession.

Perhaps the most compelling reason espoused by Virginians for staying in the Union was one of economic interests. The Border South and the Upper South were clearly becoming more tied to the Lower North than the Lower South, with the rapid growth of the railroad system in the region spurring the ties. Manufacturing was expanding, mining was expanding (especially in the western part of Virginia) and new crops (wheat and vegetables) were being grown in worn-out tobacco fields. Change was moving Virginia away from its traditional slave-based economy driven by a nonagricultural expansion. By the 1850s, "fewer than half the adult white males listed themselves as farmers," and "nearly one-third of all Virginians lived in counties that included a significant town or city, exposed to urban markets and ideas."[6] As these new nonagricultural men became the nucleus of rising Unionism in the state, they increasingly sought to challenge the political power of the planter class. Their livelihoods were not tied to slavery, and they saw no advantage to secession. During the Secession Winter, "the two leading Unionists in the Virginia State Convention [most commonly referred to as the Secession Convention], John B. Baldwin and George W. Summers, warned repeatedly that Virginia's commercial and industrial interests were 'bound up with the free states of the border.'"[7] Virginia was diversifying economically, and that diversification was connecting the state to the North, rather than the Deep South, where the black belts were most numerous and the Slave Power strongest.

The "Slave Power," the term used to describe the aristocratic planter class ("slavocracy" was used also), had from the earliest days of Virginia controlled the political apparatus of the state and, for the most part, governed as they pleased. Consequently, they shaped laws and policies for their own benefit. This caused a class consciousness to develop and, again from the earliest days of the Commonwealth, resulted in huge resentment from the vast majority of white men who were not included in the planter class and who felt they were unfairly taxed and not adequately represented in local or state government. Historian Brent Tarter describes it as "the persistence of undemocratic politics in Virginia."[8] By the late 1850s, anti–Slave Power sentiment was increasing in virtually every section of Virginia. In the western part of the state, the most rapidly growing area, this resentment had reached an almost uncontrollable level as non-slaveholders, the vast majority in the region, felt the Slave Power had rigged the system. In the view of these westerners, this was undemocratic government at its worst.

Within the anti–Slave Power movement were "green shoots" of antislavery sentiment and racial tolerance. Antislavery is more difficult to define, for not only did interest in the issue wax and wane during the decades prior to 1861, but the very nature of the institution seemed to perplex Virginians (and Americans in general) in a wide variety of ways. A brief digression is necessary to discuss the hateful institution of slavery.

At its base, slavery posed a deep-seated philosophical enigma that most in the nation, North and South, struggled with from the Revolutionary War era right up to the outbreak of the Civil War. "The institution of slavery conflicted uncomfortably with the two most cherished texts in antebellum America, the Bible and the Declaration of Independence."[9] As a result, antislavery sentiment surfaced periodically within different groups. There were those who opposed slavery for religious reasons (the Quakers and some Methodists and Baptists), those who opposed slavery on general moral grounds, those who opposed slavery for economic or societal reasons and a large group who opposed the Slave Power per se. After the legislature of 1832 sought (and failed) to eliminate slavery, many Virginians "continued for some years to believe that slavery was an evil," and they sought to emancipate slaves and remove them from the state by supporting colonization (various efforts to colonize ex-slaves outside of the country).[10]

The Quakers led one movement to eliminate slavery because they felt God opposed it. Although Quakers provided a few leaders to the antislavery movement, they were a small sect and usually considered out of the mainstream of local culture because of their secret and unusual behavior. A more central group, the Evangelicals, were temperance people by and large and included folks who regarded fighting, drunkenness and the harsh attributes of white masculinity of the era (dueling, for instance) as unacceptable behavior. This group was haunted by the immorality of slavery—because of the Bible and because it simply did not fit "their" view of Christianity. And this group included a broad cross section of the population—whites and blacks, young and old, men and women, rich and poor. The Evangelicals held revivals in ever-growing numbers during the 1840s and 1850s, some lasting for days at a time. One such meeting at Union in Southampton County, Virginia, during the fall of 1858 "started with little excitement" but "continued for nine days amid a growing outpouring of religious fervor." In the end, some "forty whites and more than a dozen blacks had experienced conversion."[11]

What is especially noteworthy is that these Evangelicals welcomed free blacks and even some slaves into their revivals and, in some cases, even into their congregations. And by the 1850s, Evangelicalism had become so central to Southern culture that the movement was no longer just for "plain folks" but had real appeal to a wide range of Southerners.[12] It had become a part of the mainstream culture, and thus Evangelicals had an enormous impact on the rigid, hierarchical Southern way of life promoted by the paternalistic planters. Here was a way for men to meet women, for poorer and Middle Americans to meet wealthy folk and, uncharacteristically for Virginia and the South in general, for whites and blacks to intermingle in a nonthreatening environment. Here, then, was a growing mainstream nucleus for antislavery thought, a clear "green shoot."

Another group opposed to slavery were those who did so for economic reasons. This large group of "Middle Americans" sought to carve out a living—indeed, to create their own economic independence—by challenging the economic system established by the aristocratic, wealthy planters that too often benefited only the planters. They were the smallholders (those who owned land and perhaps a slave or two, shopkeepers, factory workers, artisans and the rising professional class) who would become the nucleus of the Whig Party that emerged in the mid-1830s. Of significance, most of this group did not own slaves, and many would harbor—sometimes openly, sometimes quietly—antislavery views. In the North, this same class of workingmen vehemently opposed the immigration of freed slaves to their towns and cities, as they did not want competition for their jobs.

The most famous of the "beraters" of slavery for economic reasons in Virginia was Henry Ruffner, a slaveholder, Presbyterian minister and president of Washington College (later Washington and Lee) in Lexington. He published an *Address to the People of West Virginia*, in which he argued that Virginia was falling behind the free states of the North because slavery was less productive than free labor. He cited statistics from Northern states and even views of supportive large slave owners in Virginia as he urged the western part of Virginia to begin gradual emancipation. He denounced the abolitionists as those "smitten with a kind of moral insanity" and their "malignant rage against slaveholders" as most damaging to the antislavery movement in the state. Local newspapers largely supported his views, and some in the eastern part of the state even offered encouragement.[13]

Antislavery sentiment was not only complex but also very difficult to document conclusively.

Returning to the discussion of the Slave Power, the Southern aristocrat, the owners of the large plantations practiced a never-ending paternalistic behavior that constantly grated on poorer whites, free blacks and, of course, even more so on the lowly slave. A half century ago, Avery Craven, an award-winning Civil War historian, observed, "In the vast growth and expansion of the day, the wealth and power of the few grew disproportionately to that of the many. Liberty was putting an end to equality."[14] This growing economic inequality was particularly true in Virginia. In recent scholarship, Tarter exhaustively traces "the undemocratic political institutions and practices that persisted from the colonial period through the age of Jacksonian Democracy" in the state.[15]

In fact, many aristocratic planters did not favor democracy. In Virginia, they kept white men who did not own property from having the right to vote until 1851. These planters tried to control the electoral process as well as every other facet of social life in the state. During the 1830s and until the mid-1840s, the Slave Power sought to silence debate about their control of Southern society by instituting gag rules. It was at this time that "Northerners invented two words to describe slaveholders' offensive-minded defense: Slave Power."[16] The gag rules were eventually dismissed but resulted in large numbers of non-slaveholding whites in the South (and especially in Virginia) to oppose the Slave Power more and more vehemently. About this time, the Slave Power began to focus their attention on controlling the Democratic Party, which still contained large numbers of Jacksonian Democrats, those Middle Americans who so embraced Andrew Jackson's defense of the common man—a group dominated by non-slaveholders.

This resentment or estrangement resulted in these Middle Americans (and also some enlightened men from the planter class) to join a new political party to pursue their rightful place in the Virginia state government. They believed fervently in the Declaration of Independence and in the Bible and believed it was time to oppose the planters. Fewer than 25 percent of Virginians owned slaves, and fewer than 10 percent were of the planter class, defined as those owning twenty-five or more slaves. During the 1830s, the newly formed Whig Party arose to oppose the Slave Power. When the Whig Party collapsed in the mid-1850s, its members became known as "The Opposition." In her compelling work *Mothers of Invention*, Drew Faust captured the essence of the scene: "Put simply, upper-class southerners had a greater investment than their poorer countrywomen and -men in the system [slavery] that had given them their superior status." Even after the defeat of the Confederacy, "elite white women of the South held fast to the traditional hierarchical social and racial order that defined their importance."[17] Class consciousness became a rising concern among the Southern elite—could they count on non-slaveholders to defend their system of slavery in time of conflict?

As the anti–Slave Power movement gained momentum during the antebellum years, did the non-slaveholders, in fact, develop an element of antislavery sentiment?

By the early 1830s, a number of factors impacted antislavery sentiment in Virginia. First and foremost was the August 1831 Nat Turner Rebellion in Southampton County. Turner, a slave with fanatical antislavery beliefs, led a slave revolt that resulted in the "massacre of nearly sixty whites, most of whom were women and children."[18] That, in turn, led to Turner and his band being captured and brutally dealt with. The fear of more slave revolts so captivated white Virginians that it became the central public concern of that time.

Petitions from virtually every part of the state were sent to the legislature calling for action of one kind or another, usually ending slavery over time and ridding the state of blacks through some type of colonization. One petition from the Valley region is quite notable: "215 'females of the county of Augusta'…called for [the] 'extinction of slavery.'" It was "remarkable because it was brought by women, who usually stood outside the political process" and could not vote.[19] Suddenly, the time had come to debate the issue of slavery in the state of Virginia.

Consequently, a great debate did occur in the 1831–32 session of the Virginia legislature regarding the future of slavery in the Commonwealth. Then-governor John Floyd seemed intent on setting Virginia on the path toward emancipation. Young men in the legislature took the lead—three of

William Ballard Preston opposed the Slave Power throughout his long political life. He would lead the final delegation of Virginians to see Lincoln in April 1861. *Courtesy of the Virginia Historical Society.*

the most notable were James M'Dowell, William Ballard Preston and Thomas Jefferson Randolph (grandson of the revered president). M'Dowell would deliver a memorable speech declaring it was time to emancipate slaves, Randolph would propose putting emancipation with deportation in front of the voters and Preston would become famous for submitting his motion to declare it expedient to legislate against slavery. After weeks of almost continuous debate, a vote was finally taken on January 25, 1832, where the Preston motion was defeated seventy-three to fifty-eight. "The vote clearly revealed a strong sectional split." All delegates from western Virginia and most from the Valley region (with fewer slaves) supported it, while most in eastern Virginia (with more slaves) opposed.[20]

Despite the defeat, opponents of slavery persisted. Led, for the most part, by Whigs or non-slaveholding Democrats from the western part of the state, "majorities voted to declare slavery an evil and to examine ways by which the state might get rid of it." Virginians were ready to see the institution put on the road to extinction.[21] And many in Virginia were well aware of the forced migration of Native Americans, the so-called Trail of Tears, where the central government had spent millions to move the Cherokees from North Carolina to Oklahoma. Could blacks be removed from the state, they asked? "Lincoln, advocating the departure of 4 million blacks in a hundred years, sounded reasonable in an age that witnessed the arrival of 2 million Irishmen in thirty years." Henry Clay had advocated the spending of several million federal dollars annually for African colonization, and Thomas Jefferson had urged federal land revenues be used to finance black departure, so precedents were certainly set.[22]

———

Tragically for those seeking to end slavery peacefully by removing blacks, at this very moment of heightened antislavery sentiment in Virginia, radical abolitionist agitator William Lloyd Garrison appeared and launched his newspaper, *The Liberator*. A year or so later, the American Anti-Slavery Society was formed. Abolitionists now turned their provocative and ugly language on all slaveholders by denouncing them as sinners and slavery as the ultimate evil. Garrison attacked black deportation, calling it as outrageous as black slavery itself. "The black-removal idea lay forever discredited among northern antislavery extremists after Garrison's savage assault."[23] These attacks, although the product of a tiny minority of Northerners (Freehling estimated less than 2 percent of the Northern voting population were abolitionists at the height of their appeal[24]), devastated the antislavery element in Virginia.

Many thoughtful, politically moderate Northerners expressed outrage at the abolitionist assault, too. One typical example is a letter written to U.S. senator William C. Rives (Virginia) by Nathan Appleton, a leading Bostonian. Appleton wrote, "The first aggression was made by the North, or rather by a few individuals residing in the North…under the lead of William Lloyd Garrison and Wendell Phillips…At home this movement excited little attention: the few individuals comprised in it were considered fanatical monomaniacs—rather the objects of pity, than any other feeling."[25] However, many Southerners felt the abolitionist campaign encouraged racial warfare by urging slaves to revolt, and that put Southern antislavery moderates on the defensive. "Yankees desecrated southern virtue," which caused a "welling up of anti-Yankee hatred" that probably "rallied more southern folk" to the slave owners.[26] As a result, an anti-abolitionist backlash developed that was most pronounced among the antislavery men of Virginia, for "they wanted respect, not abuse."[27]

Leading antislavery Virginians turned against the abolitionists for what they considered to be outlandish, duplicitous propaganda. Southerners were now held to a higher standard, they argued, than Northerners on the black question, for most Northern states were truly hostile to black immigration, and some—such as Illinois, the Land of Lincoln—even forbade it. In southeastern Virginia, "Alexander W. Jones, the erstwhile antislavery spokesman…condemned the abolitionists who sent pamphlets to Norfolk as an 'atrocious gang of lawless fanatics' who were attempting 'to desolate the land with all the horrors of a servile war.'"[28] The leading

Whig newspaper in the state capital, the *Richmond Whig*, expressed shock and dismay at the collapse of the emancipation effort caused largely by the Garrisonian attacks. In the summer of 1835, the paper editorialized, "The friends of prospective emancipation had the weight of numbers, the youth of the country, and as they thought, all the demands of patriotism on their side. Where is that party now? Annihilated...by the interference of Garrison and Co."[29] The early abolitionist attack strengthened the proslavery element and weakened the antislavery element—certainly not what the abolitionists had in mind.

By the 1840s, though, antislavery sentiment was on the rise again, driven by the economic collapse caused by the Panic of 1837. Virginia, and the nation, had fallen on hard times. The collapse in prices for agricultural products across the board renewed calls that slavery was a real part of the problem because it depressed economic growth. "Virginians were well aware that their beloved commonwealth, once the wealthiest and most populous state in the Union, was rapidly falling behind such Northern Free States as New York in both power and prestige." Many Virginians pointed to slavery as the cause of the state's "economic stagnation."[30] Although the continued activities of the Garrisonians plagued the antislavery men in Virginia throughout the decade, "antislavery thinking nevertheless abounded."[31] Led by Virginia Whigs who "showed themselves more devoted to commerce and to the Union than to the extension of slavery," Virginia's aristocrats began to suspect Whig loyalty to the institution.[32] Typical is this statement by Rockingham County's Lunsford Lewis regarding his Whig father, Samuel Hance Lewis: "While he [his father] owned slaves, he, like many Virginians, considered the institution an evil, and he rejoiced when it ceased to exist."[33] An expanding economy—and expanding opportunities for Middle Americans to achieve economic independence—now became a central theme of the rising Whig Party.

John Zaborney and other modern historians have countered Hickin's decades-old work. In his *Slaves for Hire*, Zaborney, while acknowledging that hiring out slaves was a complex story, argues that "slave hiring...strengthened Virginia slavery because many Virginia slave owners with surplus slaves hired out those slaves within Virginia" and made lots of money with the practice. By keeping their excess slaves in Virginia, it strengthened the institution by involving more Virginians with supervising slaves—"it entailed the transfer of control from owners to countless white Virginians," and this added exposure, he claims, caused more non-slaveholding whites to understand the advantages of slavery.[34]

What took center stage, however, was not the "abstract" denouncing of slavery but the very real problem of just how to accomplish ending it. Most felt the way to accomplish this was to "whiten the republic." Removing blacks had widespread appeal both in the North and in the South. Northerners, for the most part, did not want to deal with an influx of freed slaves. Southerners, on the other hand, wanted to remove blacks so that they (whites) would be in the majority in each and every district of the South. For example, in the Tidewater region of Virginia, where blacks held a majority in many areas, no emancipation program could possibly move forward without a substantial reduction in the black population, and this was true virtually anywhere in the South where blacks outnumbered whites. Freehling summarized, "The persistent admirers of Jefferson's black removal plan included the Border South's favorite statesmen, Henry Clay; the Republicans' favorite politician, Abraham Lincoln; and the North's favorite novelist, Harriet Beecher Stowe."[35] The final word on antislavery during the 1840s belongs to Dr. Robert Lewis Dabney, the noted Presbyterian minister of Richmond and proslavery advocate: "I do believe that if these mad fanatics [the abolitionists] had let us alone in twenty years we should have made Va a free State."[36]

The 1850s found Virginia experiencing an economic boom with new industries, expanded manufacturing and mining—and record-high prices for slaves. These record-high prices pushed the domestic slave trade into high gear as slave owners now saw their excess slaves turn into "a major source of capital that could be mortgaged to produce even more wealth."[37] This caused yet another change in antislavery sentiment to emerge as many Virginians now saw slavery as a way to compete in the new

Robert Lewis Dabney, proslavery Presbyterian minister and professor at Union Theological Seminary, thought slavery could be eliminated peacefully in Virginia. For a time, he was Stonewall Jackson's chief of staff. *Courtesy of the Library of Virginia.*

economy—the hiring out of slaves to work in factories and the selling of slaves to the Deep South to raise capital. Many Virginians, led by young men of the upper class, became advocates of the proslavery argument and rejected the appeals of the more moderate antislavery men. At this time, the Democratic Party in the South began to turn away from moderation, from its Jacksonian roots, and began to focus on protecting the rights of the large slaveholders—the Slave Power. And protection of the Slave Power advanced steadily as the Whig Party collapsed in mid-decade.

As this rise in proslavery sentiment occurred, a number of social developments lent support, albeit indirectly, to the antislavery cause. Western Virginia, as noted, became the fastest-growing section of the state as the immigration of white settlers, whose interest in slavery was nil, increased the numbers of Virginians with potential antislavery sentiment. John C. Underwood spent fifteen years of his life (1846–61) trying "peaceful persuasion" by attempting to introduce new types of land use that would use free labor. He was most known for the introduction of dairy farming with "many Fauquier County farmers…going into the business of cheese-making and…'very successful—making three and four pounds a day from each cow.'"[38] Eli Thayer, a congressman from Massachusetts, was preparing to establish a colony of Northerners in western Virginia "to bring industry into the border states, to introduce antislavery forces into the states colonized, and to make a profit."[39] Several Virginia cities seeking Northern capital were reaching out to non-Southerners. The Fredericksburg City Council instructed its representative trying to find a Northern buyer for its waterpower company to tell his "northern friends the assurance of our fraternal feelings and cordial good will…say we should hail their advent into our midst with pleasure."[40] Movement on the gender front was occurring as well. Women were beginning to experience some newfound energy as a result of Virginia's diversification. Crofts noted compellingly, "White women in antebellum Virginia, even if in many ways constrained, were hardly mere putty in the hands of their husbands." Virginia women were becoming "more independent-minded, self-conscious, assertive, and even 'protofeminist'" than women in the Lower South.[41] This was driven by an increase in urbanization, the diversification of the state's economy and more contact with Northerners.

While it is unwise to underestimate the complexity of assessing the rise or fall of antislavery sentiment in Virginia during the antebellum years, it is fair to conclude that waves of new developments were at work throughout the state. New economic developments with new manufacturing and mining techniques, the rapid expansion of railroads with their unbelievable impact on the rise of small towns, diminishing growth of the plantation economy, the increase in the population of non-slaveholders, the growth in economic ties with the Lower North rather than the Lower South and even the beginning of change for the roles of women all had an impact on support for slavery. As these economic and social developments were impacting every region of the state, they portended the vanguard of modern society—a society that could not tolerate slavery.

A final factor that adds still additional complexity to the antislavery discussion is the political meaning of slavery to mid-nineteenth-century Americans. Black slavery had one meaning; white slavery had yet another. White slavery dealt with the domination of the common man by the power of a few. Ever sensitive to the European model where kings and queens and aristocrats trampled the rights of the common man, Americans of the antebellum era were constantly concerned about the consolidation of power in the hands of a privileged few. Some have argued that it was not black slavery per se but the concentration of political power in the hands of a minority of Southern aristocrats—the Slave Power—that drove so many Northerners to support the newly established Republican Party during the late 1850s. Michael Holt concluded, "Their [moderate Republicans] goal had been to save the Republic from a Southern conspiracy [the Slave Power] and to protect themselves from enslavement, not to attack or end black slavery."[42] Defining and tracking the rise and fall of antislavery sentiment in Virginia is, indeed, a challenging matter.

As the non-slaveholders continued to confront the Slave Power in the decade just prior to the outbreak of war, the central happening in the state was the Virginia Constitutional Convention of 1850–51—and it produced the first major setback for the Slave Power in the history of the state. Since the founding of the Republic in 1776, Virginia had been controlled by a slaveholding oligarchy of privileged families.[43] By 1850, this undemocratic structure was under extreme attack by liberals, moderates and conservatives—essentially all those who were excluded from the process. The people called for an election to determine if a state convention should be called—and it won by a landslide, 46,327 to 20,668, or 69 percent for versus 31 percent opposed to a convention.[44] During the summer of 1850, discussion about the election of delegates and debate on the issues coming before the convention took center stage throughout the state—the time for democratic reform had come as the aristocrats were beginning to lose their grip.

Key political issues coming before the convention included universal white manhood suffrage, more equal representation in the legislature between eastern and western portions of the state, more democratically elected state office holders (rather than legislatively appointed), more popular control of local government and, somewhat surprisingly for this era, a call for state-supported education—all opposed by the Slave Power. Underlying the political issues were economic and societal factors. The middle and western parts of the state were dominated by smallholders and non-slaveholding families, while the eastern part of the state was dominated by large slaveholders and the subsequent plantation economy, although other economic interests were on the rise in the east as well. The social factor most dominant was that the gentlemen of the slavocracy considered labor as degrading and demeaning (they promoted a life of gentility achieved through the use of slaves) while the small farmers felt working the land to be worthy and noble. "The choice between free and slave labor was one between 'the hardy, independent tenantry of our country' and 'those who have no other rule than to work as little and waste as much as they can,' an epithet that could apply as easily to slave owners as to their chattels."[45] In addition, many Virginians convincingly argued that "the labor of a free white man, in the temperate latitude of Virginia, is more productive than that of a slave—yielding a larger aggregate for public and private wealth."[46]

Underlying the slavocracy's defensive stance and their subsequent all-out push to retain control of the state government was their real fear that fellow Virginians, led by non-slaveholders, would eventually call for an end to the institution of slavery. "The east feared excessive taxation more than abolition per se, although fears of both were expressed."[47] For many aristocrats, "places like Maryland and parts of Virginia looked increasingly like Pennsylvania and Ohio, and less like Mississippi or Louisiana." The implications of this "whitening" of the state were profound for the future support of slavery.[48]

The agitation of the non-slaveholders found its way into two central issues: taxation of slave property and representation in the legislature. White Virginians, not of the planter class, saw that their time had finally come. "Virginia sustained a distorted tax system that favored slaveholders," and the majority of Virginians—not just western Virginians—demanded that it be changed. The electoral system, based on *viva voce* voting (casting a vote by stating your preference to an election judge) "favored the slaveholding elite" as their representatives could, and did, unduly influence how men voted. What had become increasingly clear was that Virginia had "never ensured the full sharing of political power among all adult, white, male citizens." In an age of increasing equalitarianism, Virginia had never embraced equal representation in the legislature. "In the final analysis, Virginia had not adopted to the main currents of American democracy to the degree that other states had."[49]

All of these attacks on the slavocracy and their weakening position among Middle Virginians made the convention of 1850–51 a watershed event for the state. And the convention, indeed, lived up to its hype by producing a new constitution that instituted truly dramatic change. It was a giant step forward for democracy, for the yeoman farmer, for the Middle Virginians as it changed the way things were done. A more equitable basis of representation in the general assembly was established; all white men were given the right to vote; the governor henceforth would be elected, not appointed by the legislature; the power of the legislature was curtailed; the judiciary of the state was reorganized and strengthened; and local government was structured so that it was responsible to the people it governed. All in all, it was a change of true substance that had lasting implications for the white people of the state.[50] It broke the hold the aristocrats—the Slave Power—had had on the state since its founding.

The new constitution represented a setback for the slavocracy and the old guard of Virginia. By granting more power to the western part of the state, it put in place the structure that had the potential to end slavery over time. Slaves were scarce in the western part of the state to begin with, and this rising resentment of the plantation elites caused "eastern slaveholders [to feel] certain the protection of slavery would not be a matter of prime concern for the west."[51] It should be noted, however, that the slaveholders were not totally defeated. As Freehling noted so cleverly, while the slaveholders "gave western Virginians their treasured one-man, one-vote legislative apportionment," they "traded one non-slaveholder resentment for another." The slaveholders imposed "no tax" on slaves under twelve years of age and no tax over $300 on any slave. "With other property assessed at its actual value and with slave prices skyrocketing in the 1850s, yeomen insisted that an iniquitous tax ceiling filled slaveholders' wallets with non-slaveholders' dollars."[52] The tensions were, of course, over money, power and paternalism, as "the color-blind argument that slaveholders must rule non-slaveholders outraged the southern (and northern) non-slaveholding majority."[53] The demand for real democracy in this age of reform became the clarion call of the non-slaveholders. Craven began this line of argument decades ago by concluding, "Gradually the effort to free the Negro slaves on Southern plantations brought to a focus most of the sentiments engendered by all injustice and set the reformer at the task of bringing low the perfect aristocrat who held these slaves in bondage."[54]

The new constitution clearly bounded the power of Virginia's elites and gave more control of state government to non-slaveholders. White men who did not own land (and slaves) were enfranchised and permitted to vote on the new constitution, and as a result, it "won overwhelming approval by a popular vote of 75,748 to 11,063." While the aristocrats still had considerable power, "the political culture of Virginia's colonial and Revolutionary past had changed…democratic government by white men in Virginia finally began in 1851, seventy-five years after George Mason and Thomas Jefferson had declared that all men were created equal."[55] Non-slaveholders were beginning to have a real voice in the politics of Virginia. Of course, neither the Whig nor Democratic Party "could claim to be the exclusive agent of change." But the Whigs gradually became identified with the political moderates, democratic reform, practical liberalism driven by the new economy of the expanding urban and commercial centers and, to some extent, temperance. At the convention, "the Whigs included a sizable moderate element and a clear majority in favor of reapportionment and white manhood suffrage."[56] The Whigs increasingly had become the party of reform and more progressive thought, while the Democrats were more the party protecting the status quo and upholding the past—and championing the cause of the Slave Power. These trends will be documented in the following chapters.

A final incident regarding anti–Slave Power sentiment in Virginia needs to be addressed, and that is the John Brown raid of October 16–17, 1859. At this moment in time, most Virginians who opposed the slavocracy in one way or another were ready to move the political process forward. Many "Whigs talked of uniting with the conservative Republicans as a means of defeating the 'corrupt' party which was then in control of the Federal Government [Buchanan and his unsavory Democrats]," and this movement seemed to be gaining momentum.[57] Hopes were quite high that the sectional crisis could be resolved peacefully if conservative Northerners would unite with the Southern opposition. These two groups, representing the great political "center" in the country, were in a decided majority across the nation during the fall of 1859.

But on the night of October 16, Brown led his "Army of Liberation" across the Potomac and captured the B&O Railroad bridge over the river. He then occupied the Federal arsenal located in the town of Harpers Ferry. At 1:30 a.m. on the seventeenth, Brown stopped the eastbound train of the B&O. "Conductor A.J. Phelps and his crew dismounted and approached the strangers along with Heyward Shepard, a baggage porter at the station. Shots rang out in the darkness with unintended consequences. Heyward Shepard, a free black man employed by the Baltimore and Ohio Railroad, was shot through the body and died a few hours later."[58] Brown next sent out parties of "liberators" to the surrounding countryside to free slaves and to capture their masters. However, Brown was quickly challenged by locals, including some hastily organized militia, and took shelter in the engine room of the arsenal, where he was surrounded. Brown and all of his followers were captured the next day by U.S. Marines led by Colonel Robert E. Lee of the U.S. Army. During the scuffle, several marines and civilians were killed or wounded along with several of Brown's band. Brown was tried by a local jury and sentenced to hang a month later.

While a day or two of extreme excitement followed, the affair seemed to have died down in a week or so as Virginians "looked apparently upon the episode as that of an imbecile and felt that after his punishment the whole affair should be dropped."[59] And it would have been dropped, except that before Brown's hanging, several Northern newspapers and several Northern political leaders called for him to be pardoned—and, of course, all of the abolitionists rallied to Brown's defense, calling him a martyr. But Brown was hanged, and the Northern press (at least some of it) condemned Virginia for hanging him. Virginians (almost all of them) and Southerners (almost all of them) reacted with total outrage at what they considered general Northern support for a fanatic murderer. Virtually all Southerners blamed radical abolitionists for inciting the raid. Conservative Northerners, who condemned Brown's raid, could not assuage Southern feelings quite enough. "As a result of Northern sympathy, or supposed sympathy, for Brown's crime, all factions in Virginia were united in their resentment."[60] Brown's raid proved a significant blow to anti–Slave Power and antislavery sentiment in Virginia.

While anti–Slave Power and pro-democracy sentiment continued to rise during the antebellum years in Virginia, the Whig Party rose, collapsed and then morphed into an Opposition Party. The Opposition would then become the Union Party during the Secession Winter. Could this Union Party of political moderates, who represented the majority of Virginians, have prevented secession?

The Opposition cannot be easily categorized, nor can its members be easily pigeonholed. As with all political parties, it was a hodgepodge of folks with many, many different points of view. But it had one essential characteristic from beginning to end: it was a coalition of folks who opposed the Democratic Party—first, the Jacksonian Democrats, and lastly, the Slave Power–controlled Southern Rights Democratic Party. The Opposition became the party of "modernization." It sought to modernize the state by diversifying its economic base; by building canals, roads and railroads; by encouraging new enterprises; and by chartering banks to make capital more readily available. It tended to attract those who were more cosmopolitan, more forward-looking, more reform-minded; it was "the party of economic development and moral uplift."[61] Most of these ideas were resisted or outright despised by the Slave Power.

While the Opposition could not be called liberal in today's sense, the party did include "the more liberal heirs of the Jeffersonian and Madisonian traditions," and they favored the more liberal thoughts of the day. They feared the arbitrary (and unchecked) power of the executive branch; they favored white male suffrage; they favored apportionment based on the white vote (thus opposing the slavocracy's insistence to count slaves); they attracted former Democrats, like the highly regarded Senator William Cabell Rives (who struggled with the evils of slavery throughout his long and distinguished career); they favored elected rather than appointed statewide office holders; and they attracted most of the rising middle class, who wanted to challenge the economic system established by and controlled for the slavocracy. Importantly, the Opposition ended up including the entire antislavery element in the state—those who opposed slavery for religious reasons, those who opposed slavery on economic grounds, the smallholders and those who opposed the slavocracy per se.

The Opposition became identified with antislavery folks and suffered from the association as its "losses in Virginia were of course connected with the slavery question."[62] William Hitchcock (and others) challenge this view, claiming that many in the Opposition (former Whigs) were still focused on protecting slavery in the years immediately prior to the war. But as the Southern Rights Democratic Party emerged in 1860, those who joined it were the uncompromising advocates of the plantation economy—they picked up the mantle of protecting slavery at all costs. On the other hand, the Opposition, which became the new Union Party, became the party of Union first, slavery second. The desertion by rank-and-file anti–Slave Power Democrats to the Union Party in February 1861 will be documented in Chapter 3.[63]

During the antebellum years, the "Democrats tended to bring together those from the bottom and top of the economic spectrum" while the Whigs "ran better among those at the middle rungs."[64] Crofts, in his study of Southampton County in the heavily slave-populated Tidewater region, found that "the fault lines that split Southampton had parallels across the South. The upper county, like most in the Upper South, had no use for secession. Upper-county non-slaveholders, who were more Whiggish and antisecessionist than upper-county slaveholders, in effect established the political tone for the region."[65] However, even some large slaveholders joined the Unionist ranks. An important example is Robert Eden Scott of Fauquier County, in the Piedmont region, the region with the second-highest percentage of slaves in the state. Scott, a staunch Whig turned Unionist, was a tall, dignified, charming man who commanded great attention in the county (and in the state) and was an outspoken opponent of slavery throughout the 1850s. In spite of his courageous stand against slavery, his constituents not only elected him to the Constitutional Convention of 1850–51 but also returned him to the legislature. Furthermore, even his "views on the evils of slavery did not prevent his election as a delegate to the 1861 secession convention." Scott not only

Robert Eden Scott would champion the Union cause at the Virginia State Convention even though one-half of the voters in his county supported the Slave Power. *Courtesy of the Library of Virginia.*

became a leader of the Unionist forces in the convention, but he also proved that anti–Slave Power (and antislavery) sentiment was even strong in some parts of the Piedmont—yet another "green shoot."[66]

No discussion of anti–Slave Power and uncompromising Unionism in Virginia can be complete without mention of John Minor Botts. A portly man of immense size, he was nicknamed "the Bison." By 1861, he had become an unconditional Unionist and would oppose the Confederate government throughout the war. His plantation was ravaged by the troops of General J.E.B. Stuart, and he was arrested and imprisoned during the war for his outspoken criticism of Jefferson Davis. After the war, he would write a famous (or infamous) treatise, *The Great Rebellion: Its Secret History, Rise, Progress, and Disastrous Failure*, in which he accused John Baldwin of not reporting Lincoln's offer of April 4, 1861, to abandon Fort Sumter if Virginians disbanded the Virginia State Convention.

John Minor Botts, "the Bison," was an unconditional Unionist who pleaded with Lincoln not to risk war by re-provisioning Fort Sumter at a private meeting in the White House on April, 7, 1861. *Courtesy of the Library of Virginia.*

But during the years leading up to the secession crisis, the Bison, a Congressman from Henrico County in the Tidewater, was a leading antislavery spokesman, noting that "slavery had been an evil for Virginia which had 'lost caste and power by holding on to the system.'" He enraged the "fire-eaters" by championing the idea that free labor was more profitable than slave. He campaigned vigorously for the Constitutional Union Party in the presidential election of 1860. As a large slave owner with a huge plantation, "in a day of almost universal Southern hysteria [about protecting slavery]…Botts retained a level head." Botts simply "was not terrified by the possible demise of slavery at some future date." He endured endless abuse before, during and after the war but should be remembered for seeing "the holocaust and disaster that ultra-Southernism was to bring to Virginia." Botts sacrificed his political career (and almost his life) to oppose the Slave Power and champion the Union cause—still another "green shoot."[67]

Botts's idea that free labor was more productive than slave labor found examples among free blacks. Instances of blacks achieving success in Virginia (and indeed throughout the South) are numerous. Crofts reported from Southampton County, "One finds instances of free black families that managed to overcome all the obstacles…Jordan Steward…owned thirty acres…on which he raised subsistence amounts of corn, peas, and hogs…James Taylor… owned almost one hundred acres…both Steward and Taylor had standing in the community…Lemuel Whitehead, a forty-nine-year-old black carpenter, apparently leased a 160-acre farm…Colegate Whitehead…leased an even more productive farm…by farming on such a scale… Colegate Whitehead ranked in a class with many white farmers of Southampton."[68] Edward Ayers noted from Stanton, "In defiance of every obstacle, some free blacks in Augusta managed to gain both property and respect. Robert Campbell, a 'black' man of sixty-five…had worked for decades as a barber. He owned five buildings near the heart of Stanton, including his shop…when he died, the last line of his substantial obituary read, 'Uncle Bob' was much respected and beliked by all our citizens.'"[69] "Green shoots" surface again.

Additionally, many enlightened slaveholders freed their slaves at time of death, as their wills would often spell out the details of freedom. In some cases, local whites would assist the process:

> *When C.C. Clarke of Hanover County died, he left eighteen slaves to be free and provided those who would go to Liberia with their expenses and one hundred dollars each. One of the woman slaves was married to a Negro whose owner was a man of limited means. His owner was unable to free him without some compensation but was willing to sell him for eight hundred and fifty dollars, considerably below his real value. His wife, who had four children, was willing to use the five hundred dollars they would inherit toward the purchase of her husband; her former master's widow gave another hundred; and the executor advanced the rest of the money needed to buy the man and send him off with his family.*[70]

Edmund Ruffin, an aristocrat who cared nothing about non-slaveholding whites, was Virginia's most radical Southern Rights activist. *Courtesy of the Library of Virginia.*

"Green shoots" of forward-looking behavior were numerous in Virginia and the Upper and Border South.

Whether the Unionists of Virginia, dominated by non-slaveholders and the more forward-looking, politically moderate men of the state, could have influenced the move to eliminate slavery over time is certainly open to endless debate. But the antithesis of the Unionists, the Southern Rights Democrats (men such as Henry Wise or Edmund Ruffin), were totally focused on preserving the past—and preserving slavery. They longed for the return of undemocratic control of the state by the slavocracy. They had never fully recovered from the universal white man suffrage granted by the Constitution of 1851. "A good many upper-class Virginians agreed with Edmund Ruffin, at least in private, that universal suffrage had corrupted and demeaned the former high tone of Virginia politics."[71] Most Virginia Unionists had had enough of the Southern aristocrats placing personal gain and their own political power above the public good.

After war began, so many Virginians seemed to unite in support of the Slave Power that the Unionist argument appears quite weak. But is it?

Many historians see the ill-advised decision of Abraham Lincoln to resupply Fort Sumter, and the equally ill-advised Confederate attack in response, as the causal factors in starting the Civil War. As will be documented in the Epilogue of this work, this was *not* the case. It was Lincoln's Proclamation of Insurrection a few days later (the proclamation was issued on Monday morning, April 15,

1861) that drove so many Virginia Unionists to support the Confederacy. Crofts so aptly named them "reluctant Confederates." But no historian has destroyed the myth of a "united South" better than William W. Freehling. For the student of the war interested in this subject, Freehling's *The South vs. The South: How Anti-Confederate Southerners Shaped the Course of the Civil War* is a must read. Following are a few highlights from Freehling's compelling analysis:

- 37 percent of Southerners lived in the Border South (Delaware, Maryland, Kentucky and Missouri) but contributed only 10 percent of the Confederacy's soldiers, a loss of some 250,000 fighting men.
- 200,000 border whites joined the Union army compared to 90,000 for the Confederate army, while 100,000 Middle South whites (Virginia, North Carolina, Tennessee and Arkansas) joined the Union army. These 300,000 Southern Union army recruits replaced every northern state Union fatality in the first two years of the war, causing the Confederate government to adopt its controversial draft a full year before the Federal government.
- After issuance of the emancipation proclamation in January 1863, some 350,000 Southern blacks joined the Union army—200,000 as un-enlisted laborers and 150,000 as soldiers or sailors.
- The 200,000 Southern black laborers were lost to the Confederacy, causing a severe manpower shortage throughout the South, and the 150,000 black soldiers and sailors tipped the number of troops scale heavily in favor of the Union army.[72]

More recent research points to an ever-increasing number of Southerners from the Confederate States who chose to fight for the Union. Below are some astounding numbers of Southerners who fought for the Union from the states that seceded, ranked from highest to lowest:

Tennessee	42,000
Virginia and West Virginia	30,000
Arkansas	10,000
Louisiana	7,000
North Carolina	5,000
Alabama	3,000
Texas	2,200
Florida	1,500
Georgia	700
Mississippi	545
Total	101,945[73]

Of the many additional examples of Southern disunity that could be cited, none is more compelling than the number of Southerners in the Union military high command. Union general Winfield Scott was a Virginian. A lesser-known but truly important example is from Southampton County. The county's most famous Civil War general was Union general George H. "Pap" Thomas, who became known as the "Rock of Chickamauga." "Thomas is now recognized as one of the ablest Union generals. He won deep respect from the soldiers he commanded, who knew that Thomas would not squander their lives impulsively."[74] Thomas paid dearly for his devotion to the Union, as many of his closest friends and family members deserted him. Still more compelling, "160 Southerners commanded federal brigades and fought with distinction, and about one-fourth of federal generals were born in the South."[75] In Virginia, thirty thousand men made the crystal clear choice to fight for the Union—and the number of "reluctant" Confederates easily doubles that. These statistics certainly support a widely divided South, even during this time of mass hysteria and intolerance of those who did not support "the cause."

The modern polling techniques in vogue today would be hard-pressed to sort out how Virginians truly felt and how their loyalties would really have panned out had Lincoln not issued his proclamation on that particular day in April 1861. The analysis presented in this work will indicate that the anti–Slave Power sentiment displayed by the Unionists of Virginia could have produced a different outcome than civil war had it been properly encouraged and supported. While it is too strong to conclude that all anti-secessionism in Virginia was connected to anti–Slave Power sentiment, for instance, Varon argues that "disunion was a far more pervasive concept than secession in antebellum politics."[76] It is fair to conclude a good part of Unionism was connected to class consciousness—the long-simmering resentment of Middle Virginians to the slaveholding aristocrats, those Tarter so intriguingly dubs "the grandees of government." Proponents of slavery—the Slave Power— were undoubtedly concerned with what troubles lay ahead for slavery if their political opponents, largely non-slaveholders, came to control the state government. In addition, Hickin's riveting conclusion to her exhaustive study of antislavery in the state is still worth noting. She stated, "There is surely sufficient evidence to lead one to consider the possibility that silent emancipationists constituted a large minority of Virginians in 1861" and that these largely non-slaveholders were "men who believed slavery in the abstract an evil."[77] "Green shoots" and the possibilities they held for solving the dilemma of slavery abounded within the Unionists of Virginia.

The often-overlooked subject of Unionism within the Confederacy is not within the scope of this work, but suffice it to say that a nucleus of "hard-core" Unionism did exist. It was scattered throughout the Confederacy, concentrated in the backcountry of the northern and western peripheries and in the towns and cities where the aristocrats were not so dominant and where modernization was taking hold. These Unionists were conspicuous and outspoken.[78] The hard-core Unionist element, combined with the "reluctant" Confederates, were sizable minorities in most Confederate states. In Georgia, for instance, 45 percent voted against secession even as Governor Brown suppressed the pro-Union vote. Michael Johnson concluded, "Far from being united, Georgia and the rest of the South was deeply divided on the question of secession." And he pins the tail squarely on the Slave Power, stating that "it was not the electorate but…the ruling class that led the state out of the Union. Secession was the ultimate test of the hegemony of the slaveholders."[79]

Another modern historian, Marc Egnal, concluded, "Serious problems, however, confront any interpretation that explains secession by reference to a single ideology or mind-set, whether rational or irrational, whether focused on slavery or republicanism. Citizens in almost every state in the Deep South were seriously divided over the wisdom of secession."[80] Again, what motivated the Unionists of the South is certainly complex, but there can be no doubt that anti–Slave Power sentiment, concentrated in the non-slaveholders, was a significant factor. Freehling's riveting conclusion rings true yet: "The tale of the southern house divided, when told in lockstep with intertwined tales of the American house divided, highlights underappreciated gems of Civil War lore."[81]

Lastly, it should be noted that several leaders of the North—William Henry Seward, Stephen A. Douglas and Charles Francis Adams, to name the most prominent—recognized the importance of reaching out to the Unionists of Virginia (and all those in the South who opposed secession). They worked diligently throughout the Secession Winter to find a compromise that would be acceptable to these political moderates so that fighting could be prevented. Seward, more than any other, saw a way to divide the South by building on the anti–Slave Power sentiment of the non-slaveholding majority.

And keeping Virginia in the Union was, indeed, the way to prevent war, or in the event of war determining a rapid and winning outcome. "One thing was certain. If the seven states of the Lower South began armed conflict against the Union without the Old Dominion, there could be little doubt as to the ultimate outcome."[82] Seward, in fact, spent most of his time reaching out to the Unionists of Virginia in a herculean effort to avert the Civil War.[83]

Three of the most important leaders of the Virginia Unionists, all slave owners, will be highlighted in this work: John B. Baldwin of Augusta County, George W. Summers of Kanawha County and William C. Rives of Castle Hill in Albemarle County.

We now turn to the two most important elections in the state of Virginia during the nineteenth century: the presidential election of 1860, held on November 6, 1860, and the election for delegates to the Virginia State Convention, held on February 4, 1861.

CHAPTER 2

THE PRESIDENTIAL ELECTION OF 1860

Sorting northerners and southerners into mutually distinct pigeonholes runs the
risk of imposing an arbitrary order on a messy irrational tragedy.
—Daniel W. Crofts, Old Southampton

During the nineteenth century, Virginians voted in dozens of elections—from presidential and gubernatorial elections to elections for constitutional conventions and special elections of one kind or another. Two of these elections—the presidential election of 1860, held on Tuesday, November 6, and the election for delegates to the Virginia State Convention, held on Monday, February 4, 1861—had the potential to position the state to play a key role in averting civil war. The presidential election, despite enflamed rhetoric and unfamiliar prospects caused by a four-way race, followed normal voting patterns for the most part. But it was the other election that would prove so portentous. The election for delegates to the Virginia State Convention was simply a monumental happening—it was an explosive turnabout for Virginia's electorate whereby previous party loyalty was discarded and a new political entity took shape. Like the phoenix rising out of the ashes, it was the most dramatic political realignment in the state's history. The election of 1860 will be analyzed here and the election of 1861 in Chapter 3.

First, a look at the role Southern Republicans played at the Republican National Convention, held in Chicago from May 16 to 18, 1860, to nominate a president and vice president and adopt a party platform for the upcoming presidential election in November. As the representatives of this new political party (this was only the second time the party would field a national ticket) gathered at the Wigwam, the structure built to house the convention in Chicago, it was a foregone conclusion who the party nominee would be. While a half dozen men had thrown their hats in the ring, most as favorite-son candidates from a given state, it was William Henry Seward whom most delegates felt would secure the nomination on the very first ballot.

A former two-term governor of New York and leading antislavery senator in the U.S Congress, Seward was widely viewed by leading citizens of all political persuasions to be the most qualified candidate in the nation, for "contemporaries regarded Henry Seward as not only a true statesman, but a true visionary."[84] New York was the leading state in the nation—the center of commerce and trade, the center of law and finance, the center of culture and the arts. New York had the largest population (and thereby the greatest number of Electoral College votes and the largest congressional delegation in the House) and was a fiercely contested two-party state. Seward, with his colleague Thurlow Weed (political boss of New York), had mastered the complexity of running a bureaucracy about as large as that of Washington, D.C. Also, they had learned how to manage a legislative body controlled partly by an opposition party. Seward had recently returned from a triumphant tour of Europe during which he was wined and dined and hailed as the new leader of the United States.

Frederic Bancroft, a postwar historian and one who had substantial interactions with actual participants at the convention, observed, "The fact that Seward had been prominent so long; that for a decade he had had no rival in the opinion of the progressive people of the North; that he had been in perfect harmony with the changing tendencies, first of the best Whigs and then of the best Republicans—these furnished opportunities for dangerous attacks upon him. Notwithstanding the numerous objections—some sincere but many specious—Seward was still the favorite of a very large majority of the Republican voters and politicians."[85] Seward losing the nomination was the greatest political upset in the history of the Republic up to that moment in time. Abraham Lincoln, the favorite-son candidate from Illinois, was a dark horse candidate at best. Most Republicans (including the assembled delegates), as well as most citizens of the country, had, in fact, never seen him or heard him speak and had read very little of what he had written. His nomination occurred because of a fortuitous series of events (some planned, some serendipitous) at the convention, events that ended up hurting Seward and helping Lincoln.[86]

Freehling, in his insightful analysis of voting at the Republican nominating convention, illustrated how the leading Southern Republican, Missouri congressman Frank Blair Jr., helped engineer Lincoln's grand success—a success aided and abetted by Southern Republicans. Frank, an antislavery apostle, was one of the nation's true characters of that era who would come to an early end by smoking and drinking himself to death. Before he died, however, he led Border South Republicans on a wild and woolly chase to end slavery in the Border South by deporting emancipated blacks—and he had some followers not only in Missouri but also in Virginia, Kentucky, Maryland and Delaware. At the Republican nominating convention, he was the undisputed leader of Border South Republicans. On the first ballot, Blair secured 10 percent of all Republican votes for a Southerner, Missouri's favorite-son candidate, Edward Bates, who would later become Lincoln's attorney general. Surprisingly, both Seward and Lincoln received substantial Southern support, with Lincoln receiving an astonishing 20 percent of his vote from the South. The balloting continued through an inconclusive second round, but on the third ballot, where Lincoln eked out a narrow victory, Blair, with his father and brother, maneuvered Maryland's vote to Lincoln, giving him forty-two votes from the South—almost half of the total Southern vote at the convention and a full 18 percent of Lincoln's final tally.[87] Without this Southern support, Lincoln likely would not have secured the nomination. These Southerners who played such a key role in the nomination of Abraham Lincoln were, first and foremost, anti–Slave Power men of the first rank, and some even could be classified as antislavery.

Not surprisingly, the group included several prominent Virginians. The Republican Party of Virginia was centered primarily in the Panhandle region of the far Northwest (present-day West Virginia) but included pockets in other sections, too. It held a one-day convention on May 2 in Wheeling, the largest city in the Panhandle. Frank Blair was the principal speaker. The party sent twenty-three delegates to the Chicago convention, where their credentials were challenged, but after a brief debate they were all seated. The delegation was considered solidly for Seward, but after being plied by Lincoln delegates in a series of late-night encounters, they gave fourteen votes to Lincoln and only eight to Seward, one of the major shifts in state voting that ended up giving Lincoln the nomination. The delegation included John C. Underwood, a controversial New Yorker who had moved to Virginia, married into the Stonewall Jackson family and spent years trying to encourage Northerners to emigrate to the state; John G. Jacob, editor of the influential *Wellsburg Herald*; Alfred Caldwell, a native of Ohio who had become the popular mayor of Wheeling and was elected as a Republican to the Virginia State Senate; and Archibald Campbell, a former Whig and editor of the powerful *Wheeling Intelligencer*.[88]

While disdained and chastised by eastern Virginians of the Slave Power and the newspapers controlled by them, this small but growing group of Virginians brought the Slave Power issues (the previously mentioned issues of taxation and representation) before the electorate and at times were rather visible. Although Caldwell may have been an abolitionist, most Virginia Republicans were anti–Slave Power and had no use for the abolitionists of New England. The *Wellsburg Herald*, in Brooke County of the Northwest, captured the view of Virginia Republicans in its editorial of March 31, 1860, as "to break the slavocracy's hold and to 'do battle for the cause of equal rights, and the elevation of the white race, the protection of white labor and the carrying out of impartial justice for all.'"[89] This view focused on freedom for the white man from dominance by the Slave Power and mirrored the national Republican Party platform that could be characterized as more anti–slave owner than antislavery.

However, Virginia Republicans did berate slavery when it suited their purposes. On economic grounds, they proclaimed that slavery penalized the white workingman by causing him to subsidize taxes for the slave owner and suppressed land values and the output of free labor. Thus, "limiting slaveholders' political ascendancy became the Virginia Republicans' primary message, and they attached greater importance to the 'liberties of the white man than to the slavery of the black.'"[90] The intra-South debate that sprang up during the presidential campaign increasingly pitted slave owners against non–slave owners and focused on limiting the political power of the aristocratic planters and creating a fair, more democratic system of taxation and political representation—issues that transcended the small Republican Party in the state.

While the Republican Party was nominating its second national ticket for the 1860 campaign, an even newer party was coming together. During the winter of 1859–60, venerable Kentucky senator John J. Crittenden had summoned "opposition" members of Congress together, and they formulated plans to create a new party. Opposition was defined as those who favored neither the Republicans nor the Democrats, for many Americans "looked for a party that truly embodied Union and compromise; in their eyes, the Democrats talked of Union but favored the South while the Republicans talked of Union but only on Northern terms."[91] On Washington's Birthday in 1860, they announced their new Constitutional Union Party, stating that both existing parties were capable of tearing the nation apart, and called for a spring convention in Baltimore. First and foremost, those joining this effort were Union men who rejected the extremist politicians found in both the newly formed Southern Rights Democratic Party and the Republican Party. They truly believed that moderates, both Northern and Southern, held to the same political principles: Union first, sectional considerations second.

A week before the Republicans gathered in Chicago, representatives of the newly formed Constitutional Union Party gathered in Baltimore on May 9. Murat Halstead, a well-known newspaper editor and journalist, covered every political convention of that spring, and his observations are cited frequently by historians. Halstead was an eyewitness participant and a fairly impartial reporter. Therefore, several of his comments about the Constitutional Unionists Convention will be cited. First, he reported, "The turnout of delegates is larger than was expected. I believe there are really as many people in attendance here, as there were at Charleston [where the Democratic Party had first met in early May]."[92] Primarily former Whigs, nationalistic Whigs, they came from North and South, but the Southern Whigs seemed to dominate. They were a distinguished group to be sure, as "every body is eminently respectable, intensely virtuous, devotedly patriotic, and fully resolved to save the country," Halstead reported.[93]

As the Democratic Party had failed to produce a ticket at its Charleston convention in early May and was scheduled to meet again in Baltimore that June, the Constitutional Unionists suddenly felt they had a fighting chance with the Democrats badly split and the Republicans purely a sectional party. If they could win the Upper and Border South along with the Border North (sections that were more connected to and attuned to one another), they might just be able to capture enough Electoral College votes to throw the election into the House of Representatives (assuming no candidate received a majority). In the House, they thought they had a much better chance to win the presidency outright. "The delegates seem to be in high spirits," Halstead noted from the convention floor, "and to be confident of their ability to make at least a powerful diversion. The general foolishness of the two great parties has given the third party unusual animation."[94]

For their presidential candidate, they passed over aging Texan Governor Sam Houston and the aged Kentuckian John Crittenden and nominated former senator John Bell of Tennessee, a large slaveholder but one who would have been open to compromise on slavery extension (as with many former Whigs). Bell had the right credentials for political moderates, as he had been the leader of the old Whig Party in Tennessee and one who rejected the extremists in both the Republican and Democratic Parties. Bell received the nomination on the second ballot when the Virginia delegation swung to his support. For vice president, they nominated, by acclamation, one of the greatest Americans of the era, Edward Everett of Massachusetts. Everett, a former Congressman, U.S. Senator, governor, minister to Great Britain and president of Harvard, totally overshadowed the diminutive and uninspiring Bell; nevertheless, the team seemed very impressive. They set about producing a campaign strategy that downplayed agitation over slavery and focused on preserving the Union "as it was." They hoped to appeal to Northerners and Southerners who were fed up with the slavery debate and wanted the Union saved from more civil turmoil that, they felt, could lead to armed conflict. Halstead concluded after the convention had ended, "It was remarkable, and I shall not say it was not a refreshing fact, that the Convention avoided altogether the discussion of the slavery question… Not a word was said from first to last about the question of slavery in the Territories, or the execution of the Fugitive Slave law, and old John Brown was only referred to a couple of times."[95]

This was a time of rapid economic growth in the borderland, propelled by the rapid development of the railroad system in the region as previously noted. The Constitutional Unionists hoped to tap the theme that, in the long run, protecting and expanding the economic prosperity of the region was more important than protecting slavery. And to accomplish this they proposed restoring the Compromise of 1850, which would reestablish the line running from the southern border of Missouri to California whereby slavery would be permitted south of that line and prohibited north of the line. This would be the Constitutional Unionists' supreme effort to end the slavery debate and thereby save the country from further strife. Slavery was not suited for the western territories, they claimed, because of climate, geography and soil conditions, so their strategy was to settle the issue and move forward. The party did attract a group of distinguished politicians who many believed were capable of guiding the nation through the current crisis.

Virginians took an active role in the Constitutional Union convention, sending fifteen delegates to the meeting in spite of the fact that many Old

Line Whigs had not yet joined the Constitutional Union Party. For instance, John B. Baldwin, who would become one of the key leaders of the Virginia Unionists, attended the Whig convention in Richmond even though the Whigs had disintegrated as a national party some years before. In addition to the fifteen delegates, William Cabell Rives and John Minor Botts were among the nominees for the presidential spot on the ticket, along with delegate William L. Goggin, the unsuccessful Opposition (Whig) candidate for governor in 1859.

The Virginia delegation included: Samuel Watts (Norfolk County), Robert E. Scott (Fauquier County), Travis H. Epes (Nottoway County), N.B. Meade (Alexandria), William Martin (Brunswick County), A.H.H. Stuart (Augusta County), Edward D. Christian (Richmond County), James Witherow, (no county), William L. Goggin (Bedford County), William J. Dickerson (Russell County), Marmaduke Johnson (Richmond City), George W. Summers (Kanawha County), George T. Yerby (Northampton County), Waitman T. Willey (Monongalia County), and E.T. Taylor (Roanoke County).

These Virginians were front and center at the convention. William Goggin was elected one of the permanent officers of the convention, Alexander (Sandy) Stuart was elected one of the vice-presidents of the convention and it was George W. Summers who delivered Virginia's vote on the second ballot that gave Bell the nomination (Virginia cast thirteen votes for Bell and two for Botts on this final ballot). At the end of the convention, A.R. Boteler, the newly elected congressman who defeated the favored Democrat in the 1859 Virginia congressional election, was appointed to the National Central Executive Committee of the party, a prestigious and important post. Six of these men would go on to play crucial roles in the upcoming Virginia State Convention.

Alexander H.H. "Sandy" Stuart, a distinguished politician from the Valley Region, would not yield to the Slave Power. He voted against the Ordinance of Secession on April 17, 1861. *Courtesy of the Library of Virginia.*

By early 1860, the Democratic Party in Virginia had morphed into the party of the Slave Power and was dubbed the Southern Rights Democratic Party. Most large slave owners in the state were either in it or moving into the ranks. The party took up the challenge of protecting the Slave Power, espousing the virtues of slavery and protesting Northern abolitionist interference. "They attempted, with considerable success, to lead the rising generation of Virginians toward a South Carolina perspective, militantly assertive of southern rights."[96] During the decade, they had controlled the legislature (and thereby the two U. S. Senators from the state, who were appointed by the legislature), most of the congressmen and the governorship as well. It is fair to conclude that the Democrats should have been able to carry the state in the 1860 presidential election—in fact, very few living Virginians at the time could ever remember when the Democrats had lost a presidential election.

But the Democrats of 1860, in a spectacular example of "shooting oneself in the foot," became so bitterly divided at their conventions during that spring that they formed two parties: a Southern Democratic Party, or Southern Rights Democratic Party, and a Northern Democratic Party. In Virginia, the Democrats had gradually weakened over a number of years as a result of intraparty factionalism, spearheaded by Governor Henry Wise on the one hand and Senator R.M.T. Hunter on the other, over control of the party. The final breach occurred in February 1860 at the party's state convention when the party ruptured over the election of delegates to the national convention. Prior to this breakup, the party had lost several seats in the state legislature and a congressional seat in the June 1859 elections. One historian observed that "a common thread in the results of the elections of 1859 appeared to be a popular backlash against southern extremism."[97] Nevertheless, the extremists seemed to gain control of the party in the state.

The Opposition politicians, who were experiencing something of a revival at this time, were laser-beam focused on Southern extremism and would attempt to exploit it to the fullest in the coming presidential election. Opposition Virginians came from every corner of the state, and while a rather diverse group, they were held together because they despised the Democrats. The lead sentence in the editorial of the *Staunton Spectator*, the Unionist paper of that city, of March 6, 1860, observed, "The movement of patriotic and conservative men against the Black Republican and Democratic parties, both of which are alike sectional and tending to disunion, is gathering strength in all quarters, and is destined, we trust, to become a power that will be felt in the land."[98] Most in this group were the leading anti–Slave Power voices in their respective communities, and they became the leaders of the Constitutional Union Party.

These anti–Slave Power men were faced with an extremely delicate task, though. As a result of John Brown's raid the previous year (and the response to it by some Northerners), many Virginians had become obsessed with the future of slavery—and of slaves. Slaves began to challenge their owners in all sorts of ways, causing an unprecedented unease to grip the state, driven by white fears of slave insurrection or just slave insubordination. The insecurities of slaveholding Virginians skyrocketed. They began to take action against non-slaveholders, the bulk of the anti–Slave Power group, men who were viewed as potential nonsupporters of slavery. The Slave Power hired "mobs" to confront the Opposition, and they even hired detectives to see if any in the group might be aiding slaves.

Although his raid was a dismal failure, John Brown transformed his defeat into something much, much bigger as he accepted his death sentence. "I am ready for my fate," he declared, in an attempt to seek martyrdom. Brown truly believed he was chosen by God for his mission.[99] Henry Wise, then governor of Virginia, had met with Brown, developed an affinity for the man and considered sparing his life. Wise would be haunted by his decision to hang Brown for the rest of his life, as he "never forgot Brown and consistently testified to his greatness." When Wise reflected on Brown, "he felt nostalgia over a missed opportunity and regret about a road not taken."[100] Indeed, had Wise spared Brown's life, the events that led to civil war, and certainly Virginia's role, could have unfolded very differently or even not at all.

But the impact of Brown's death on the Constitutional Unionists, as they began their

Henry A. Wise, a former governor, would lead the Slave Power at the Virginia State Convention. He would employ "extra-legal" tactics to ensure Virginia's secession. *Courtesy of the Library of Virginia.*

campaign in the summer of 1860, was to force them to express support for their "peculiar institution." They had to counter the Southern Rights Democrat attack on their "soundness" on the slavery issue, although "they were poorly positioned to compete in a proslavery shouting match." They countered the soundness attacks by insisting the issue of slavery in Virginia be dealt with by Virginians, a popular stance. While in the long run the Constitutional Unionists knew that slavery would not work, which was "broadly consistent with Whig-style economic and moral development," they could not be seen as abolitionist-friendly because "Democrats routinely denounced all Whigs as abolitionists."[101] Even so, within this broad group of mostly former Whigs, some antislavery sentiment did exist; it was just quiet. The *Wellsburg Herald*, for instance, "believed that there existed throughout Virginia a 'strong undercurrent of sentiment' against slavery that only awaited some 'proper occasion to wake into life and overwhelming activity.'"[102]

What took the place of any outright antislavery talk in the campaign, however, was the Constitutional Unionist charge that the Southern Rights Democrats were the party of disunion, the party of the uncompromising secessionists. They claimed in no uncertain terms that Southern Rights Democrats were engaged in a "disunionist conspiracy" in an attempt to reestablish their former dominance of state politics and society. In Frederick, Maryland, the leading Unionist newspaper heralded a typical broadside of the campaign: "If you desire dissolution of the Union, vote for Breckinridge; if you desire the disruption of democracy, vote for Breckinridge."[103] The Unionists coupled, quite successfully, the argument that secession was a rebellion that meant war —and that war meant the destruction of Virginia. Dr. Thomas J. Pretlow, a leading Unionist in Southampton County, in the heart of the Tidewater region, spoke passionately to county residents: "Let me tell you my friends, if Virginia secedes from the Union your houses will be burned, your firesides will become desolate, your very hearthstones will be torn up. Virginia must sweat great drops of blood…If my voice is unheeded, I call God to witness that I discharge my duty to the utmost of my humble ability, that no man's blood may be on my head."[104] Of course, Pretlow's prescient words did go unheeded—and Virginia would indeed sweat great drops of blood.

Equally important to branding the Democrats as disunionists, the Constitutional Unionist strategy to brand the Southern Democratic Party the proslavery party—the party of the Slave Power—parried the "soundness on slavery" charge. The party of the Slave Power claimed it would do anything to promote the return of unlimited (and undemocratic) power to the aristocratic planters. Just before the election, the *Staunton Spectator* trumpeted, "Gov. Wise [who had become a staunch secessionist] is even now, at this very time having companies of 'Minute Men,' organized as they are doing in South Carolina. Treason has doffed its mask, and is now stalking undisguised over the sacred soil of Virginia itself. It is time the patriotic masses of the people were aroused to a proper sense of the danger which is now impending over their heads and households."[105] The Constitutional Unionists had drawn their line in the sand.

This strategy appealed not only to the non-slaveholding bloc per se but also to the equalitarian bent in the party, centered in the rising middle class that so resented the elitism of the paternalistic planters. Appealing to such men not only caused a significant number of traditional Democratic voters to stay home, but it probably caused a few to vote for the Constitutional Unionist, in spite of the *viva voce* voting procedure. In Democrat-leaning Southampton County, the Constitutional Unionist Bell lost to the Southern Democrat Breckinridge by a scant eighteen votes out of well over one thousand cast. Crofts makes the compelling point regarding Southampton Whigs (using as an example the Southampton Whig Elliott L. Story) that "Story…was one of a good many southern Whigs who shared a mentality that was in many ways progressive and was certainly nonconfrontational."[106]

During the election campaign, a contentious debate occurred regarding the effects a Republican win could have on the Border and Upper South. Federal patronage was a truly big deal in mid-nineteenth-century America. The jobs were not only well paying in a time when there were not that many such jobs, but they also carried a degree of prestige that government jobs no longer hold. Great concern was expressed, especially by the Southern Rights Democrats, of a Republican president distributing jobs throughout the South that could establish an anti–Slave Power or even an antislavery base in every city and town. A report in the *Delaware Republican* predicted that "slaveholding gentlemen will cross the Potomac in swarms and clamor at the Capital for the privilege of serving their country in public office—Slavery or no Slavery."[107] So this was a real concern and a very real possibility in the eyes of slave owners. The slave owners further opined that once the Republican Party took control of the Federal government, it would surely embolden those with antislavery sentiments to come forward.

In addition, a growing economy in non-plantation-dominated areas would only increase anti–Slave Power sentiment, many warned. Georgia's J. Henley Smith, a Treasury Department appointee of President Buchanan, forewarned Georgia congressman Alexander Stephens (later vice president of the Confederacy) that antislavery sentiment would swell in the Border South after a Republican victory "and bring debates about slavery's sins to the respectable center of Border South public life."[108] As the Border South, including the western part of Virginia, continued developing its diversified economy, the "sins of slavery" could become paramount. In fact, this was already happening in western Virginia, where there were few slaves and where the argument that free labor was more productive than slave labor was proving true.

After the party conventions had ended in late June, the political canvass opened with some fanfare—and some real confusion for the electorate. For the first time in its history, the country was presented not with two major choices but with four. This caused some confusion in Virginia, for sure, but it had much greater implications for the country at large. Historian Edward Ayres observed, "The American party system had evolved to hold things together, cementing the locality to the state and the state to the nation." Furthermore, he noted that "normal politics had come to be based on fervent competition between two, and only two, national parties." In Washington, "the replication of the two-party system" kept things intact. He concluded that "if the parties became sectional, if the parties abandoned any effort to reach across the border, there was little else to keep things from shattering."[109] While few Americans living through the turmoil could see these broader developments, the presidential election of 1860 was shaping up to be a watershed event for the country.

Voting for one of the four parties can be summarized as follows:

VOTE REPUBLICAN—While Republicans sought to present themselves as a moderate party and their candidate as a moderate, they were not so perceived by the electorate. Many in the North and an overwhelming majority in the South thought of them as radicals. Throughout the South, most Southerners referred to them as "Black Republicans," meaning they stood for the black man. Some viewed the Republican platform as radical for the time, as it "denied that slavery was based in the common law, denied the right of Congress or of a territorial legislature to establish it in any of the territories, denounced the principles of non-intervention and popular sovereignty as deceptions and frauds, and defined the doctrine of the right of secession as treason."[110] While many historians argue to the contrary, Republicans needlessly offended moderate Southerners by their harsh rhetoric against all Southerners and their uncompromising stance on the territorial extension of slavery issue. Moderates saw the territorial extension issue as a red herring. John Gilmer, congressman from North Carolina and leader of the Southern Unionists in the House of Representatives, pleaded on the floor of the House, "Why, sirs, do you think these ultra men [Southern Rights Democrats] insist on what they call protection [protection of their rights to take slaves into the territories], because it is any value to them?... They demand it because they think you will refuse it, and by your refusal, they hope the South will be inflamed to the extent of breaking up this government…the very thing the leaders desire."[111] A vote for the Republicans was first and foremost a vote against the Slave Power and the dominance this minority group had held over the majority of white Americans for several decades. Unfortunately, many Americans of the era felt a vote for the Republicans was a vote for the North only and a vote against the South.

VOTE NORTHERN DEMOCRAT—After the Democrats reconvened in Baltimore after the breakup in Charleston, they still could not agree and decided to form two parties. The Northern wing adopted the Democratic platform of 1856, which opposed congressional interference with slavery, supported decisions by the Supreme Court on slavery extension, called for stronger enforcement of the Fugitive Slave Law and supported Douglas's doctrine of popular sovereignty, whereby voters of a given territory would determine if slavery was to be permitted. They had won the 1856 election on this platform and felt, as the only true national party, they would win again. Unlike the Republicans, they were open to compromise on slavery extension and were willing to cooperate with moderate Southerners. However, they fiercely condemned the Southern Rights Democrats and hurled their most harsh criticism at their former party members for breaking up the party and for their uncompromising stance on slavery. A vote for the Northern Democrat was viewed as a vote for the moderate Democrat. The party had some support in the South, but the vast majority of support came from the North.

VOTE SOUTHERN RIGHTS DEMOCRAT—The other part of the Democratic Party became known as the Southern Rights Democratic Party or the Breckinridge Democrats, and they stood for an aggressive defense of slavery and Southern rights. They endorsed the Dred Scott decision, proclaimed the Constitution gave them the right to take their slaves anywhere in the territories of the United States, harshly protested the agitation of some Northern states against slavery and insisted that states had rights that superseded the central government. "They regarded the Constitution as an instrument of the union between states" with the "states, and not the government so created…the final judges of the extent of their reserved powers."[112] A vote for the Southern Rights Democrats was a vote to protect slavery and to oppose the Republicans and all that they stood for. The Southern Rights Democrats were at the other end of the political spectrum from the Republicans but were equally radical. Other than some marginal support coming from "fusion tickets" in the North, their support came totally from the South.

VOTE CONSTITUTIONAL UNIONISTS—This newly formed party sought to avoid the slavery debate and promote national harmony by appealing to political moderates who were fed up with the constant agitation produced by the Republicans and Southern Rights Democrats. They called for preserving the Union, first and foremost, by strictly following the Constitution and by strictly enforcing the laws of the land. The party included many well-known senior statesmen and appealed to those who believed in the public good. It was a party that appealed to moderate Southerners, the former Whigs, who supported a more limited version of states' rights, but favored the right of slave owners to take slaves into the territories, knowing full well that no slave owner wanted to do it. Unlike the Southern Rights Democrats, however, they were open to compromise, and they were not confrontational. They opposed both popular sovereignty and the aggressive stance of the Southern Rights Democrats, especially their proposal to reopen the African slave trade. Their support was centered in the Upper and Border South and scattered throughout the North.

The candidates of the four parties were as follows:

Republican—Abraham Lincoln of Illinois for president, Hannibal Hamlin of Maine for vice president

Northern Democrat—Stephen A. Douglas of Illinois for president, Hershel V. Johnson of Georgia for vice president

The Presidential Election of 1860

Southern Democrat—John C. Breckinridge of Kentucky for president, Joseph Lane of Oregon for vice president

Constitutional Unionist—John Bell of Tennessee for president, Edward Everett of Massachusetts for vice president

The presidential election of 1860 then turned into two elections—an election in the Northern states between Lincoln and Douglas and an election in the Southern states between Breckinridge and Bell. The election in the Northern states quickly developed with the Republican Party centered on restricting the spread of slavery into the territories as a way to eventually eliminate the institution. They appealed to the more progressive men of the North but, ominously for maintaining peace in the nation, included the most radical abolitionist element as well. The Northern Democrats centered a campaign on downplaying the slavery debate by favoring Douglas's popular sovereignty, and this argument appealed to the more moderate men of the North, among them a large bloc of very wealthy businessmen who controlled much of the nation's commerce and who, for business reasons, did not want to risk the disruption of war.

The election in the Southern states developed quickly also. From the outset, the Southern Democratic Party of John Breckinridge was the choice of the proslavery Southerner, who demanded the protection of slavery unconditionally, including the right to carry slaves into any territory in the country. In a move to enrage the more liberal Republicans, some in the party even proposed reopening the African slave trade. As a result of Southern delegates walking out of the Democratic Convention in Baltimore, the party was clearly captured by the more extreme, uncompromising wing of the Southern rights crowd, led by "fire-eaters" such as William Yancey. The Constitutional Unionists with their lackluster candidate Bell sought to downplay the slavery question and focus voter attention on preserving the Union to foster economic prosperity. They appealed to political moderates both North and South, but especially to the Southern man who could be defined as progressive.

The focus of the remainder of this chapter will deal with the election in Virginia, particularly the role of the Constitutional Unionists and their campaign strategy.

At the outset, it should be noted that in the nineteenth century, political campaigns were wildly popular events that were heavily attended. In an era without radio, television, professional sports or the Internet, life was tedious and often downright boring—men and women working from dawn to dusk every single day. Political campaigns, with their rallies and stump speeches, provided great relief for all. More importantly, perhaps, they offered free barbecues, plenty of liquor and other entertainment of all kinds. Folks could dress up and go see their neighbors and friends under the guise of being a responsible, patriotic citizen. Politicians took every advantage of this "social nature of a campaign" and used it effectively to spread their view of the state of the nation. Consequently, voter turnout was usually very high, sometimes reaching as high as 90 percent of the electorate.

The Constitutional Unionists started their campaign with great hope for the outcome. They freely discussed the election being decided by Congress and pledged to work to that end. Newspapers also spoke freely about it, as "the *Louisville Journal* expressed optimism that Bell and Everett could win if Lincoln failed to gain an outright victory."[113] In Virginia, highly regarded men, such as elder statesmen William Cabell Rives, led the Unionist charge. Rives campaigned throughout the state and in every speech attacked the Slave Power. What was driving men of Rives's rank was the chance for non-Democrats to regain political dominance in Virginia. Out of power for far too long, they saw the breakup of the Democratic Party as their big chance. "A glorious hour is at hand for the Whigs of Virginia," proclaimed the *Staunton Spectator*. Indeed, many thought "the great talents of Southern Union men, squandered for the last decade, would finally have a chance to save the entire country, steering it between the detested Republicans and the reviled Democrats."[114]

John B. Baldwin, who had left the Whigs and now come over to the Constitutional Unionists, campaigned with all his vigor, going from Lynchburg to Richmond to Alexandria—even to areas with strong Democratic roots—to encourage support for the Union. His speeches were hailed everywhere as Union-saving addresses. He ridiculed the Democratic Party's position on unconditional support of slavery and for proposing a reopening of the African slave trade and accused its chief spokesman, Alabama's William L. Yancey, of being an outright disunionist. "He called on 'all good citizens to rally to the support of the Constitutional Union ticket' appealing alike to Whig, Democrat, and Republican." He denied the right of secession, stating that all should look to the Constitution for solutions to the sectional troubles.[115] Baldwin gave a rousing speech in Richmond that September that lasted over two and a half hours. He electrified the crowd by blasting the proslavery disunionists and called all to stand by the flag of the country. In its editorial that week, the *Richmond Whig* (the Constitutional Union newspaper of the city) stated, "It was empathetically the speech of the canvas...It places Col. Baldwin in the front of the debaters, not only of Virginia, but of the entire Union..."[116] Baldwin would campaign long and hard for the Union cause, and only with great hesitancy would he don Confederate gray.

John Brown Baldwin, the rising young star of the Virginia Unionists, came from a distinguished family of Augusta County. He would serve on the board of visitors of the University of Virginia early in his career. *Courtesy of the Library of Virginia.*

Likewise, the highly regarded George W. Summers sprung to the support of the Constitutional Union ticket. Hailing from large and populous Kanawha County, which Bell would carry handily in the election, he knew his constituents. He campaigned across the state and bitterly denounced the Southern Rights Democrats as the party of the past, the party of the status quo and, most importantly, the party out of step with the changing economic climate in Virginia. He denounced the Democrats for holding back Virginia's economy and loudly promoted expanding roads, banks, railroads and canals to foster economic growth. He appealed to the workingman, the rising Middle Americans, former Whigs, moderate Democrats and all those opposed to the slavocracy.

An example of the wide-ranging nature of those opposed to the Slave Power is the little-known case of John Minor Botts. During the fall of 1859 and early winter of 1860, "the Bison" launched a spirited campaign to establish a "national" Republican Party (one that would include the Border South) with none other than himself as its presidential nominee. During this time, he lashed out at the Southern Rights Democrats. "With 'utter loathing and contempt,' he termed the secessionists 'enemies,' 'insane,' 'infamous'" and sought to couple his moderate antislavery views with those of moderate

Republicans.[117] Botts insisted that Republicans stop "indiscriminately insulting all Southerners," and that, along with his refusal to publicly call slavery evil, cost him so much Republican support that by late winter of 1860, his campaign had failed. By early April, he would not only throw his support to the Constitutional Unionists, but he would throw his presidential hat in their ring as well. Botts came to believe that the best chance for Virginia and the Upper South to win the election was with the Constitutional Union Party.

On Monday, October 1, Botts addressed an "immense audience" at the Bell-Everett rally in Richmond, where "over 4,000 persons, of both sexes, were present," reported the *New York Times*. He accused the Southern Rights Democrats of planning to break up the Union for their own political gain, he spoke against the right of a state to secede and he planted himself squarely in the Constitutional Unionists' camp. He concluded, "As to Mr. Bell, all knew him to be an old-line Whig, a Union man and a conservative in sentiment. The object of Mr. Bell's friends is to put down fanaticism at the North, and treason and disunion in the South."[118] His speech was a powerful denunciation of the Slave Power.

Nationally, and in Virginia, the Democrats had their political apparatus intact during the campaign, but it was bitterly divided. The Douglas wing denounced the Southern Rights wing even more harshly than they denounced the Republicans. The Douglas men accused the Southern Rights men of not only being disunionists at heart but also deliberately breaking up the party, as "the convention dissolved without naming anyone as its candidate, a humiliating failure for the most powerful party in the nation."[119] Most Democrats in Virginia supported Breckinridge, with only the German-dominated areas supporting Douglas.

Intriguingly, the Douglas Democrats now began an accommodation with the Constitutional Unionists. They sought, to some degree, to form alliances or "fusion tickets" in an attempt to find a winning combination. Most of these efforts met with only lukewarm support, as long-held animosity between the Whigs and Democrats was difficult to overcome in a heated political campaign. The Constitutional Unionists, however, scrambled throughout the race to hold a fragile political apparatus together. The Whig Party had disintegrated years before, as had the subsequent American or Know-Nothing Party, and what the Constitutional Unionists had left was little more than fragments from dissolved political machines. What held the fractured party together, though, was unyielding opposition to, if not downright hatred of, the Southern Rights Democrats, John Minor Botts being a prime example.

The four-way race ended in early November, and election day was not marred by any unusual activity to intimidate or discourage voters, other than the *viva voce* procedure that so influenced like-minded voting in each community. Interest in the election was very high, and "the excitement about the presidential election in Richmond, according to one account, was 'so pervasive and intense, that business has been wholly neglected by the mass of the community.'"[120]

The election results for Virginia by region are as follows:

Region	Bell	Breckinridge	Douglas	Lincoln
Trans-Alleghany Northwest	14,316	17,425	3,946	1,402
Southwest	9,578	10,456	857	403
Valley	12,315	11,318	4,753	13
Piedmont	20,240	19, 891	2,661	12
Tidewater	18,232	15,233	3,091	99
Total	74,681	74,323	15,308	1,929

While Bell won the state by the narrowest of margins—358 votes out of over 166,000 cast—there are other stories of interest. Douglas had his greatest success in the Valley, where there were lots of Germans who were turned off by the anti-immigrant faction in the old American Party (now part of the Constitutional Unionist). In the Northwest, where there were lots of anti–Slave Power folks, Democrats, who just could not bring themselves to vote for Breckinridge, stayed home. Lincoln and the Southern Republicans did about as expected, receiving the vast majority of their very small vote in the Northwest, with Ohio County in the Panhandle giving him the largest vote.

A further review of the above numbers, however, poses two fundamental questions regarding the thesis presented in this work. First, if the anti–Slave Power sentiment was strongest in the Trans-Alleghany Northwest, where slaves were so scarce, then why did Breckinridge, the candidate of the slavocracy, carry the region? Secondly, and conversely, why did Bell carry the Tidewater region with the highest population of slaves and supposedly the region controlled by the slavocracy? The answer to both lies not in the anti– or pro–Slave Power sentiment of voters in particular regions but in other factors.

Factor number one was party loyalty. In the Trans-Alleghany Northwest, where only very large Kanawha County had more than 10 percent slaves, the populace had long roots to the Jacksonian-principled support of the plain and simple ways of the past—they were Jacksonian Democrats. As a result, many counties in the region had voted Democratic for years—and the 1860 election would prove no different. Shanks concluded in his mid-twentieth-century study, "The organization, press, and most of the trusted leaders of the Democratic party supported Breckinridge. Party loyalty to most Virginia Democrats, therefore, required them to support him."[121] A quarter of a century after Shanks, Freehling noted, "As the New Political History has demonstrated, 90 per cent of mid-nineteenth-century voters, unlike more independent-minded twentieth-century voters, remained virtuously loyal to their party…a moral man with ethically steady opinion was expected to cast the same straight party vote in election after election, whatever ephemeral event transpired."[122]

Factor number two was the previously mentioned *viva voce* voting procedure, in which every man had to state before an election judge who he voted for, sometimes in front of a hostile audience. Typical is this letter from a mountaineer of Giles County in the Southwest region, who wrote to the governor before the election, "I would like to Know from you what is to prevent me from Voting for Lincoln. as he is the man I prefer. the reason for this letter is that there is a great deal of threatening on the part of Slave holders in regard to poor men exercising the elective franchise…I think it hard if I should be prevented from execiseing [*sic*] the wright [*sic*] of suffrage that other men do in selecting any one of the four candidates."[123] Thus, in spite of the Constitutional Unionist campaign that tried in every possible way to focus voter attention on the changing nature of the new Southern Rights Democratic Party—the movement to support the Slave Power unconditionally—party loyalty, the tradition of voting for the same party, and *viva voce* voting trumped the rising Unionist sentiment in the region.

However, the Trans-Alleghany Northwest, similar to all other regions in Virginia, was not monolithic. A group of counties in the southern part of the region—Mason, Putnam, Kanawha, Clay and Nicholas—had been Whig strongholds for years, and they remained so in this election, giving Bell a majority of their votes. Immediately to the north of this string of counties was a set of counties that had been traditionally Democratic—Jackson, Wirt, Roane, Calhoun, Braxton, Lewis, Upshur, Barbour and Tucker, to name the most prominent—and they, too, remained loyal to their roots and gave Breckinridge a majority of their votes. Southerners had a strong sense of feeling "that danger could be overcome by voting for familiar and trusted party nominees," and "that conviction drew them to the polls on November 6."[124] While party loyalty was key in this election, such loyalty was about to change dramatically.

In the Tidewater region, the same factor, party loyalty, held true. In counties with large towns or cities and in counties experiencing new types of economic development—the counties around Richmond and Norfolk are prime examples—the Whigs had usually dominated. Even though the Whig Party had morphed into a loosely held Opposition, now the Constitutional Union Party, it was still able to command a majority of votes in those formally Whig strongholds where "ex-Whigs usually voted for the so-called Opposition Party—so called because it opposed the hated Democracy."[125] It is important to mention that in the *viva voce* voting era, party loyalty had a neighborhood loyalty factor as well. Many factors were at play in determining how a neighborhood, a county or a region voted, but none was more important than "antebellum southerners [who] voted more as members of a community than as individuals."[126] Local leaders, local press, neighbors, ministers and "the community" all were certainly driving factors in how a man voted. When voting in front of all his friends and neighbors, a man's loyalty "inspired" by *viva voce* likely trumped specific campaign rhetoric tied to various campaign issues.

In the Tidewater region with its high percentage of slaves, the same theme persisted as in the Northwest region with very few slaves; that is, the region was divided by traditional party loyalties. Counties that surrounded Richmond (Henrico, New Kent, Charles City, Prince George and Surry) and Norfolk (Nansemond, Norfolk, Princess Anne, Warwick and Elizabeth City) typically voted for the Whigs and gave the Constitutional Unionists a majority of their votes in the presidential election of 1860. Traditional Democratic counties in the region—Hanover, King William, Caroline, Essex, Middlesex and Gloucester—gave a majority of their votes to Breckinridge. Here, too, party loyalty was about to change.

Did owning slaves influence the way in which a man voted? Crofts has demonstrated that it did *not*, as the percentages for high and low slaveholding for Virginians in the presidential election demonstrate.

	Whig	Democrat	Nonvoting
Entire State	30.3%	36.8%	32.2%
High Slaveholding	34.1%	38.9%	27.0%
Low Slaveholding	27.9%	35.5%	35.3%

In ten Tidewater counties that held between 30 percent and 60 percent slaves (high-slaveholding counties), five counties—Surry, Prince George, James City, New Kent and Henrico—were carried by Bell, while the five neighboring counties of Hanover, Caroline, King and Queen, King William and Gloucester were carried by Breckinridge. Crofts concluded, "The pattern of partisan allegiances that developed bore no uniform relationship to slaveholding or to the conspicuous regional divisions."[127] Again, the relationships that mattered seemed to be driven by community, by family, by political organizations, by churches and by *viva voce*, not by slaveholding.

However, the most dramatic number above is that over 35 percent of smallholders (those owning a slave or two—Nonvoting in the Low-Slaveholding column above) did not vote. In an era when voter turnout was usually very high, many times in excess of 80 percent, this number is noteworthy, especially for a presidential contest. Did the Constitutional Unionists' campaign to paint the Democrats as the party of the Slave Power play a role? Certainly, it appears some smallholders who had traditionally voted Democrat decided to stay home rather than stand in front of their neighbors and vote for the Slave Power. Some of the nonvoting could have been driven by the changing nature of the state—the move to more modern ways and means. Crofts's landmark study concluded, "Mounting evidence suggests that southern partisanship pitted those who welcomed 'the social and economic changes associated with the Transportation Revolution' against those who were ambivalent about change or opposed to it—and unhappy about the use of government power to promote it."[128] The Constitutional Unionists drew their greatest strength from folks focused on modernization, a group dominated by non-slaveholders (or smallholders). Had the Constitutional Unionists gained control of the Virginia state government, as they were strongly favored to do in the upcoming election of May 1861, they could have pushed their modernization agenda forward—and that agenda, quite likely, would have focused primarily on the future expansion of Virginia's economy, an economy not based on large slave gangs.

But did the Constitutional Unionists' campaign strategy have any real impact on the electorate? Shanks compared the vote for John Letcher, the successful Democratic candidate for governor in 1859, with the Democratic vote for Breckinridge in the 1860 presidential election. Letcher was from the western part of Virginia, had espoused antislavery views (now refuted because of the John Brown raid) and was known to oppose the Slave Power and what they represented—so he was very popular in the western part of the state. On the other hand, Breckinridge was connected to the Slave

Power and favored the aristocratic planters, as the Constitutional Unionist campaign so vigorously portrayed. So what happened to the Democratic vote in Virginia in these two elections?

There were some real differences between the two outcomes in races just a year apart. In the Tidewater region, Breckinridge received 9.0 percent fewer Democratic votes than Letcher; in the Valley region, he received an astonishing 20.0 percent fewer; and in the Northwest, he received 8.0 percent fewer. In what is now West Virginia, Breckinridge received 11.3 percent fewer Democratic votes than Letcher compared to what is now Virginia, where he received just 5.6 percent fewer. Something was going on within the Democratic Party, and that something was partly the Slave Power's attempt to take over the party so that they could reassert control of the state government. It appears the Constitutional Unionists' strategy to tie the Southern Rights Democrats to the aristocratic planters did have an impact, as thousands of traditional Democratic voters turned away from Breckinridge by simply not voting.

While it certainly can be argued that all Constitutional Unionists were not opposed to slavery, it cannot be argued that they were not against the Slave Power. They opposed the Slave Power over representation in the legislature, they opposed the Slave Power over universal white man suffrage and they opposed the Slave Power over the privileged position of the slavocracy, whether on the taxation of slaves or some other long-standing benefit. Shade, in his study of the democratization of Virginia, concluded, "The conflict over secession pitted a party dominated by slaveholders against one representing men with no direct stake in the peculiar institution." Equally important, he noted that "those portions of the state that had opposed democratic reform of representation and the suffrage now advocated secession."[129] Secession was unquestionably the *sine qua non* of the Slave Power, for they saw it as the only way to maintain their position of power in a state where non-slaveholders were not merely increasing their majority but gaining political power ever so steadily.

—————

The presidential election of 1860 in Virginia concluded with Breckinridge receiving 44.6 percent of the vote versus 55.4 percent of the vote for Bell, Douglas and Lincoln (the anti–Slave Power vote). The Southern Rights Democrats, unlike in the Lower South, where Breckinridge rolled to victory after victory and where he received all of his Electoral College votes, were rebuffed for the most part in the Upper and Border South. Virginians voted against the Slave Power by a wide margin, and "for Virginia's southern extremists, the elections brought gloomy news indeed, for they indicated the ascendancy of a new Union coalition."[130] The Constitutional Unionists' campaign to portray the Slave Power for what it was produced real results.

Intriguingly, on the national level, the Constitutional Unionists narrowly lost their opportunity to have the race decided in the House of Representatives. While Abraham Lincoln won an impressive 180 Electoral College votes (27 more than he needed to win the election) by carrying the populous states of the North, his victory was very shallow. Ayres's arresting conclusion of the Republican victory is striking: "The Republicans, though, knew the fragility of this stirring victory: if one-half of 1 percent of Northern voters in crucial places had voted differently, the election would have been thrown in to the House of Representatives, where Republicans were a minority. Abraham Lincoln, who won less than 40 percent of the popular vote in the country as a whole, would not have become president."[131]

For Abraham Lincoln, the political gods had smiled twice—first at the Republican National Convention when he won the nomination by a series of events that bordered on happenstance and then in the general election when the dominant national party fractured and a new party emerged, dividing the electorate even further. Abraham Lincoln, in fact, received fewer votes in winning his election than most previous unsuccessful presidential candidates had received in losing theirs.

A mere three months later, however, as Virginians went to the polls to elect delegates to the Virginia State Convention, called by the legislature to determine Virginia's future course regarding secession, the anti–Slave Power campaign of the Constitutional Unionists produced astoundingly different results. The portent of things to come was at hand.

We now turn to the election of February 4, 1861, an election that had the most profound implications for Virginia and the nation.

CHAPTER 3
THE SEA CHANGE

I have only time in reply to your inquiry, to say that there is hope of preserving peace and the Union. All depends on the action of Virginia and the Border States. If they remain in the Union and aid in a fair and just settlement, the Union may be preserved. But if they secede under the fatal delusion of a reconstruction, I fear that all is lost. Save Virginia and we will save the Union.
—*Stephen A. Douglas, letter published in the* Staunton Spectator, *February 12, 1861*

Virginians, for the most part, were very disappointed by Lincoln's Electoral College victory. All could clearly see it was a Northern victory. Although Lincoln was a dark horse candidate at the Republican National Convention, where he unexpectedly received the party's nomination, he was favored to win the general election as a result of Republican victories in several congressional elections in Lower North states during the fall. David Donald made this insightful observation: "In the days before the election, as Republican victory seemed increasingly likely, Lincoln's basic pessimism reemerged as he began to fully realize that a campaign initially undertaken primarily for local political reasons was going to place him in the White House."[132] And into the White House he would go, politically inexperienced at the national level and virtually unknown by the vast majority of the nation's leaders—political, business, finance, whatever.

In Richmond, the Constitutional Unionists immediately began to speak about the "good news"; that is, the very marginal victory achieved by the

Republicans. They received less than 40 percent of the popular vote in the presidential election and did not gain control of either the House or the Senate. In the House, they won 108 seats to 129 for the opposition; in the Senate, they won 29 seats to 37 for the opposition. The Constitutional Unionists in Virginia began to argue that Lincoln's election was not cause for secession in part because the Congress was controlled by non-Republicans. There was certainly no mandate from this election, they claimed.

In Charleston, South Carolina, November 7 dawned cloudy and gray, in line with the mood of the city. As news spread about Lincoln's victory, the Palmetto Flag, the state's symbol, was raised over virtually all government buildings. A sitting federal judge in the city told his courtroom, "So far as I am concerned, the Temple of Justice raised under the Constitution of the United States is now closed."[133] Within hours, perhaps minutes, of confirmation of Lincoln's election, South Carolina aristocrats began the process of calling a state convention to consider secession. "As A.P. Aldrich, one of the most important South Carolina secessionists, exclaimed, 'whoever waited for the common people when a great move was to be made—We must make the move and force them to follow.'"[134] There would be no democratic processes adhered to in slavocracy-dominated South Carolina.

In the Lower South, a decided minority—in some states probably a majority—was opposed to immediate secession. The Slave Power, in characteristic style, attempted to suppress dissension by threatening opponents with mob violence or expulsion. One Lower South congressman, Alexander Stephens of Georgia, spoke passionately against the immediate secessionists. Addressing the Georgia legislature, he pleaded, "Good governments can never be built up or sustained by the impulse of passion…Let the fanatics of the North break the Constitution, if such is their fell purpose."[135] A careful, studied response was called for by the state, he pleaded.

Although chance occurrences and the disorganization of the opponents of secession contributed to the final outcome, in Slave Power–dominated South Carolina, the planters were determined to break up the Union— and to do it without delay. On November 10, the legislature passed a law calling for a state convention to meet on December 17 in Columbia, the state capital. It met on that day and passed a resolution stating, "That it is the opinion of this Convention that the State of South Carolina should forthwith secede from the Federal Union, known as the United States of America."[136] Three days later, after the convention had moved to Charleston because of an outbreak of smallpox in Columbia, the ordinance of secession was ratified 169 to 0. No debate was permitted, no dissension was tolerated. "Amid extraordinary scenes of marching bands, fireworks displays, militia calling themselves Minute Men, and huge rallies of citizens waving palmetto flags and shouting slogans of southern rights," the Union was dissolved.[137] South Carolina was gone.

Judge James Louis Pettigru, one of South Carolina's most well-known and highly respected jurists and a stout Union man, issued this prescient statement: "I tell you there is a fire; they have this day set a blazing torch to the temple of constitutional liberty, and, please God, we shall have no more peace forever."[138] Four long years later, tens of thousands of its young men lay dead; thousands of its civilians, including many slaves, lay dead; and much of the state lay in ruins. The flag-waving and slogan-shouting had ceased.

———

In Virginia, the scene was much more complex, as there would not be a 169 to 0 vote supporting secession in this state. Most of the Union newspapers in the state were dismayed by South Carolina's precipitous action. Charlestown's *Virginia Free Press* captured the mood of many in Virginia regarding South Carolina, stating that the action of that state "is beginning to excite disgust every-where, and is fast destroying the sympathy which naturally existed among Southern men."[139] Most Virginians, indeed, were genuinely dismayed by Lincoln's victory, but most felt also that it meant nothing but more debate and contention over slavery—and slaves. Slaves learned of the outcome of the election by word of mouth and began to sense a great change was in the works. Slaves began to challenge slave owners more directly, slave owners began to become more insecure about slave loyalty (slaves were accused of setting fires to barns or poisoning food, for instance) and whites generally became overly suspicious about blacks. Rumors circulated that Northern abolitionists had been dispatched to Maryland and Virginia to incite slave uprisings, the worst fear of all whites.

As a result, "soon after Lincoln's election in November 1860, a *New York Daily Times* correspondent reported that vigilance committees outside Richmond were alert to strangers. Outsiders with unclear origins or intentions could easily face mob violence."[140] Any white man found associating with slaves was subject to questioning and possible arrest. It was a scene that heightened tensions in every town and city. And it was a scene that played into the hands of the secessionists, who now organized meetings in town halls in virtually every corner of the state. In meeting after meeting, the secessionists were enthusiastically applauded when accusing the Black Republicans of promoting equality of the black and white races and of failing to protect Southern property rights by not enforcing the Fugitive Slave Law and by subverting the Constitution to benefit the North exclusively. Although these radical secessionist claims were either untrue or wildly exaggerated, they garnered real attention.

As the secessionists' appeal expanded during late November and December, the Constitutional Unionists launched a campaign based on moderation and reason. They argued that Virginia was more aligned economically to the Border North than the Cotton South, that Virginia would become the battleground if armed conflict between North and South ensued and that Virginia should exercise caution and conservatism. In addition, they positioned Virginia as the great mediator—the state that could find a common ground. They characterized the South Carolinians as "disunionists," "extremists" and, most importantly, the Slave Power. Thus positioned, the secessionist appeal began to wane, and many Virginians adopted a "wait-and-see" approach. On Thursday, December 13, 1860, "seven senators and twenty-three representatives from the South issued a manifesto which urged secession and the organization of a Southern Confederacy."[141] Virginia's Constitutional Unionists now had their "smoking gun."

Indeed, the "manifesto" put the secessionists in Virginia on the defensive as the Constitutional Unionists released a veritable barrage of attacks on those pushing a Southern Confederacy, coupling them very neatly to the Slave Power. This attack had real appeal to the non-slaveholding workingman and the rising professional class who now made up the bulk of the Unionist movement. At a mass meeting in Richmond in late December where all parties were invited, the *Richmond Inquirer* commented that "an assemblage embracing all classes of our citizens—including the sturdy laborer and the industrious mechanic, the physician, the lawyer, and the solid man of business" were present.[142] The Constitutional Unionists, now dubbed "Unionists," dominated, and their proposals of moderation were adopted despite strenuous objections from the secessionist minority.

While former Whigs, such as the highly respected John Brown Baldwin, William Cabell Rives and George W. Summers, were the centerpieces of this new "Union" party, most Douglas Democrats joined its ranks, too. In

December, Rives called for representatives from the Border North and the Border South to meet and develop compromise proposals—and to reject the now branded disunionists of the Lower South. Augusta County's leading Douglas Democrat, William H. Harman, joined with Rives, calling for "reasoned rather than mob action." "Harman favored a state convention as a way to moderate local radicalism and to restrain expression of 'extreme opinions, for or against the Union.'"[143]

But as the Unionist momentum gathered strength east of the Blue Ridge, it swept away virtually all opposition in the west. In the Southern Republican stronghold of the Panhandle, where most counties gave Lincoln a sizable vote, almost every man joined the new Unionist movement, as could be expected. It was in the Democratic stronghold counties of the Northwest region—those counties just to the south of the Panhandle where Breckinridge and the Southern Rights Democrats rolled to impressive victories in the November election—that a political sea change occurred. Lifelong Democrats—again, those who had just voted for Breckinridge in November—now deserted the Democratic Party in astounding numbers and joined the Unionist movement, the movement sponsored by and controlled by Constitutional Unionists, most of whom were former Whigs, the lifelong opponents of these Democrats. Here is the story.

In early January 1861, the Unionist movement continued to gain strength throughout the state, but it was still not clear which side, secessionist or Unionist, would prevail. Governor John Letcher, a Douglas Democrat (and Unionist), was the governor and gave his annual address to the legislature at its opening on January 7. It was a moderate statement that met with great praise in the press from west of the Blue Ridge but was roundly denounced by the press controlled by Virginia's secessionists, for Letcher called for a studied, careful approach to the sectional crisis. Secessionists soon branded him the "Tortoise Governor" for not joining in the immediate secession movement.[144] In addition, Letcher called for a national conference of all states to meet in Washington to find a workable compromise. On January 19, the national conference resolution was approved, and the legislature appointed some of its most eminent men as delegates: John Tyler, former president of the United States; William Cabell Rives, former U.S. Senator and French ambassador; John W. Brockenbrough, federal judge for western Virginia and founder of the law school at Washington College;

John Letcher, governor of Virginia in 1861, was a Unionist who bitterly opposed former governor Wise and his radical Southern Rights followers. *Courtesy of the Library of Virginia.*

George W. Summers, former U.S. congressman, gubernatorial candidate and state judge; and James A. Seddon, Richmond lawyer, former U.S. congressman and soon-to-be secretary of war in the Confederate government. The national conference would convene in Washington and become known as the Peace Conference.

Great excitement ruled the hour in Richmond as the legislators gathered that January. Since their defeat in the November election, radical secessionists had tightened control over the Democratic Party. At first, it appeared the secessionists had the upper hand. Sandy Stuart, the staunch Unionist from Augusta County, stated, "Madness rules the hour. You can hardly imagine the extent of the insanity. I have scarcely a ray of hope left."[145] But Stuart misjudged the moment, for many legislators from western Virginia were still arriving—and these were the men who opposed secession most strongly and who commanded a majority in the lower House.

As the legislative session settled into its routine, it became clear that the Democratic Party was becoming more and more deeply divided as moderates resisted the overtures of the radical secessionists. Three long-standing Democratic congressmen broke with the party and openly opposed secession. Congressman Sherrard Clemens (his first cousin was Sam Clements, i.e. Mark Twain) from the Panhandle was first to break, driven by his constituents' fierce opposition to secession. He stated that if he had to be a disunionist to be a Democrat, then he was no longer a Democrat. Clemens's departure could be expected, but when Congressmen John T. Harris from the Shenandoah Valley and John Millson from Norfolk bolted the party to join the Unionists, it portended real trouble for the Democrats.

The legislature approved calling a state convention to consider secession, which was a defeat for the Unionists, but otherwise the Unionists scored two major victories. First, the legislature approved apportioning delegates to the just-called state convention on the "white basis" as the lower house of the legislature was proportioned, and that gave the Unionists great hope because western Virginians would dominate. Secondly, the legislature gave voters the right to approve or disapprove the action of the convention by popular referendum, an action the secessionists opposed with all their might, for it was "too democratic" for their taste (and they knew they would lose).

The legislature then scheduled election day for delegates and for the referendum initiative on Monday, February 4. The Unionists and secessionists immediately launched aggressive campaigns to sway voters to their respective positions. Despite winter weather and a hastily called election, the two sides went at it with true gusto. Both sides drew men of real distinction to their camps. "The men who traveled throughout Augusta [County] in the cold of late January 1861, putting themselves before the people and debating the future of the county, state, and maybe nation, fitted the profile of what leading men of Augusta—and Virginia and the South—looked like: lawyers, slaveholders, members of prominent families, wealthy and well connected."[146] The five candidates from Augusta County traveled as a group and spoke to large and intensely interested crowds every day except Sunday throughout the short campaign. John Baldwin was the most outspoken Unionist, condemning the "absurd demands of hot-headed agitators [abolitionists and secessionists]."[147]

The press naturally bent to their task, and sharp divisions in the pro- and anti-secession papers developed rapidly. Large and important Augusta County provides a relevant example. The leading Democratic paper, the *Staunton Vindicator*, proclaimed, "It will not do to sing paeans to the Union and the stars and stripes when waves of revolution and disunion are surging all around us." The leading Unionist paper, the *Staunton Spectator*, countered with the choice of "whether we will remain in the Union which has made us a great, free and happy people or fall into secession and thus into the bogs of anarchy and the bloody quagmire of civil war." Every paper in the state had an opinion—and none proved shy in expressing it.

The early election date seemed to favor the secessionists, who now urged immediate secession as the only way left for Virginia. The Virginia congressional delegation, controlled by the Southern Rights Democrats, put its weight behind the secessionist candidates, "declaring that Congress would not enact a suitable compromise, and strongly implying that the Union could be reconstructed only if Virginia seceded quickly."[148]Additionally, it put its weight against the popular referendum that was now part of the legislature's convention bill, bitterly denouncing it as "stupid." The Slave Power had money (lots of it), political clout (lots of it) and a long-standing tradition of winning statewide elections (lots of them). Many Virginians thought they would win handily.

But the Unionists parried the secessionist thrusts by circulating a letter, dated January 31, 1861, from Stephen Douglas that suggested a fair and just settlement was possible. The letter received wide circulation and was written to a Virginia gentleman from Petersburg. Douglas proclaimed, "I have only time in reply to your inquiry, to say that there is hope of preserving peace and the Union. All depends on the action of Virginia and the Border States. If they remain in the Union and aid in a fair and just settlement, the Union may be preserved. But if they secede under the fatal delusion of a reconstruction, I fear that all is lost. Save Virginia and we will save the Union."[149] The letter had great appeal to those favoring the Union.

John J. Crittenden likewise counseled that patience would be justly rewarded. He promoted his Crittenden Compromise throughout the month, and it was warmly received by the Union men of Virginia. William Henry Seward, Lincoln's secretary of state-designate, began to reach out to Virginia Unionists with ideas for a settlement. On January 12, Seward delivered a powerful speech in the Senate. Some contemporaries said it was the most important speech ever delivered to the Congress, and it packed the Senate chamber with over two thousand spectators that included virtually all the movers and shakers of Washington. "As Seward rose to speak, the chamber turned deathly quiet and all strained to hear every word…He insisted that saving the Union was paramount, 'Republicanism is subordinate to Union, as everything else is and ought to be'…and concluded 'Still my faith in the Constitution and in the Union abides, because my faith in the wisdom and virtue of the American people remains unshaken.'"[150]

Henry Adams, whose father, Charles Francis Adams, led the conciliatory Republicans in the House and was a close ally of Seward, was an eyewitness to the stirring speech. He recorded this observation: "The effect of the speech was instantaneous. From that day the rumors began to subside; the Union men in the South took new courage; public confidence began to re-establish itself, the country breathed more freely and hope rapidly rose. Letters poured in on him from the South, and he received as many from Virginia alone, as he did from his own State."[151] Douglas's letter, Crittenden's compromise proposal and Seward's words resonated with Virginians and had a marked impact on the electorate. The immediate secessionist momentum in the campaign began to weaken.

In northwestern Virginia, where there were so few slaves and even fewer large slaveholders, a game-changing awakening seemed to be occurring, driven by a tide of anti-secessionism. It developed so rapidly and was so deep rooted that the *Wellsburg Herald* predicted "a breakup of the state if Virginia adopted an ordinance of secession." Most importantly, the *Herald* proclaimed that the Slave Power—and their obsession with protecting slavery at all costs—was what was driving this anti-secession phenomena for northwesterners. These non-slaveholders "had no more real interest in the institution of slavery in any part of Virginia than they had with slavery in Brazil," it proclaimed.[152]

In addition, the calling of the Peace Conference turned out to be of great benefit to the Unionists. The Washington meeting not only raised hopes throughout the state that a Union-saving compromise was now possible, but it also put the secessionists in a compromised position. "The Unionists who devised the idea of a Peace Conference thus laid a clever and effective trap for secessionists, who found themselves in the awkward position of asserting the state's peacemaking efforts were futile" even before they began.[153] So momentum continued to build for the Unionist coalition.

During the last few days of January, the Unionists, now sensing a possible victory, unleashed their most virulent attack on the Southern Rights Democrats, expounding the message that the Democrats were the Slave Power and were the disunionists. As the "moderate Breckinridge men, especially those from the West" became disenchanted with the overwhelming spirit of disunionism in the party, the Unionists reached out to them in politically astute ways, the most astute being to do away with old party labels—Constitutional Unionist, Southern Rights Democrat, Whig, American, Opposition, whatever. They suggested that all previous labels be abandoned and that a new label, "Union," be adopted. This new Union Party, then, attracted virtually all Constitutional Unionists, virtually all Douglas Democrats and, most significantly, a group of moderate Breckinridge men as well. Suddenly, the Union Party's numbers began to mount substantially.

Sensing a rising wave of opposition to their position, the secessionists launched a final counter-offensive just days before the election. Led by Virginia's two U.S. Senators, R.M.T. Hunter and James Mason, plus eight of the twelve congressmen from the state, they put their reputations and political future on the line by issuing a statement on January 26 endorsing all of the Southern Rights candidates to the state convention and condemning the popular referendum initiative as inexpedient. While some historians view Hunter as a moderate, his "moderation" was a smokescreen at this time, as he was "adamantly opposed to federal union in which the South was not dominant." As a representative of the Southern Rights Democrats, he "sought special privileges, not equal rights, for the slaveholding section."[154] Following the issuance of the statement, a great meeting was held in Richmond on January 28 at the African Church, where all parties were invited. While in a slight majority at this meeting, the Democrats succeeded in nominating three secessionist candidates for the state convention, but the meeting was so raucous that it ended in a fistfight between secessionists and Unionists.

While many slaveholders responded with enthusiasm to this statement from Virginia's congressional delegation, the great bulk of non-slaveholders did not. James B. Dorman wrote to Governor Letcher from Lexington, "The people here are thoroughly Union in feeling. They will not follow the lead of South Carolina, but will struggle honestly and with determined purpose for the continuance of the confederacy [the United States]."[155] In Southampton County, "to a greater extent than usual, slaveholders and non-slaveholders voted on opposite sides, the latter opposing secession," and it "was accompanied by a record polarization between slaveholders and non-slaveholders."[156] So even in this southern Virginia county, in the heart of the Tidewater region, the non-slaveholders were striking out on a more anti–Slave Power path. It was a vote driven by class resentment, by the rapidly rising egalitarian nature of the Union Party and by the underlying theme that "plain country people" were not about to fight to "protect rich men's negroes."[157]

Also of note, this election was not "rigged" to favor the aristocrats, as no region was given more than its fair share of votes, the number of delegates now based on the total white population in each county. Tarter observed, "The election of 4 February 1861 was the first statewide election of a constituent assembly in which the members might have reasonably well represented the opinions of the whole white male population of Virginia."[158]

Election Day, February 4, was a day to remember for Virginians of all stripes. In Richmond, the day began with a snow shower, but the skies had cleared by midafternoon. Voters turned out in large numbers despite the adverse weather, and as usual, liquor flowed freely. "Intense excitement prevailed to a greater extent, according to the *Dispatch*, than 'any election within our memory,' as sporadic fistfights broke out across the city."[159] The city, the state and indeed the nation were all tuned in. While winter weather curtailed voter turnout in some parts of the Commonwealth, all in all, voter participation was fairly good.

A review of the election results of February 1861 follows. The review is in three parts: first, a look at the election of Union versus Secession delegates to the Virginia State Convention; second, an examination of the votes "for" or "against" requiring the electorate to approve or disapprove the passage of a secession ordinance; and third, a comparison of the votes for Breckinridge (the Southern Rights Democrat) in the 1860 presidential election with the votes for or against the referendum in the 1861 election.

DELEGATES TO THE CONVENTION BY REGION[160]

REGION	UNIONIST (%)	SECESSIONIST (%)
Northwest	28 (90%)	3 (10%)
Southwest	14 (56%)	11 (44%)
Valley	22 (85%)	4 (15%)
Piedmont	14 (39%)	22 (61%)
Tidewater	16 (50%)	15 (50%)
Total	94 (63%)	55 (37%)

As illustrated, only in the Piedmont region, with the largest number of "black belt" counties in the state (sixteen)—a black belt county being defined as a county where over 50 percent of the population was enslaved—did the secessionists win a majority of delegates. Even in the Tidewater region, dominated by the "old Virginia aristocrats" and with a large slave population, the secessionists could win only 50 percent of the delegates. In the Valley region, long dominated by the Opposition and where slaveholding was more modest, the Unionists won by a huge majority, selecting 85 percent Union men, nearly matching the Northwest. In the Northwest region, the Unionists carried every single county by a large majority, sending 90 percent of their men to the convention as Unionists (and it should have been 100 percent, as will be discussed below). Drawing conclusions from the delegate election is complicated because of the "human factor." A popular or well-known man could be elected from a county who, for personal reasons, did not represent the views of a majority of his respective county voters. Two clear examples of delegates not representing their constituents are cited from the Northwest region.[161]

In Wetzel County, located just below the Panhandle counties, 99 percent voted for the Unionists, yet their county representative, Leonard Hall (who was the commonwealth's attorney for the county), was an out-an-out secessionist. Hall never wavered in his support of the secession movement and consistently voted against the best wishes of his constituents. In fact, he was so appreciated by Richmond secessionists that they gave him an award for standing up against the folks in his county. During the war, when Wetzel County became a part of the new state of West Virginia, Hall continued to represent the county in the Confederate Virginia Legislature, which did not recognize the new state. He died at the relatively young age of fifty-one in 1875.

The same can be said of Sam Woods, a Canadian who had moved to Barbour County to practice law before the war. Barbour County, located close to the Valley region in the eastern part of the Northwest, voted 90 percent for the Unionist cause, yet Woods, a popular lawyer in Philippi, one of the largest towns in the county, was an ardent secessionist, too. He voted for the Ordinance of Secession on both April 4 and April 17, against the clear and unmistakable wishes of his constituents, and went on to serve as an officer in the famous Stonewall Brigade in Lee's Army of Northern Virginia. Interestingly, after the war, he returned to Barbour County, where his constituents evidently forgave him for his secessionist stance, and was elected a member of the West Virginia Constitutional Convention of 1872. Woods had a long and highly successful life, ending his career as a judge on the West Virginia Supreme Court of Appeals. He died in 1897, some thirty-two years after the war ended.

While Hall and Woods were clearly anomalies in the Northwest region, it should be noted that, for the most part, delegates did represent their constituents in a fair and reasonable way. As an example, from large and populous Augusta County, which was entitled to three delegates and where 93 percent voted for the Unionist ticket, all three delegates were strong Unionists. "The three most fervent Union candidates won in a landslide in Augusta. Stuart, Baldwin and Baylor each took more than 3,000 votes; Imboden and Harman won only a few hundred each."[162] In some counties where the vote was evenly divided—Fauquier County in the Piedmont region, for instance—anomalies occurred as well, as both of its delegates were Unionist even though the Unionists outpolled the secessionists by a mere thirty-three votes out of over one thousand cast. But this was the exception rather than the rule.

To repeat for emphasis, the short but intensely fought campaign of late January 1861 turned out to be a tremendous victory for the political moderates of Virginia, represented by the Unionists. They carried three regions of the state handily; evenly matched the secessionists in what should have been a secession stronghold, the Tidewater region; and lost only the heavily slave-populated Piedmont region. In the Northwest, a watershed event had occurred, which will be analyzed below. For the Slave Power, though, the delegate election was a bitter loss. Potter observed, "During December and early January, secessionists had kept up a vigorous activity and had developed appreciable strength in Virginia…[but] when the votes were counted, the secessionists had incurred a stunning defeat."[163] That stunning defeat was felt not just in Virginia but throughout the entire country, especially in the Lower South. "Observers in the seven states that had already seceded glumly interpreted the vote as a rebuke to the Cotton South."[164] The Slave Power, and their highly organized and heavily funded campaign, had been trumped by non-slaveholders. Given these results, there should have been no "rich man's war, poor man's fight" in Virginia.

***

We now turn to an analysis of the vote for or against the referendum. As mentioned earlier, a "for" vote means a secession ordinance, if approved by the convention, would require the electorate to vote to approve or disapprove, while an "against" vote would mean it would *not* be put before the electorate. The Southern Rights Democratic Party called for a vote against the referendum in the strongest possible terms—the referendum must be defeated at all costs became their mantra. But here again, the non-slaveholders rose to the moment and defeated the Slave Power overwhelmingly. The vote on the referendum is as follows.

REFERENDUM VOTE BY REGION[165]

REGION	FOR (%)	AGAINST (%)
Northwest	34,343 (94%)	2,248 (6%)
Southwest	13,593 (68%)	6,397 (32%)
Valley	20,706 (81%)	4,852(19%)
Piedmont	16,194 (50%)	16,386 (50%)
Tidewater	15,700 (51%)	15, 278 (49%)
Total	100,536 (69%)	45,161 (31%)

The referendum vote can be considered a more "pure" indication of how Virginians felt—support for or against the Slave Power—for the local personality, the "human factor" found in the delegate selection process, was taken out of the equation. As noted in the prior analyses, in a few cases, a very popular man was elected to be a delegate to the convention and may or may not have represented the views of his county's citizens, for or against secession. The referendum vote was positioned by both parties as straight up or down—a Unionist vote was "for" referendum, while a secessionist vote was "against" referendum.

In the Northwest region, the vote was simply astounding. Not a single Democratic county stayed loyal to the party. Every county in the region gave the Unionist a lopsided victory, with the secessionists barely able to garner 6 percent of the vote overall, with some counties giving them as little as 1 percent. In previously Democratic strongholds of the region—Preston, Monongalia, Wetzel, Tyler, Doddridge and Ritchie Counties, to name just a few—the upland Democrats, now turned Unionists, totally obliterated the Southern Rights Democratic Party. Fed up with the Slave Power, with their defend-slavery-at-all-costs mantra, the non-slaveholders of the region stood up to challenge the slavocracy and voted overwhelmingly for the referendum. This "sea change" will be analyzed in more detail below.

In the Southwest region, 68 percent of the votes were for the referendum, with all but four of the twenty-five counties giving them a majority. Greenbrier, Fayette, Boone, Raleigh, Mercer and Monroe Counties, in the northern part of the region, gave the referendum over 80 percent of the vote, with large and heavily populated Greenbrier County giving it over 90 percent. Only the four counties in the southern part of the region along or near the North Carolina border—Carroll, Grayson, Smyth and Tazewell—voted against the referendum.

Parenthetically, of the twenty-five delegates the region sent to the convention, only 56 percent were Unionist (fourteen Unionists versus eleven secessionists). As it turned out, the Southwest region was more divided than the Northwest, and when the moment of truth came on April 17, most of the Unionist delegates joined with the secessionists and voted to leave the Union after Lincoln's call for troops. Shanks concluded, "The delegates from the southwest were almost as unanimous for secession as those from east of the Blue Ridge. The valleys there were fertile, slaves were numerous, the plantation system prevailed, and the Southern Methodists were strong."[166] Shanks might be correct in stating that the valleys were fertile and the Southern Methodists strong, but he does not seem to be correct about numerous slaves and the plantation system, as sixteen of the twenty-five counties had less than 10 percent slaves, the other nine had less than 30 percent. The plantation system was not as prevalent, for the vast majority of white men living there were small, non-slaveholding farmers.

In the Valley region, long a Whig or Opposition stronghold, the referendum received a full 80 percent of the vote, with Augusta County, the most populous in the region, giving it a monstrous 93 percent. The Valley region was much more heavily populated with slaves than the Southwest, with twelve of the eighteen counties having 10 to 30 percent slaves and two counties with 30 to 50 percent. The two small counties with a high concentration of slaves, Clarke and Roanoke, characteristically gave the secessionists the highest percentage of votes in the region. (As an aside, the Valley region was so strongly pro-Union that twenty-two of the twenty-six delegates from the region were Unionist, almost matching the count from the Northwest region. The Valley region was Unionist through and through, and after the war began, many joined the Confederacy with great misgivings. The Lincoln administration had only to reach out to these staunchly Union men in a small way to keep them loyal.)

The Piedmont region, with thirty-two counties, and the Tidewater region, with thirty-nine, were the regions with the highest concentration of slaves in the state—and thus the regions most dominated by the plantation system. They should have been controlled by the Southern Rights Democrats because secession sentiment was strongest in counties with high concentrations of slaves. They should have carried these counties against the referendum. But surprisingly, in both regions, the vote for or against the referendum was split almost evenly.

The central/southern part of the Piedmont region was home to the great black belt of Virginia. Eight counties—Brunswick, Mecklenburg, Lunenburg, Charlotte, Prince Edward, Cumberland, Powhatan and Louisa—held more than 60 percent slaves. All eight counties voted against the referendum, with Lunenburg County leading the way. The Piedmont region sent the largest number (and largest percentage) of secessionist delegates to the convention, twenty-two, or 61 percent. Again, black belts and a vote against the referendum went hand in hand.

In the Tidewater region, although heavily populated with slaves, the Whig Party had been very strong during its heyday, and the Opposition was still strong. They lobbied hard for the referendum, and the region narrowly voted in favor. Counties with large towns and the large cities themselves (the more cosmopolitan centers of the state) gave the referendum its greatest support. Alexandria County, Norfolk County and the large cities of Norfolk, Richmond and Petersburg all voted for the referendum. In the central part of the region, a grouping of counties with high slave populations—Caroline, Essex, King and Queen, King William, Hanover, New Kent and Gloucester—voted against the referendum.

Two concluding comments regarding the analysis of the referendum vote are axiomatic. First, as with the delegate election, the Slave Power suffered a staggering loss. "A Charleston, South Carolina paper bemoaned the fact that the Old Dominion 'would never secede now, and even though the convention should pass an ordinance of secession the people would vote it down.'"[167] Most political moderates in the country, North or South, viewed the results as a strong repudiation of the secession movement. Second, the Unionists achieved a momentous victory that even surmounted their wildest dreams. "The success of the friends of the Union, has really astonished us all…The Gulf Confederacy can count Virginia out of their little family arrangement—she will never join them," observed a prominent Virginian.[168] Indeed, the margin of victory was historic.

When the final vote was counted, fully 69 percent of Virginians rejected the position of the Southern Rights Democratic Party and voted for the referendum. Usually an election is considered a "landslide" when a party wins by a 10 percent spread or more, 55 percent to 45 percent being a landslide. A result of 69 percent to 31 percent almost defies description—it is a margin rarely seen in any type of free election. As a consequence of Virginia's vote, Unionism in the Upper South states of North Carolina, Tennessee and Arkansas, as well as the Border South states of Maryland, Kentucky and Missouri, soared. Moderate Northerners, even some in the Republican Party, were greatly heartened by the vote, and the moderate Northern press renewed its call for an accommodation with these true Union men of the South.

A fundamental political realignment had occurred in Virginia, where anti-secession Democrats had joined with the Constitutional Unionists to form a new political entity, quickly dubbed the "Union Party" by the press. This new party was, in fact, dedicated to keeping the Union intact, but even more so, it was dedicated to opposing the Slave Power. William Henry Seward, the new secretary of state, was the first national politician to see the implications of this movement. "Seward and Weed, now realizing this new development had true appeal—where economic differences, geographic differences, and slave owning differences were merging to create a sea change—sought ways to exploit it."[169]

Finally, an analysis of the referendum vote of February 1861 with the vote for Breckinridge in the 1860 presidential election.[170]

REGION	NOVEMBER 1860 PRO–SLAVE POWER	NOVEMBER 1860 ANTI–SLAVE POWER	FEBRUARY 1861 PRO–SLAVE POWER	FEBRUARY 1861 ANTI–SLAVE POWER
Northwest	47%	53%	6%	94%
Southwest	51%	49%	32%	68%
Valley	38%	62%	19%	81%
Piedmont	48%	52%	50%	50%
Tidewater	41%	59%	49%	51%

The percentages in this table are defined as follows. The November 1860 Pro–Slave Power vote is the vote for Breckinridge and the Southern Rights Democratic Party; the Anti–Slave Power vote in that election is the vote for all other parties (Constitutional Unionist, Northern Democrat and Republican). The February 1861 Pro–Slave Power vote is the vote against the referendum (as championed by the Southern Rights Democratic Party), while the Anti–Slave Power vote is a vote for the referendum (as championed by the rising Union Party).

As illustrated, the most dramatic shift in the Pro–Slave Power vote occurred in the Northwest region, where only 6 percent of the men voting supported the Slave Power in February 1861 as opposed to the 47 percent who had supported them in November 1860. In the Southwest and Valley regions, the Slave Power lost substantially also, with decreases in support of 19 percent in both regions between November and February. Only in the Piedmont and Tidewater regions, again with their large black belts and dominance of the plantation system, did the Slave Power vote hold up. It is important to note that even in these two Slave Power–dominated regions, fully one-half of the voters failed to support them in the referendum vote. Across the state, the Slave Power suffered a staggering loss by any statistical comparison.

A second chart looks at the number of votes, rather than percentages, for and against the Slave Power in the same two elections. This comparison produces even more pronounced results.[171]

REGION	NOVEMBER 1860 PRO–SLAVE POWER	FEBRUARY 1861 PRO–SLAVE POWER	DIFFERENCE	FEBRUARY 1861 ANTI–SLAVE POWER
Northwest	17,425	2,248	15,177	34,343
Southwest	10,456	6,397	4,059	13,593
Valley	11,318	4,852	6,466	20,706
Piedmont	19,891	16,386	3,505	16,194
Tidewater	15,233	15,278	(45)	15,700
Total	74,323	45,161 (31%)	29,162	100,536 (69%)

The numbers in this table are defined as follows. The November 1860 Pro–Slave Power vote is the vote for Breckinridge and the Southern Rights Democratic Party; the February 1861 Pro–Slave Power vote is the vote against the referendum (the position of the Slave Power as noted above), the Difference indicates the loss of Slave Power support in each region, and the February 1861 Anti–Slave Power vote is the vote for the referendum (the position of the new Union Party as noted above).

While the first chart illustrating the percentages is indeed dramatic, the actual numbers presented in the second chart (above) are truly stunning. The Slave Power lost votes in four out of five regions between the November 1860 presidential election and the February 1861 referendum vote, while the difference in the Tidewater region is insignificant. In spite of an intensely fought campaign, with a party organization basically intact and with huge sums of money invested, the Slave Power could not sway voters to support their "no referendum" appeal. Only 31 percent of Virginians bought their argument, while 69 percent rejected it. Virginians just said NO to the Slave Power.

In the Northwest region, support for the Slave Power disappeared almost completely. In the traditional Democratic-stronghold counties of the upper Northwest—Preston, Monongalia, Marion, Wetzel, Tyler, Doddridge, Ritchie, Wirt, Calhoun, Gilmer, Lewis, Upshur, Barbour and Tucker—where Breckinridge received over 60 percent of the vote in November 1860, just three months later, the Democratic party line vote was totally gone with less than 6 percent staying loyal to the party. In highly populated Wetzel, Monongalia and Preston Counties, over 99 percent of the voters said NO to the Slave Power. Wetzel County provides the most striking example of the total collapse of the Southern Rights Democratic Party in the Northwest. There, Breckinridge received 72 percent of the vote in the presidential election (607 votes out of 850 cast), but in the February election, only 7 voters followed the party line, while 937 rejected it. Crofts concluded from his multiple regression that "an antisecession surge in low-slaveowning regions in February 1861 disrupted patterns of party loyalty that had endured for a generation."[172] In the Northwest region of Virginia, it is fair to say the voting patterns were destroyed in the February election.

The fifty counties that would secede from Virginia and form the state of West Virginia in 1863 included all of the counties in the Northwest region, nine counties in the Southwest region and six counties in the Valley region. In these fifty counties, the vote against the Slave Power was 45,819 to 3,706, as fully 92.5 percent of the men voted against the Slave Power. Link concluded correctly, "The largest concentration of unconditional Unionists existed in the northwestern counties. Residents there believed in the motto 'Union first, Union last, Union forever.'"[173] It is little wonder, then, that the white men of the Northwest moved to form a new state.

Many historians have analyzed the results of the Virginia elections of 1860 and 1861 from many different perspectives and thus have produced different conclusions—the old adage that there are "statistics, damn statistics and lies" comes into play. Crofts produced the most thorough analysis of Virginia voting patterns ever but cautioned that "multiple regression alone has the potential to mislead."[174] In an effort not to mislead, the central conclusion of the votes analyzed above follows.

How the delegates voted on April 4 and April 17, for or against the Ordinances of Secession, was driven in large part by external developments, in particular by Abraham Lincoln's Proclamation of Insurrection, as will be analyzed in the chapters that follow. Men did change their minds over time, and as a result, some conclude that the Unionists' strength was not as strong as originally thought.[175] However, the election on the referendum—where changing opinions of individual delegates were not involved—the electorate, as a whole, spoke loud and clear. There was no conditional vote—a vote against the referendum was a vote for the Slave Power, while a vote for the referendum was a vote against the Slave Power. There is no question how the two sides positioned the vote. No one misunderstood what the vote stood for, and the result was unquestionably one-sided—a stunning defeat for the Slave Power. Potter called it a "smashing blow" to the secessionists.[176] Edward Ayres, a leader of Virginia's Civil War historians, observed, "The secessionists of the old plantation regions of the east had been handed a defeat they could barely stomach."[177] A newspaper editor in southwestern Virginia announced, "The immediate secession candidates have been badly whipped—in fact almost annihilated…"[178] However one chooses to describe it, the referendum election was a watershed event—a "sea change." Never in any election in the history of Virginia had such an overwhelmingly lopsided result been recorded. Non-slaveholding Virginians simply rejected the Slave Power and in so doing opened the door to solving the secession crisis by keeping Virginia in the Union.

Gabor Boritt, longtime head of the Gettysburg Civil War Institute, observed, "It is too easy for historians to merely ratify the past and suggest what happened had to happen."[179] Given the "sea change" analyzed above, could the Unionists of Virginia have sustained their vote against secession had they been engaged by more enlightened political leadership in the nation's capital?

CHAPTER 4
FEBRUARY, A TIME FOR HOPE

Gentlemen, the eyes of the whole country are turned to this assembly in expectation and hope. I trust that you may prove yourselves worthy of the great occasion.
—John Tyler, president of the Peace Conference and former president of the United States

February 4, 1861, was a cold and blustery day in the nation's capital. But it was also a day for sunny optimism, as delegates to the Peace Conference began to assemble in Willard Hotel's Dance Hall, the grand ballroom in downtown Washington donated for use of the conference by the prominent Willard brothers. The conference had been called by the legislature of Virginia to propose constitutional amendments and other remedies to solve the national crisis. Other states responded to the call of Virginia because it was the most populous, wealthiest and historically important state in the South. Seven states in the Deep South had seceded from the Union and were busily forming a new government. President-elect Lincoln was due to arrive in Washington by the end of the month, his inauguration scheduled for Monday, March 4. President Buchanan seemed confused—his cabinet was shattered by partisan wrangling, his efforts to blame the crisis on both North and South made him few friends and his policy of abandoning Federal properties in all of the seceded states outraged many in the North, especially the Radical Republicans. Both the House and the Senate had failed to produce any remedies from their respective committees appointed to find such.

The conference was called to order at noon by Charles S. Morehead, former governor of Kentucky, who proposed that the distinguished Judge John C. Wright of Ohio be made temporary chairman. Wright was approved unanimously and proceeded to address the assembly: "We have come together to secure a common and at the same time a most important object—to agree if we can upon some plan for adjusting the unhappy differences which distract the country."[180] Wright, almost blind and just shy of his eightieth birthday, would die just nine days later, on February 13. His death would not only bring accolades from all present but would also spur delegates to action. Ominously for the success of the convention, the Radical Republican Salmon Chase convinced Ohio governor Dennison to replace the moderate Wright with a militant hard-liner, Christopher P. Wolcott.

Delegates from eleven states—New Hampshire, Rhode Island, New Jersey, Pennsylvania, Delaware, Maryland, Virginia, North Carolina, Kentucky, Ohio and Indiana—were present at the opening. Ten additional states—Vermont, Maine, Massachusetts, Connecticut, New York, Tennessee, Missouri, Illinois, Iowa and Kansas—would send delegates over the next few days (except for Kansas, whose delegates would not arrive for weeks). After substantial intrastate debate, four states chose not to send delegates (Michigan, Wisconsin and Minnesota bowed to Radical Republican demands and Arkansas to secessionist demands), and two others (California and Oregon) chose not to send delegates because they were just too far away from Washington. Of course, the seven states of the Deep South that had seceded were not present.

"Eventually, 132 delegates from twenty-one states arrived to take their seats at the conference. Some owed their appointments to their respective governors and others to their legislatures, but all held official credentials duly

John Tyler, tenth president of the United States, became the permanent president of the Peace Conference held in Washington during February 1861. *Courtesy of the Library of Virginia.*

certified by administrative authorities in the several states. It was a distinguished group."[181] In all likelihood, no group of such credentialed people had come together in the nation since the Continental Congress of 1787. John Tyler of Virginia, former president of the United States, would become permanent president of the convention, which included a half dozen former cabinet members, nineteen former governors, eleven former U.S. senators, fifty former congressmen, five former ambassadors, ten circuit court judges and twelve state supreme court justices.[182] If a constitutional amendment was to be proposed, this was certainly the group that could do it.

Most of the 132 delegates could be called political moderates (and indeed many were former Whigs), and they were ably led. Among the notable moderate leaders were the distinguished Maryland lawyer Reverdy Johnson; former Kentucky senator James Guthrie; Kentucky's highly regarded Whig statesman, Charles A. Wickliffe; former Virginia congressman and state judge George Summers; Virginia's elder statesmen, former ambassador and former cabinet minister William Rives; New York businessman William Dodge; Missouri war hero Alexander Doniphan; and North Carolina's great jurist Thomas Ruffin. As the *Cincinnati Enquirer* proclaimed on February 13, "among conservative men, the Convention [is] the hope of the country."[183]

However, several Northern states sent hard-line "ultras" as delegates, and as it turned out, they were present in sufficient numbers to cause real problems. The ultras were mainly those formerly associated with the Liberty or Free-Soil Parties and were vehemently opposed to any compromise with the South—and tragically, when it suited their purposes, they would lump all Southerners together and brand them as members of the Slave Power. A prominent leader of the Northern ultras was none other than former Ohio governor Salmon Chase, who would shortly become secretary of the treasury in the Lincoln administration. For years, he had viciously attacked slave owners in particular and Southerners in general, and he had not a tiny bit of compromise spirit in his heart. He was determined to defeat the Slave Power and break their dominance of the Federal government, and to him, that meant defeating any compromise proposal at this conference, even one supported by Southern moderates.

While the Slave Power was not represented in any strength, a few ultras from the South were present also. One of the most prominent Southern ultras was Virginia's own James A. Seddon. From Stafford County, in the black belt of the Tidewater region, Seddon had been a Democratic congressman from Richmond and was a strong Southern Rights advocate. He saw no way to work with the Republican extremists and, typical of the Southern Rights advocates, branded all Republicans as radicals. Actually, his heart was with the new Southern Confederacy, for which he would be appointed secretary of war by Jefferson Davis in a few weeks. Both Chase and Seddon (and their followers) were opposed to the very nature of the Peace Conference.

The hard-line Northern press, led by Horace Greeley, editor of the *New York Tribune*, took every opportunity to castigate the conference and its members. He called them "political fossils" and claimed they were out of touch with the country and could never be trusted with devising a plan of action. The hard-line Southern press, led by the *Charleston Mercury* and its editor, fire-eater Robert Barnwell Rhett, was equally obnoxious. They demanded the Peace Conference be "smashed up" and that Virginia secede immediately. Sadly for the work of the conference, the ultras and the hard-line press, both North and South, wanted nothing else than for all compromise efforts to fail.

But at this point in time, political moderates still were in the majority throughout the country, and the Peace Conference was hailed by most Americans as a truly great event.

The Peace Conference met every day but Sunday for the balance of February. The moderates held the balance of power, and some progress was made. Many important speeches by important people took place, and the delegates gradually began to coalesce around a set of articles that they hoped could be placed in a constitutional amendment that could be presented to the House and the Senate for consideration. The press reported steady progress with many leading political moderates in the country holding out real hope.

Of importance at this point in time, William Henry Seward, secretary of state-designate, had become the leader of the moderate Republican forces in Washington and was beginning to push for compromise. "By early February Seward had come full circle from his thinking in early December and now felt saving the Union was of ultimate importance. If a compromise on slavery extension had to be made, so be it."[184] Seward met with James Barbour, George Summers and others to establish contact with Virginia Unionists and to promote the activities of the pro-compromisers in the Peace Conference. The new Union coalition in Virginia, the rising Union Party, held great promise for leading the nation toward compromise. Barbour, an astute politician, had written to Seward about the new coalition, "You may lose a portion of your own party North. But you place yourself and the new administration at the head of a national conservative party which will domineer over all party organizations North and South yet many years to come."[185]

By mid-February, Seward's compromise policy and his now unending preaching of "we must save the Union" was resonating with Upper and Border South Unionists, whose political beliefs were nicely aligned with Seward's policy. Virginians had elected a Unionist-dominated convention, and the entire Upper South had swung decidedly against the secessionists. On February 9, "Tennessee voters decided not even to call a convention [to consider secession]. Two days later the Kentucky legislature adjourned without calling one, and a week after that Arkansas

William Henry Seward as he began his second term in the U.S. Senate. He would lead the pro-compromise forces in the Republican Party and developed a plan to divide the South. *Seward House, Auburn, New York.*

and Missouri voters elected unionist-dominated conventions. The wave of secession that had swept away the cotton states had broken against large unionist majorities in the Upper South."[186] Seward now saw a real chance to solve the national crisis by dividing the South. Henry Adams reported in his diary that Seward had said, "The storm is weathered."[187]

———

As the Peace Conference was working toward approving articles for an amendment, on February 23, a number of Peace Conference delegates met with President-elect Lincoln in his suite at the Willard Hotel. Rives, the most distinguished of the group, was acknowledged by Lincoln and led off the discussion by commenting on his crusade to save the Union, ending with, "I can do little—you can do much. Everything now depends on you." Lincoln replied, "I cannot agree to that. My course is as plain as a turnpike road. It is marked out by the Constitution. I am in no doubt which way to go.

Suppose now we all stop discussing and try the experiment of obedience to the Constitution and the laws."[188] Many Southerners viewed Lincoln's remarks as warlike and, led by hard-liner James Seddon, began a heated exchange with him regarding the need for compromise. Later, Lincoln made it known he would not endorse the Peace Conference Amendment, so the delegates decided to move ahead with their plan to submit the amendment to the Congress.

The Peace Conference ended with an amendment that consisted of seven articles:

Article 1 reestablished the Missouri Compromise Line.

Article 2 provided that no new territory could be acquired without a majority of senators from the slave states and free states approving.

Article 3 forbid Congress from interfering with slavery within any state.

Article 4 provided for strict enforcement of the Fugitive Slave Law.

Article 5 prohibited the foreign slave trade forever.

Article 6 stated that all states must approve amendments.

Article 7 stated that Congress would pay slave owners for slaves prevented from return by violence or intimidation. (Radical Republicans called for this article's immediate defeat, stating the amendment was too pro-Southern.)

The Virginia delegation was made up of two strong Unionist (Rives and Summers), one strong secessionist (Seddon) and two leaning toward secession (Tyler and Judge John Brockenbrough). Rives and Summers were true to their constituents, as were Seddon and Tyler. But it was Brockenbrough, the swing vote, who abandoned the wishes of the men in his region. A delegate from Lexington in the Valley region of the state, Brockenbrough represented an area of overwhelming Unionist sentiment. He betrayed his constituents because, for the most part, he voted with Seddon and Tyler. As a result, Virginia voted against the majority of the articles and against Article 1, the key to the overall amendment as it reestablished the Missouri Compromise line. Brockenbrough's siding with the secessionist-leaning contingent was roundly (and rightly) criticized by the local press in Lexington. The Unionists, who had captured a huge majority of the vote for delegates to the Virginia State Convention, were dismayed by the vote of the Virginia delegation at the Peace Conference, as it did not reflect the wishes of the vast majority of Virginians at that point in time. It was a vote too much in line with the Slave Power.

———

Just before adjournment, President Tyler addressed the conference a final time. "Gentlemen of the Conference: The labors of this Convention are drawing to a close…We came together at a most important and critical time…I go to finish the work you have assigned me, of presenting your recommendations to the two Houses of Congress, and to ask those bodies to lay your proposals of amendment before the people of the American Union…So far as in me lies, therefore, I shall recommend its adoption."[189] Later, Tyler would pronounce the amendment as incomplete and disjointed.

The heavy-handed presence of Northern radicals and the seething presence of pro-secession Southerners did little to aid the debates of the conference. Both groups of extremists were content to draw their respective lines in the sand and let "come what may." The moderate Republican Tom Corwin had observed earlier, "Southern men are theoretically crazy. Extreme Northern men are practical fools. The latter are really quite as mad as the former."[190] The essence of the extreme Northern position was expressed by some in the New York delegation when they denounced the "odious doctrine of property in man," stating, "We do not believe that the people of New York will, under any pressure of circumstances, however grave, recognize a claim so repugnant to humanity, so hostile to freedom." James Seddon, Virginia's Southern Rights man, proclaimed at the conclusion of the convention, "We have been defamed by the people of the North…You have educated your children to believe us monsters of brutality, lust and iniquity."[191] But in spite of the extremists and their constant blustering, the moderates of the convention held firm and produced an amendment to the U.S. Constitution that had some real merit—although some argued it was too accommodating to the Southern moderates.

The amendment was a direct challenge to the aristocratic planter class in the seceded states, and it coincided with the fundamental realignment of political parties in the borderland—the rising new Union Party. Crofts was the first to observe that "the challenge to the Democrats came from new political entities, the emerging Union parties, whose most distinguishing characteristic was a base of support in which slave owners were incidental and irrelevant."[192] This new Union Party was the antithesis of the Slave Power, for sure, and the Peace Conference Amendment was in line with the Union party's central principle—to avoid a military confrontation with the seceded states at this moment in time. The amendment—and the new party—held great potential for solving the slavery problem over time because the slave owners were indeed "incidental and irrelevant" to the men in this new party. These Unionists were committed not only to saving the Union but also (and importantly) to building a new economy with government-funded infrastructures—an economy that was not based on slavery. The Unionists needed time to consolidate their newfound political power, and this amendment gave them just that.

William Henry Seward, who had become the leader of moderate Republicans by the time the Peace Conference ended, saw the possibilities of this new Union coalition better than anyone, and he sought to develop a "Southern strategy"—a strategy of accommodation—that would exploit it. He only had to persuade Abraham Lincoln that it would work.[193] David Donald concluded, "Seward...was confident he could persuade the President-elect to agree that the fever of secession should be allowed to run its course in the Deep South while Unionism should be fostered in the Upper South by avoiding all provocations...he counted on his enormous intelligence and undeniable charm to win over the President-elect."[194] Seward's failure to convince Lincoln, and the tremendous implications it had for preventing war, will be explored in Chapter 6.

John Tyler did as he promised and presented the proposed amendment of the Peace Conference to the House and the Senate. Then he returned to Richmond and expressed his displeasure with the proposed amendment and urged Virginians to prepare for conflict. Fellow Virginians Seddon and Brockenbrough, who had sided with Tyler and voted against some of the articles, denounced the amendment, too. Rives and Summers, who strongly favored the amendment, launched a spirited defense of the Peace Conference and promoted adoption of the amendment. Rives would deliver a great speech at Metropolitan Hall in Richmond on March 8, stating, "As a whole, [it is] the most comprehensive and satisfactory settlement...that has emanated from any quarter."[195]

The House at once began to debate just how to receive the Peace Conference amendment, and partisan bickering prevailed. Illinois congressman John McClernand, a Democrat and a key ally of Senator Douglas, sought to have the amendment read on the House floor as a way to merely receive it. The Democrats had developed a strategy to place the disunionist label on both secessionist and Republicans, with McClernand exclaiming, "'Open the eyes of the people to the effects of Lincoln's election,' thereby pinning responsibility for the crisis right where it belonged."[196] Radical Republicans would have none of it, though, as abolitionist Congressman Owen Lovejoy objected to receiving the amendment in any way, stating, "It is not a peace congress at all. There is no such body known to this House."[197] Indeed, both secessionists and Radical Republicans opposed any compromise effort, as compromise would undermine their respective agendas.

Finally, McClernand and other moderates introduced a motion to suspend the House rules in order to take up the amendment; such a motion would require a two-thirds majority. Not surprisingly, moderate Republicans, such as Thomas Corwin, William Kellogg and the eminent Charles Francis Adams, strongly supported the move. Secessionists openly opposed it, as did the vast majority of Radical Republicans. When the final vote was tallied, it failed the required two-thirds majority—93 to 67 (107 votes were needed)—so the House never even discussed the Peace Conference proposal. Reuben Hitchcock, a member of the Ohio delegation, stated in a letter to his brother, "Indeed, there is too general a feeling that party is paramount to the Union—I fear that this feeling or rather the apprehension of injuring the party will lead to a policy which will destroy both it & the country."[198]

The Peace Conference proposal had a somewhat different run in the Senate. Senator Crittenden, its leading backer, succeeded in having the amendment referred to a select committee on February 27 for review and endorsement. The committee was appointed by Vice President Breckinridge and consisted of Crittenden, Seward, Trumbull, Bigler and Thompson, all leading figures. They endorsed the proposal the next day by a three to two vote, with Seward voting against it for several reasons. Seward had been the leader of the pro-compromise Republicans and had implied to more than one observer that he would support a Crittenden Compromise–type proposal. "He [Seward] led them to suppose that he would do something in the way of conciliating the South. Perhaps he designed to do so; but finding that he could not get his party to follow him, he forfeited his promise and took ground against Crittenden and against the Peace Conference."[199]

Nevertheless, Crittenden, Douglas and other leading compromisers pushed ahead with the amendment, and Crittenden, in a final effort to secure a compromise, substituted the Peace Conference Amendment for his own compromise proposal. Crittenden pleaded with his colleagues, "I shall vote for the amendments proposed by the Convention, and there I shall stand. That is the weapon offered now, and placed in my hand, by which, as I suppose, the Union of these States may be preserved; and I will not, out of any selfish preference for my own original opinions on this subject, sacrifice one idea or one particle of that hope. I go for the country; not for this resolution or that resolution, but any resolution, any proposition, that will pacify the country."[200] The venerable Crittenden was the man of the hour, imploring his countrymen to vote for peace.

But despite the heroic efforts of the compromisers, extended debate erupted in the final hours of the Senate session with Radical Republicans and uncompromising secessionist senators combining forces to argue for defeat of the amendment. "In a vote that came after four o'clock on the morning of March 4, radicals like Bingham, Chandler, Fessenden, Grimes, Sumner, Trumbull, and Wade voted with fire-eaters like Wigfall. Only seven Senators supported the amendment; twenty-eight opposed it. Senator Seward was absent."[201] If avoiding war was the goal, these names should be remembered as the villains.

So the Peace Conference Amendment, put together by the most impressive gathering of political giants since the Constitutional Convention of 1787, was rejected by a congress so divided and so partisan that it could not see the great swell of moderation and support for compromise that was sweeping the country, both North and South. If put to popular vote, the Crittenden Compromise or the Peace Conference Amendment would most likely have received a substantial majority of votes in most Northern states and an overwhelming majority in virtually every state of the Upper and Border South. As a dismayed James Guthrie observed after the defeat of the Amendment in Congress, "If Virginia plays the fool now the whole South is lost to the Union."[202]

Allen Nevins, one of the foremost American historians of the twentieth century, concluded, "So far as the actual diffusion of slavery went, the Republicans could have afforded to swallow the Crittenden Compromise— for the possibilities of slavery expansion were near the end."[203]

Delegates to the Virginia State Convention gathered at noon on February 13, 1861, in the capital at Richmond. As analyzed in the previous chapter, they had been elected from each county of the state in a special election called by an act of the legislature. The delegates could be divided into three broad groups: immediate secessionists, unconditional Unionists and conditional Unionists. Some thirty (20 percent) were immediate secessionists, a larger group of about fifty (33 percent) were unconditional Unionists and a still larger group of seventy-two (47 percent) were conditional Unionists.[204] Delegates did not stay firm to these groupings throughout the convention, and thus some are difficult to categorize. As an example, James Barbour, in the conditional Unionist group at the outset, switched to the secessionist group after the failure of the Peace Conference.

The immediate secessionists were representatives of the Slave Power who had supported Breckinridge in the election. They were led by Lewis E. Harvie, representing Amelia and Nottoway Counties in the black belt of the Piedmont

The Confederate capitol at Richmond, Virginia, at the end of the Civil War. Steeped in history, the building was the central gathering place for all things political. *Courtesy of the Library of Virginia.*

Lewis E. Harvie, an aristocratic slave owner from the black belt of the Piedmont Region, led the secessionists at the Virginia State Convention who felt that slavery could be saved only by combining with other black belts of the South. *Courtesy of the Library of Virginia.*

region, and former governor Henry A. Wise of the Tidewater region. They sought to have Virginia secede and join the Southern Confederacy without delay. The unconditional Unionists were primarily from the Northwest and Valley regions, which favored staying in the Union and denied the right of secession. They were led by George W. Summers of Kanawha County and by the brilliant constitutionalist John B. Baldwin of Augusta County. The conditional Unionists were a mixed bag of states' rights Whigs and Douglas Democrats who believed in the right of secession but favored staying in the Union until all avenues of compromise had been explored. They were led by Robert Y. Conrad of Frederick County, Robert E. Scott of Fauquier County and William B. Preston of Montgomery County.

The convention would meet each weekday from February 13 until May 1, when the first session adjourned. The deliberations of the convention were opened to the press, and by the end of February, a contract had been signed with the *Richmond Enquirer* to "publish full official reports of the proceedings of the State Convention." On April 17, the convention passed an Ordinance of Secession by a vote of eighty-eight to fifty-five. The incredible events that occurred in the convention, and in Washington, D.C., between February 14 and April 17 will be discussed in the next two chapters.

As the Unionist delegates gathered on the thirteenth, spirits were high and the mood ebullient, for they were in total control. Governor Letcher was in a great mood, too, as "the moderates had scored a clear victory, and Letcher made no effort to hide his delight."[205] Former governor John Floyd, however, was in a terrible mood, as noted in a privately written letter on February 7. Commenting on the election of delegates, he said, "The southern cause has sustained a fearful defeat," and as a result, the emancipation of the slave will become "almost irresistible."[206] George Summers nominated John Janney of Loudoun County, a firm Unionist, as president of the convention, and he was quickly elected by a vote of seventy to fifty-four. The next day, the convention met in the Hall of the Mechanics' Institute as the legislature was still in session, occupying the capitol. The third day saw Janney appoint a Committee on Elections and a Committee on Federal Relations. The later would become the key committee of the convention and dealt with evaluating all the proposals set forth by various delegates. Robert Y. Conrad, from Frederick County in the northern part of the Valley region, was appointed chairman. The committee, composed of twenty-one delegates, was dominated by Unionist, as only four secessionist were appointed as members.

Political posturing between the secessionists and unconditional Unionists began immediately with Sandy Stuart challenging Henry Wise to explain his supposed statement that Virginia militia would be used to seize Federal facilities. Wise vigorously denied that he had made any such statement on February 15. However, Virginia militia, instructed by Wise, would in fact seize Federal facilities in Norfolk and Harpers Ferry just two months later, on April 16–17. While not militia, groups of young men (some contemporaries stated they were hired by the Slave Power) began to roam the streets of Richmond, promoting secession and threatening those who opposed.

John Janney, a Unionist from Northern Virginia, was elected president of the Virginia State Convention. He appointed fellow Unionists to most key leadership positions. *Courtesy of the Library of Virginia.*

John Brown Baldwin had set the stage for the argument against secession with a series of speeches during the fall campaign for Bell and the Constitutional Unionist ticket. He attacked the Southern Rights Democrats for promoting secession because, they claimed, the Republicans would refuse to let them take their slaves into the Western Territories—the territorial expansion of slavery issue. Slavery would not work in the West, Baldwin argued, for the soil, climate and other natural conditions there prohibited it. And as slavery now stood, there would never be enough slaves to move out west in the first place. The *Staunton Spectator* captured his reasoning during October: "He [Baldwin] showed that the principle upon which that party [Southern Rights Democrats] had staked the very existence of the Union and the preservation of the Government was a worthless abstraction—that there was no territory where slaves could be taken…it was madness [Baldwin claimed] to stake the existence of the only Government of free institutions in the world upon the recognition of a principle which could be of no practical benefit to us."[207]

Baldwin and the vast majority of Southern Unionists viewed the territorial expansion issue as a classic red herring. The Southern aristocrats were first and foremost focused on maintaining power and control over the South; taking slaves into the territories was a mere ruse. To repeat for emphasis, John Gilmer, congressman from North Carolina and leader of Southern Unionists in the House of Representatives, had taken the floor in January to proclaim, "Why, sirs, do you think these ultra men [the radical secessionists] insist on what they call protection [the right to take slaves into the territories], because it is any value to them?…They demand it because they think you will refuse it, and by your refusal, they hope the South will be inflamed to the extent of breaking up the government—the very thing the leaders desire."[208] Henry Seward bought this argument, and it became one of the drivers for his pro-compromise efforts. Sadly, Abraham Lincoln, busily making his way to the nation's capital, was not a major player in this debate.

The immediate secessionists could not counter Baldwin's argument effectively because it was essentially true—no one wanted to take slaves into the western territories, for it was unclear whether the institution would be profitable in an arid, inhospitable region. Nevertheless, the secessionists continued to push their agenda that Virginia would be better off joining the Southern Confederacy rather than staying in a Union dominated by Northern states that were more and more opposed to slavery. The Slave Power of Virginia, now convinced they would be a minority in their own state, felt they had no choice other than to team up with the Slave Power in the Lower South.

But the Unionist delegates, most of whom represented a majority of anti–Slave Power constituents, would have none of this argument and dismissed the secessionists outright. On February 25, an exchange between Samuel McD. Moore and Thomas F. Goode set the stage for the secessionist/Unionist debate for the entire convention. Moore, from Rockbridge County in the Valley region, where only 20 percent (on average) of the population was enslaved—and where non-slaveholders were in a decided majority—denounced the Slave Power and their penchant for joining the Southern Confederacy. He saw it for what it was—a pure power grab. He went on to condemn the slavocracy for causing Virginia's economic stagnation. Goode, from Mecklenburg County in the black belt of the Piedmont region, where over 60 percent of the population was enslaved, leapt to his feet to protest Moore's persuasive argument. Virginia must take its place at the head of the states in the Southern Confederacy and do it now, he proclaimed. Waiting would never do, and he demanded immediate action. Delay, as everywhere in the South, favored the Unionists, and virtually all secessionists argued for immediate action.

At this time, another issue confronted the Virginia Unionists—and it was none other than Abraham Lincoln himself. Lincoln had left Springfield on February 11 and was stopping in various Northern cities and towns on his way to Washington to introduce himself to the people of the country. At most stops, he delivered some remarks, some short, some long. His speeches were construed by many as combative. For instance, in Indianapolis, he spoke of his right to retake government property and enforce the laws in the seceded states. He made no mention of the compromise efforts that were going on in either Washington or Richmond. One of the most highly regarded Americans of the era, Edward Everett of Massachusetts (as previously noted, vice presidential candidate on the Constitutional Union Party ticket), recorded in his diary, "These speeches thus far have been of the most ordinary kind, destitute of everything, not merely of felicity and grace, but of common pertinence."[209]

The secessionists, of course, seized on Lincoln's remarks, claiming they represented the uncompromising views of the Radical Republicans and portended what the South would face. Their argument was effective and damaging to the position of the Unionist majority. Sherrard Clemens, former congressman from Wheeling and delegate from Ohio County (the county that gave Lincoln his highest number of votes in the state), had become one of Henry Seward's key contacts at the convention. He wired Seward, "We are struggling here against every obstacle, and Mr. Lincoln, by his speech in the North, has done vast harm. If he will not be guided by Mr. Seward but puts himself in the hands of Mr. Chase and the ultra Republicans, nothing can save the cause of the Union in the South."[210]

Many other issues were debated, including various resolutions recommending different ways to settle the sectional crisis, the requirement to have the people vote on amendments to the state constitution, declaring Virginia's right to secede, arming the state's militia, calling a national convention of states, proposals to create a confederacy of border states (free and slave), a call for an audit of State bonds and the state's finances and the calling for a status report on Virginia's military preparedness.

As February was drawing to a close, the leadership of the three factions in the convention began sharpening their respective arguments—and determining who in their group would be the strongest voice. Shanks recorded, "The most forceful of the prepared speeches in the Convention were probably those of W.T. Willey, representing the Unionist party, W.L. Goggin of the moderates, and George W. Randolph of the secessionists."[211] Goggin, of Bedford County, who had lost the gubernatorial race to Letcher in 1859, led off with a formal speech on February 26 that did not end until the session of the twenty-seventh. He denied the right of secession and argued forcibly that Virginia would be better off, economically, trading with the North rather than with the Cotton South. He called for a conference of the border states to address the national crisis and urged a cautious, steady approach. In his opinion, hasty, thoughtless secession was not the answer. Goggin, a former Whig and firm moderate, would end up voting for secession on April 17 after Lincoln's call for troops to wage war on the South.

Also during the last days of February, the Unionists were anxiously awaiting word from the Peace Conference that some sort of compromise settlement had been reached. When word arrived late on the twenty-seventh that an amendment to the U.S. Constitution, containing seven articles, had been passed by the conference and sent to the House and Senate for action, Unionists were encouraged. The secessionist delegates ridiculed the Peace

Conference proposal, calling it a "sham," and welcomed the vote of the Virginia delegation, calling it "in the best interest of the state."

At the convention, on the last day of the month, Jeremiah Morton, from the heavily enslaved Piedmont region and a large slave owner himself, took the floor to speak for the secessionists. In typical style of the Slave Power, he sought to exaggerate Northern hostility to the South and to portray Abraham Lincoln as a fanatical radical, while downplaying the more obnoxious features of the new Confederacy (for instance, he strongly denied that the Confederate government would reopen the African slave trade). Morton wailed, "Mr. President, by the election of Mr. Lincoln, the popular sentiment of the North has placed in the Executive Chair, of this mighty nation a man who did not get an electoral vote South of the Mason and Dixon's line, a man who was elected purely by a Northern fanatical sentiment hostile to the South...The Government is no longer a Government of equal rights. Our enemies have now command of the Executive Department, they have command of both branches of Congress."[212] Again, the Slave Power's *modus operandi* was simply to ignore the fact that the great bulk of Northerners were political moderates. Mostly Democrats, but a large number of Republicans too, were indeed moderate; nevertheless, the Slave Power constantly referred to all Northerners as extremists.

In Richmond, February ended with the administrative machinery of the convention in place, with the Unionist majority assuming leadership roles in virtually every key post, with acrimonious debate raging between uncompromising secessionists and unconditional Unionists and with conditional Unionists striving to find an acceptable way out of the impasse.

In Washington, on the last day of the month, clouds were darkening as Henry Seward's compromise plans began to unravel. Few Republicans had joined him in the House or Senate to support compromise, both houses of Congress were rejecting the Peace Conference Amendment and, unbelievably from Seward's point of view, Lincoln began to reject overtures of compromise as well. In addition, over his strenuous objections, the president-elect prepared to appoint Chase and Montgomery Blair—two hard-liners—to his cabinet. These moves, when reported at the Richmond convention, weakened the Unionist position because it made it appear as though the Republicans were moving away from compromise. Indeed, confusion reigned. For as David Donald concluded after Lincoln was elected, "All eyes now turned to Springfield, where an inexperienced leader with a limited personal acquaintance among members of his own party groped his way, on the basis of inadequate information, to formulate a policy for his new administration."[213]And nowhere was this groping for policy and the consequent confusion emanating from the nation's capital as crucial as with the Unionists of Virginia.

But then a light for peace occurred on the afternoon of February 27. William Cabell Rives, still in Washington pushing the Peace Conference Amendment and still smarting from Lincoln's tactlessness on their first encounter ("You are a smaller man than I supposed—I mean in person," Lincoln had said[214]), received a message from the president-elect asking him to come to his suite at 9:00 p.m. for a meeting with Alexander Doniphan, Charles Morehead and James Guthrie. Lincoln again was awkward in his opening remarks to the delegation; nevertheless, Rives rose to speak and, "with dignity and eloquence," pleaded that just a few concessions would save Virginia and the Upper South from seceding. He spoke candidly about coercion, stating it must be avoided or Virginia and other border states would secede. Fighting must be avoided at all cost, he urged. It is reported that Lincoln then stood and said, "If Virginia will stay in, I will withdraw from Fort Sumpter [*sic*]." Rives is reported to have responded, "Mr. President, I have no authority to speak for Virginia. I am one of the humblest of her sons; but if you do that it will be one of the wisest things you have ever done."[215] Here was one of the nation's elder statesmen, counseling the untested and untried new leader to take the high road and avoid risking war.

On the last day of February, another light for peace appeared when Congress finally produced something that many moderates felt was long overdue. "The House passed and sent to the Senate the Constitutional Amendment proposed by Thomas Corwin of Ohio, as devised by the Committee of Thirty-three [the committee of the House charged with finding a settlement to the crisis] and approved by President-elect Lincoln, that slavery could not be interfered with by the Federal government in states where it already existed."[216] Had this amendment been sent to the states and ratified, it would have become the Thirteenth Amendment to the U.S. Constitution, precisely the opposite of the Thirteenth Amendment that was passed near the end of the war.

So February ended with the nation in a state of great hope—hope that a compromise would be forthcoming to stave off armed conflict. The Peace Conference had produced an amendment that was being hailed as an "harbinger of peace," Congress had produced an amendment to protect slavery in all states where it existed, the Virginia State Convention was in session to consider secession but was in the firm grip of Unionists, both North Carolina and Tennessee had rejected calling state conventions to even consider secession and the Border South states were experiencing a surge in Unionist sentiment. Even the moderate Northern press was trumpeting hope. Earlier in the month, the *New York Times* had run an editorial stating, "We have evidence now of a Union Party in the Southern states. The government has friends, the Constitution has supporters there with whom to treat. Conciliation and compromise become now acts of friendly arrangement, instead of surrender to open and defiant enemies."[217]

While "hope springs eternal" and most in the country were still looking for a peaceful settlement, most Republicans in Congress were not moving to support any of the compromise proposals. Elated with their election victory (even if it was very narrow), they sensed it was their time to quash the Slave Power, and for some, their time to push an antislavery agenda. And behind the scenes, Abraham Lincoln was supporting the congressional Republicans by making it increasingly clear he was not in favor of real concessions to the South, especially on the crucial but worthless (as Baldwin put it) territorial expansion-of-slavery issue. And as Henry Seward was beginning to realize, "the final decision regarding compromise lay in the hands of one party, and ultimately of just one man: Abraham Lincoln."[218]

We now turn to March 1861, a month of true madness for the Unionists of Virginia.

CHAPTER 5

BEWARE THE IDES OF MARCH

Without the enthusiastic support of the border states, the Cotton States' 10 percent of the nation's white population could not hope to hold out for long.
—*Edward L. Ayers,* In the Presence of Mine Enemies

March 1861 would prove to be the last month of peace the country would experience for four long, arduous years. Excitement ruled the day as newspapers in every section of the country produced headlines and editorials that alarmed citizens. No one seemed to know what to do to calm the nation. Seven states of the Lower South had seceded from the Union and established a government with a constitution, president and vice president, cabinet officers and a congress modeled after the United States. Nothing, absolutely nothing, had ever happened like this before. What did it all mean?

In Washington, the month began with extreme tension as rumors abounded that the inauguration of Abraham Lincoln would be prevented by force. General Winfield Scott had the military on high alert; soldiers roamed the streets in large numbers, and cannons were posted on high ground. Congress was winding up its troublesome session, the Peace Conference had adjourned and the president-elect was beginning to make decisions about his cabinet and policy matters that would begin to signal his course of action. The month would end more calmly in the capital, as nothing dramatic happened. Rumors swirled that something would be done to preserve the peace. This was a "do-nothing" administration barked the

New York Times. Behind the scenes, however, the now President Lincoln was making decisions that would risk war.

In Richmond, the month began with the Virginia State Convention continuing to meet with few major decisions reached. The Committee on Federal Relations was continuing to receive and evaluate proposals submitted by members on behalf of their constituents. Contentious debate between the secessionists and the unconditional Unionists went ahead unabated, with the Unionists castigating the Slave Power at every turn. Several secessionists called for Virginia to secede immediately, while unconditional Unionists called for a convention of the border states.

The galleries of the Mechanics' Institute Hall were crowded, often with boisterous pro-secession folks, and gangs of youths paraded around town, calling for secession. Many Unionists claimed both of these groups were paid by the Slave Power to stir up trouble, for everyone knew "the slave traders were spending money freely, in order to influence the public mind in favor of immediate secession." It appeared the Slave Power would stop at nothing to achieve their aim as "slave traders were pressuring Union newspapers to change their editorial stance or deliberately buying them out to achieve the same goal."[219]

While partisan, heated exchanges occurred in and out of the convention, early March was not a time of extreme tension. However, by the end of the month, Richmond witnessed tensions rising by the hour. Fort Sumter had not been evacuated, as promised, and rumors began to surface that Lincoln might take a more "determined" stance with regard to the seceded states. The Unionist coalition in the convention was beginning to show signs of cracking. "Where was the conciliatory policy from Washington?" the Unionists asked. It was never coming, retorted the secessionists.

———

Friday, March 1, the fourteenth day of the Virginia State Convention, was a good day for the Unionists. George Summers had returned from the Peace Conference in Washington and was busily putting together a report of its deliberations to present to the convention. He had let it be known that William Rives was coming to Richmond to address the convention. Rives did come as he hoped to further unite the Unionists of the convention and "to persuade them to accept the proposals of the Peace conference...He held long conversations with friends, especially R.Y. Conrad, chairman of the Federal Relations Committee."[220] By this time, a wave of Unionism was sweeping the Border South states. Unionists were growing more confident that an accommodation would be forthcoming when the new administration took office in a few days. The secessionists were despondent. In the convention, proposals were made to adjust taxes on slaves and to approve the contract with the *Richmond Enquirer* for reporting the proceedings of the convention, as general procedural matters took too much time.

On Monday, March 4, returns of the election in North Carolina had been reported, as the Carolinians had rejected calling a convention to consider secession. This was another stinging blow to the secessionists, as it was clear they were not connecting with men in the Upper South. Strengthened by this rising Unionism, Waitman Willey took the floor to deliver the first major pro-Union address. Willey, a popular and skillful politician from the Northwest, would become one of West Virginia's first U.S. Senators after statehood was achieved in 1863. Willey took apart the secession argument, piece by piece, and then discussed the evils of secession, principally the placing of Virginia on the border of a country with a seacoast and hundreds of miles of northern border, all impossible to defend. The economic advantages of staying in the Union, where it would be a central state, included new avenues of expanded trade with North and South, but especially the North. Even the real possibility of a terminus of an Atlantic-Pacific railroad in Virginia was likely. He concluded, "Let Virginia secede and all these bright prospects are forever dashed to pieces...Let Virginia maintain her position; let her stand fast where she ever stood, and this Union can never be permanently dissolved."[221] It was a magnificent speech, regarded by observers as one of the best of the convention.

With the secessionists on the defensive in Richmond, the eyes of the convention turned to Washington, where Abraham Lincoln was being sworn in as the sixteenth president of the United States. Unionists were eager to read his Inaugural Address.

In Washington, March 1 was not a good day for President-elect Abraham Lincoln or for his secretary of state-designate, William Henry Seward. Lincoln was struggling mightily with his cabinet appointments and in trying to sort out the political scene in the nation's capital, issues where his lack of experience and unfamiliarity with key figures exacerbated the roiling confusion. After weeks of highly charged and contentious intraparty (indeed, intrastate) debate, he offered the secretary of war post to Senator Simon Cameron, Pennsylvania's Republican political boss (or one of them, as it turned out). Working eighteen hours per day, he was virtually besieged by delegations and prominent individuals offering him "advice" regarding each and every aspect of his presidency. William Henry Seward, the nation's foremost Republican leader, was in a quandary, too. He had not been able to persuade enough Republicans to accept his "Southern Policy," a conciliatory policy toward the Upper South. Lincoln had not supported him on either his Southern Policy or on his cabinet recommendations, nor had the president-elect responded to his strongly worded note of concern regarding the draft Inaugural Address. "Friday, March 1, was a day of unimaginable tension for Henry Seward. He now faced the real prospect of losing his political status in the administration, in Washington [and], indeed, the nation."[222] Seward summoned his political partner, New York State political boss Thurlow Weed, to Washington for "consultation."

For pure political excitement, March 2 ranks with the most notable days in the nation's history. On this Saturday, Congress wound up its work and sent to President Buchanan three measures: (1) to create two new territories, Nevada and Dakota; (2) the Morrill Tariff Act, which would substantially increase the tariff; and (3) a proposed constitutional amendment to prohibit Congress from interfering with or abolishing slavery where it already existed (the original Thirteenth Amendment). Both the House and the Senate failed to approve the Peace Conference Amendment. In Montgomery, Alabama, the Provisional Confederate Congress admitted Texas as the seventh state in the new Confederacy. President

Thurlow Weed, political boss of New York State, was a heavy hitter is Washington as well. The lifelong political partner of Seward, Weed was extremely active during the Secession Winter. *Seward House, Auburn, New York.*

Buchanan, frightened by the rumors of imminent invasion, ordered up troops for the preservation of peace in the nation's capital. Lincoln was receiving only "special" guests in his suite at the Willard when, late in the afternoon, a bombshell from Seward arrived: "Circumstances which have occurred since I expressed…my willingness to accept the office of Secretary of State seem to me to render it my duty to ask leave to withdraw that consent."[223] Less than forty-eight hours before his inauguration, Lincoln's senior cabinet officer, "Mr. Republican," withdrew from the cabinet.

On Sunday, March 3, Seward called at the Willard, where a huge crowd had gathered hoping to see the two men leave together for church. But on this Sunday "11 o'clock came and passed and no 'Uncle Abe,'" as Seward "was seen going in, but as time passed it became probable that the visit of Mr. S had another object, and the crowd melted away."[224] Lincoln and Seward conferred secretly for much of the day. Lincoln held a dinner that evening for his cabinet, and surprisingly, Seward attended. Earlier that day, General Winfield Scott, commander-in-chief of the U.S. Army, had sent Seward a note stating it was "impractical" to relieve Fort Sumter. "For Scott…to write Seward instead of the president-elect is just extraordinary. Seward's stature and presence within the Washington establishment was second to none; indeed, General Scott evidently viewed him as the 'the premier.'"[225] Also on this day, Brigadier General P.G.T. Beauregard of the new Confederate States army assumed command of the South Carolina militia in Charleston Harbor.

For pure political drama, March 4 was unsurpassed. It was Inauguration Day for Abraham Lincoln. It was reported at the time (and most likely true) that Lincoln rose before dawn to alter the Inaugural Address. In the end, he "accepted Seward's advice to delete both a reaffirmation of Republican orthodoxy on the territorial issue and a threat to recapture federal property in the seceded states." He used Seward's exact phraseology to seek "a peaceful solution of the national troubles, and the restoration of fraternal sympathies and affections."[226] Seward had won the initial confrontation with Lincoln, as the inaugural address became nonconfrontational and conciliatory. Prior to the inauguration, Seward had met with Lincoln again, and the soon-to-be president asked Seward to reconsider his resignation. Lincoln then, accompanied by President Buchanan, rode in an open carriage down Pennsylvania Avenue to the Capitol. Troops lined the streets, riflemen were seen on the rooftops and cannons were posted on the Capitol grounds. But the inauguration went off smoothly. Lincoln delivered his half-hour speech, which was applauded lightly, and was then sworn in by Chief Justice Taney.

He walked back to the White House as part of the Inaugural Parade and hosted the Inaugural Ball that evening.

March 5, Lincoln's first day in office, found the tired new president reading Major Anderson's stark message that it would take twenty thousand troops to successfully reinforce Fort Sumter. Anderson stated he had just six weeks of supplies left. Joseph Holt, the outgoing secretary of war, who delivered the message, said it was a "total surprise" to him that Anderson had so few supplies. But Holt had received constant communications from Anderson throughout the month, and it could not have been a surprise. Holt was desperately trying to "cover his reputation." But it was a total surprise to the new president, as he thought Anderson could hold out for an extended period of time. Unsurprisingly, General Scott concurred with Anderson's assessment. Pulitzer Prize–winning historian David Donald poignantly observed that "Lincoln was not prepared for this emergency. As yet there was no executive branch of the government. The Senate had yet to confirm even his private secretary, John G. Nicolay. None of his cabinet officers had been approved."[227] On March 6, Lincoln held his first cabinet meeting and chose not to inform the cabinet of the momentous news from Anderson.

In Richmond, the Unionists were lukewarm to Lincoln's Inaugural Address, while secessionists condemned it as a war message (as did some Unionists). Although Unionist newspapers in the state gave it some support, it was Seward's effort (his promise of a conciliatory policy) that kept the Unionist momentum in the convention on track. On March 6, secessionist delegate John T. Thornton of Prince Edward County in the black belt of the Piedmont region spoke to denounce the Inaugural Address, as expected. Unionist delegate Jubal Early of Franklin County in the Piedmont countered with a message urging caution and moderation. Amid some rancor, President Janney called the attention of the assembled delegates to the fact that the report of the Peace Conference was ready for distribution.

March 7 and 8 found the Unionists on the offensive. On the seventh, former congressman John S. Carlile, from Harrison County in the Northwest, where 92 percent voted for the referendum, gave a speech ridiculing the secessionists. He challenged them to read any war message in Lincoln's Inaugural Address: "Sir, is there anything in this Inaugural Address to justify for a moment the assertions that have been made upon this floor, that it breathes a spirit of war? Read it again, gentlemen…Mr. Lincoln…has told you, in effect, and told you in pleading, begging terms, that no war will be made upon you, that no force will be used against you-none whatever." He blasted the Confederacy as a government of the aristocrats, controlled exclusively for the benefit of the Slave Power. He ended his warmly received address by stating, "I protest against this wicked effort to destroy the fairest and freest government on the earth. And I denounce all attempts to involve Virginia to commit her to self murder as an insult to all reasonable living humanity, and a crime against God."[228] Here was an unconditional Unionist at his best.

Jubal Early was a strong Unionist who opposed immediate secession and voted against the first Ordinance of Secession on April 4, 1861. Later, he would become a legendary general in Lee's Army of Northern Virginia. *Courtesy of the Library of Virginia.*

On March 8, George Brent, a relatively rare Unionist from the Tidewater region, rose to denounce secessionism on economic grounds. A young lawyer representing Alexandria City, he possessed great oratorical skills and sound reasoning. He outlined the conditions for a just settlement, a Crittenden-like plan, and called for a border state convention. "It is due to the Border States that we should meet in convention. I would not rashly and precipitately rush out of this Union, or first undertake this settlement without the counsel of these Border States. We have condemned the cotton States for their action. We should not imitate the same action on our part, but we should call them into counsel." He called coercion wrong, recognized the right of secession and stated he would stand by his state, whatever its choice. He would vote against the Ordinance of Secession on April 4.

Throughout the Upper South, virtually all Unionists were preaching the same message about coercion, i.e. the use of force to bring back a seceded state(s). Leave it alone, they begged, for a military confrontation was all that the secessionists had left to hope for. The previously mentioned John Gilmer of North Carolina had written Seward many times in early March

THE CAPITOL

THIS BUILDING WAS ERECTED 1785-9. IT WAS PLANNED BY THOMAS JEFFERSON ON THE MODEL OF THE MAISON CARRÉE AN ANCIENT ROMAN TEMPLE AT NÎMES FRANCE.

IN THE ROTUNDA IS THE FAMOUS HOUDON STATUE OF GEORGE WASHINGTON ERECTED IN 1796. IN THE NICHES ARE THE BUSTS OF THE SEVEN OTHER VIRGINIA-BORN PRESIDENTS AND THE HOUDON BUST OF LAFAYETTE ORDERED BY THE COMMONWEALTH IN 1781.

IN THE HALL OF THE HOUSE OF DELEGATES AARON BURR WAS TRIED IN 1807. HERE ROBERT E. LEE ACCEPTED THE COMMAND OF THE ARMED FORCES OF VIRGINIA IN 1861 AND THE CONFEDERATE CONGRESS MET 1861-5.

IN THIS BUILDING MEETS THE GENERAL ASSEMBLY OF VIRGINIA THE OLDEST LAWMAKING BODY IN AMERICA, AND THE FIRST IN THE WORLD TO FUNCTION UNDER A WRITTEN CONSTITUTION OF A FREE AND INDEPENDENT PEOPLE.

THE EAST AND WEST WINGS WERE ADDED IN 1905.

The bronze plaque at the Virginia State Capitol describing the history of the building. Virginians truly thought they were key to saving the nation from war. *Courtesy of the Library of Virginia.*

with essentially the same message, stating, "There must be no fighting, or the conservative Union men in the border slave states…will be swept away in a torrent of madness."[229] Counseling against coercion so strongly had an ulterior motive for the Unionists of Virginia—they sought time to regain political power. "Former Whig leaders in Virginia, for instance

George W. Summers, Alexander H.H. Stuart, John Minor Botts and John B. Baldwin, were more than anxious to resume their political careers. The huge majorities they commanded after the election in February delighted them beyond belief. These were politically astute men, they were practical politicians, they relished political power and clearly saw the stakes…avoid a confrontation with the new confederacy, and the moderates of the South [especially Virginia] would regain political dominance."[230]And it should be noted again that the Unionists of Virginia truly thought their efforts were key to saving the nation from civil war. The stakes were indeed very high for these Virginians.

By the second week in March, Henry Seward had taken command of the new Lincoln administration. While the president was spending the vast majority of his time seeing office seekers and well-wishers, Seward was running the show. All cabinet meetings were scheduled through him, most one-on-one meetings with the president were scheduled through him and he was interacting with all the major players. He was coordinating activities with General Scott, coordinating meetings with conciliators in Congress and delegations of compromisers coming to Washington to plead for restraint and he even began interactions, through intermediaries, with the Confederate commissioners sent to Washington. He was so bold that he began to advise Lincoln on senior appointments. On Saturday morning, March 9, he sent a message to Lincoln regarding George Summers: "What do you think of George W. Summers for Justice of the Supreme Court. The vacancy is produced by the decease of Judge Daniels of Virginia. Summers nomination, being from the same state, would be well. It would totally demoralize disunion in the Border States. Pray think of it."[231] Seward was everywhere, and his presence was both felt and resented. Fellow cabinet members were more than irritated because of his dominance of the president's time, and hard-line Republicans viewed him as a turncoat for "selling out" the principles enunciated in the Chicago Platform of the party.

General Scott had replied to a request from the president for his views on Fort Sumter and stated that the fort could not be defended and must be abandoned. This advice was concurred in by General Totten, chief engineer of the U.S. Army, and virtually all of the senior naval officers in Washington. As the "military necessity" advice dovetailed so neatly with

Seward's political calculations, Seward moved forward with his Southern Policy with renewed confidence. Despite his confidence, anti-Seward machinations were going on.

March 13 found a former navy officer, Gustavus Vasa Fox (Postmaster General Montgomery Blair's brother-in-law) at the White House to brief Lincoln on a plan to resupply Fort Sumter by sea. The plan, originally proposed in early February a few weeks after Anderson had first moved his command to Sumter, was to send in small boats with supplies at night. The exact wording of Fox's memorandum follows:

> *I propose to put the troops on board of a large, comfortable sea steamer and hire two powerful light draft New York tug boats, having the necessary stores on board. These to be convoyed by the USS* Pawnee, *now at Philadelphia, and the revenue cutter* Harriet Lane...*Arriving off the bar, I propose to examine by day the naval preparations and obstructions. If their vessels determine to oppose our entrance, and a feint or flag of truce would ascertain this, the armed ships must approach the bar and destroy or drive them on shore. Major Anderson would do the same upon any vessels within the range of his guns and would also prevent any naval succor being sent down from the city. Having dispersed this force, the only obstacles are the forts on Cummings point, and Fort Moultrie, and whatever adjacent batteries they may have...Two hours before high water, at night, with half the force on board of each tug, within relieving distance of each other, should run in to Fort Sumpter* [sic].[232]

General Scott had originally looked favorably on the plan in early February, largely because the guns to be aimed at Sumter (and the boats) were not yet in place. By mid-March, the guns were in place, and Scott (and the navy high command) now did not think it could work. Major Anderson had been keeping Washington fully informed through his normal chain of command. A typical message (and a very important one) was sent from Fort Sumter on March 9, arriving at the War Department on the twelfth: "I have the honor to report that we can see the South Carolinians engaged this morning strengthening and extending considerably what we supposed to have been intended for a mortar battery at Fort Johnson...One of my officers reports that he has counted nine 24-pounders which have been landed at Cummings Point within a week...It appears to me that vessels will, even now, from the time they cross the bar, be under fire from the batteries on Morris Island until they get under the walls of this work."[233]

Notwithstanding the new guns, Scott approved Fox briefing the president; Blair arranged the meeting. Lincoln reacted to the plan with some interest. Also on this day, Seward received a telegram from Thurlow Weed in Albany that the New York State legislature was increasingly upset with the rumored plans to abandon the fort. But Seward continued to push for abandonment because it had become the centerpiece of his Southern Policy, again because virtually all Southern Unionists were urging him to prevent a clash of arms with the Confederates. Lincoln, after the briefing by Fox, sought the advice of his cabinet on whether to resupply or abandon Sumter. The cabinet met twice on the fourteenth to review the situation. Seward took the lead in discussions and promoted the General Scott memorandum that the fort must be abandoned because of "military necessities"—essentially it was too late to attempt to run in supplies, and there were not twenty thousand trained troops to attempt an assault.

March 15, the Ides of March, found the President briefing the cabinet on the Fox plan to resupply Fort Sumter. He asked each cabinet minister to give him an opinion, in writing, on the following question: "Assuming it to be possible to now provision Fort-Sumpter [sic], under all the circumstances, is it wise to attempt it?"[234] Seward went to "work" immediately and counseled Smith, Cameron and Bates to carefully review the memorandum from General Scott. To repeat for emphasis, virtually the entire military high command, dominated by army men, thought the plan from Fox (a navy man) would not work. They all felt it would risk war, and they all knew how unprepared the armed forces were to engage in battle.

Montgomery Blair's father, Francis, had burst into Lincoln's office a few days before to exclaim that abandoning the fort would be "treasonous." Montgomery, now solidly behind the plan, pushed Fox to brief Lincoln again. Salmon Chase, the Radical Republican who would oppose just about anything Seward supported, stiffened also. On March 16, Lincoln received the responses. "As requested, the members of the Cabinet returned somewhat elaborate replies, Chase and Blair, agreeing with the President's own inclinations, responded in the affirmative; the five others, Seward, Cameron, Welles, Smith and Bates, advised against the measure."[235] While John Nicolay recorded the above observation years after the fact, the words he used—"the President's own inclinations"— suggest he felt Lincoln was moving away from Seward's Southern Policy by mid-March. In any event, a few days earlier, Seward had General Scott draft an order for the evacuation of Sumter, and the order was placed on Lincoln's desk for signature.

Seward was ebullient after the cabinet meeting, feeling he had now "won" the battle. He so notified his close friend Henry Raymond, editor of the *New York Times*. He also notified George W. Summers in Richmond. The word now got out that the administration was going to evacuate Fort Sumter and opt for a peaceful settlement of the crisis. But Lincoln was not quite ready to give up on the Fox plan. So he asked that someone be sent to Charleston to visit Sumter, consult with Major Anderson and report back to him. Cameron and Scott chose Fox, no doubt under pressure from Blair and Chase, and Fox went off to Charleston under the guise to "prepare the fort for evacuation." Charleston authorities, although suspicious, permitted Fox to visit the fort. At the same time, Lincoln sent two emissaries, Stephen Hurlbut and Ward Hill Lamon, to Charleston to "sample public opinion" in the city. Hurlbut, who was born in Charleston, was an Illinois lawyer who had worked with Lincoln; Lamon, also a friend from Illinois, had become his bodyguard.

When news spread that Sumter was to be evacuated, it was initially greeted by much public support. "Neal Dow, the Republican leader from Maine, wrote that evacuation of the fort would be 'approved by the entire body of Republicans in this State' because it was 'undoubtedly a Military necessity.'"[236] Such a message from Dow, an uncompromising temperance man and ardent abolitionist, was significant. Thurlow Weed reported from New York that it had been well received in the state capital. "Only the most radical no-compromise Republicans adhered to resupplying the fort, including the Blairs, Salmon Chase, Zach Chandler, Ben Wade, Thaddeus Stevens, and a few others. But even some Radical Republicans saw the military necessity and grudgingly supported abandonment, Charles Sumner a notably example."[237] Seward was so confident that he had won the argument over Sumter—Lincoln's agreeing to follow his Southern Policy in early March, Winfield Scott's military necessity reasoning for abandonment, the Cabinet vote and now the positive public reaction—that he secretly notified the Confederate commissioners in Washington that the fort would be evacuated in a few days. Peace seemed to be at hand.

In Richmond, the second week of March began just as the first week had ended, with lengthy debates between the secessionists and unconditional Unionists and no signs of either side moving toward any sort of "middle ground." On the contrary, the debates seemed to harden the respective positions. On March 8, Benjamin F. Wysor, of heavily enslaved Pulaski County in the Southwest region, proposed an Ordinance of Secession. Likewise, John A. Campbell of Washington County, on the border with North Carolina in the Southwest, presented resolutions from his constituents asking for immediate secession. The Unionists parried these efforts for the most part and pushed on with their agenda to find a settlement. They had crushed the Slave Power in the February election and were not about to relinquish their political advantage.

And the Unionist plan began to take shape on March 9, when the Unionist-dominated Committee on Federal Relations presented the first part of its report favoring a settlement along the lines of the Crittenden Compromise. Former governor Henry Wise, speaking for the secessionist faction, offered a long statement of dissent from the committee's report. Wise, from Princess Anne County of the historic coastal section of the Tidewater region, spoke of Southern rights and the need to join the Southern Confederacy. The previously mentioned secessionist leader Lewis Harvie immediately took the floor to support Wise. It was now very clear that those representing the most highly enslaved regions of the state—the black belts—were the most avid secessionists. They had lost so much public support (only 31 percent of Virginians had voted with them in the February election) that they had nothing left but to connect with their fellow Slave Power advocates in the Lower South.

March 11 was a pivotal day for the Unionists. George Summers spoke to defend and promote the Peace Conference proposal. His magnificent speech did not end until the following day, as he captivated the convention. He mentioned the problem of border state (as opposed to Cotton State) slaves escaping, he reiterated the red herring issue of the territorial question, he positioned Virginia as the border in a Southern Confederacy with all the problems that that would cause, he noted the weakness of the Lincoln presidency to threaten the South and, most importantly, he spoke to the need for a convention of border slave states. "The Frankfort Conference will, upon full consultation, agree upon guaranties which will be satisfactory to the slave States now remaining in the Union, and will devise the plan of bringing them to consideration of the other States. Let an appeal be made, not to the politicians, but to the people of the nation."[238] And the people of Virginia were kept fully informed of the activities in the convention by the local press. The *Richmond Whig* of March 12 summarized Summers's speech: "On motion of Mr. Summers, the report of the Commissioners to the Peace Conference was taken up, whereupon, he proceeded to address the convention in explanation and support of the plan of adjustment proposed by said Conference, showing that it was not only the equivalent of the Crittenden proposition, but to some extent, in advance of it."[239]

In January, John Crittenden had urged that his compromise plan be put to the voters for approval. The Radical Republicans vehemently opposed such a vote because they knew they would lose, and most likely lose by a wide margin. Summers, just returned from the Peace Conference in Washington, where he had been exposed to the debate regarding putting a compromise plan before the electorate, now promoted it wholeheartedly. Summers, too, knew such a plan would pass overwhelmingly, especially in Virginia. Summers, as previously mentioned, had begun secret exchanges with the secretary of state—exchanges that have been verified by numerous sources, none more important than *The Diary of a Public Man*. "The diary…calls attention to the then-secret history of Seward's outreach to Virginia's Unionists during the early days of Lincoln's presidency. The diarist noted on March 6 that 'a messenger enjoying the direct personal confidence of Mr. Seward' had just headed to Richmond with assurances that the administration would neither reinforce nor attempt to hold Fort Sumter."[240] The diary contained insights that only the most well-connected insider could have possibly known. John Janney wrote to his wife after Summers's great speech, "The little pigmy secessionists with their clap-trap nonsense have been reduced to the size of small mice."[241] Summers, indeed, had scored a major victory.

On March 13, John Tyler responded to Summers's speech, pointing out the weakness of the Peace Conference Amendment, but his remarks did not garner great support. Secessionist delegates from Caroline, Lunenburg, Northampton, Mecklenburg, Buckingham and Wythe Counties presented resolutions in favor of immediate secession. The Unionists tabled the secession resolutions. The Committee on Federal Relations had produced its full report by March 14, and Chairman Conrad moved that it be considered in the "Committee of the Whole." Henry Wise moved that the minority report of the committee be considered likewise. The convention agreed to both motions, meaning the full convention would consider the reports.

March 16 was the high point so far for the secessionists in the convention. George Wythe Randolph, grandson of Thomas Jefferson, delivered a rousing pro-secession speech. He defended slavery, he defended the largely agrarian Southern economy, he blamed "Northern exploiters" for Southern economic woes and he cited a long series of statistics showing why Virginia would be better off trading with the Lower South rather than the Lower North. He ended with the clarion call of the secessionists, "View the question before us as you will, and a withdrawal from the present Union seems to be the safest and best course for us to pursue. Let us not hesitate to take it and to submit our action to the people for their approbation."[242] Randolph's forceful speech was totally blunted, however, for at this very time, news reached the convention that Sumter would be evacuated shortly. "Seward empowered at least two individuals [James C. Welling, editor of the *National Intelligencer*, and New York congressman John Cochrane] to inform George W. Summers that the fort soon would be evacuated." This news "acted like a charm" and gave the Unionists "great strength" as Summers reported back to Seward.[243] The secret messages between Seward and Summers were having their desired effect. Incredibly, Seward also notified the Confederate commissioners in Washington through another secret intermediary that the fort would soon be evacuated. Debate continues to this day regarding whether Seward kept Lincoln fully informed of these developments, and although it is impossible to know for certain, it appears that Lincoln knew what was going on.

By mid-March, the scene in the nation's capital had gone from bad to worse—confusion reigned. But it was the scene in the White House that would prove so critical for the peace of the nation. And the scene in the White House was simply total chaos. The president had but two personnel secretaries at this time, John Nicolay and John Hay, neither of whom knew what to do. They were working eighteen hours per day amid a crush of visitors—folks standing in line to see the president by the hundreds. The pressure was so great, Nicolay wrote, that "we have scarcely had time to eat or sleep or even breathe."[244] The president, too, did not know what to do. As mentioned, he spent most of his time greeting well-wishers and interviewing folks wanting (or expecting, in the case of campaign workers) political appointments to government jobs, some important but mostly minor posts. "Sometimes the petitioners were so numerous that it was impossible to climb the stairs." [245] Donald insightfully noted, "As he [Lincoln] freely admitted later, when he became President, 'he was entirely ignorant not only of the duties, but of the manner of doing business' in the executive office…he tried to do everything himself." Charles Sumner, the irascible Radical Republican Senator from Massachusetts, observed after visiting with the new president, "The difficulty with Mr. Lincoln is that he has no conception of his situation…and having no system in his composition he has undertaken to manage the whole thing as if he knew all about it."[246] Lincoln, hopelessly inexperienced, "untested and untried," as his contemporaries claimed, was beginning to waver in support of Seward's conciliatory policy and risk war "as if he knew all about it."

And the chaos at the White House was exacerbated, to the extreme, by Mary Todd Lincoln. A "friendly" biographer called her an "emotionally unstable girl"; her contemporaries called her "slightly insane."[247] The latest research confirms she suffered from manic-depressive illness, now called bipolar disorder, with symptoms of depression, delusions and violent mood swings. "The signs of her mental illness began long before her 1875 commitment...

Looking out the front door of Seward's home in Washington, the entrance gate to the White House can be seen in the left-center background. *Seward House, Auburn, New York.*

These early manifestations later developed into full-blown Manic-Depressive episodes...she suffered numerous episodes throughout her life...[and] her intellect and emotions were overwhelmed by mental illness."[248]

Mary's instability added much complexity to an already overwhelmingly difficult scene. She had frequent temper tantrums, constantly meddled in the president's affairs (especially in regard to political patronage) and "at times would, in effect, blackmail her husband by behaving like a spoiled child." At one point, she forced him to give one of her friends a lucrative job by locking herself in her closest with his pants, causing Lincoln to exclaim, "How do you reckon I can go to a Cabinet meeting—without my pants?" She hated William Henry Seward with an unusual passion—"Seward is worse than Chase," she screamed—and "she declined to make an appearance when Seward, accompanied by his wife and children, called at the White House in September 1861." Senator Charles Sumner claimed Mary meddled in nearly all patronage affairs early in her husband's administration—and in early March, he was spending most of his time dispensing political appointments, so she most likely was heavily engaged. Outrageously jealous, she would fly into a rage when any pretty woman would pay attention to her husband. The president was under constant strain from his wife. At times, Mary Todd's behavior was simply ugly, and "even more embarrassing than her tactlessness was Mary Lincoln's dishonesty." She taxed the limited emotional energy Lincoln had left after enduring the eighteen-hour days of his early presidency.[249]

William Henry Seward, who lived just across the street from the entrance to the White House, was keenly aware of the scene on Pennsylvania Avenue. He pushed ahead with true gusto to save the nation from war by implementing his Southern Policy—the centerpiece of which was now the abandonment of Fort Sumter, so as to avoid any military confrontation with the new Confederate States of America.

In Richmond, no one had an inkling of the chaotic scene at the White House, but there was chaos enough in the state capitol. Debate continued, nonstop, between the secessionists and the unconditional Unionists. On Monday, March 18, Waitman Willey's resolutions were read into the record of the convention. As mentioned, Willey was from the Northwest, where a long-standing and bitter intrastate feud simmered over taxation. So, realizing the

Unionists were in a substantial majority, he introduced resolutions calling for equal and uniform taxation of all property (including slaves) at its fair value and called for the two Houses of the legislature to be apportioned on the basis of qualified voters—the "white basis"—which meant slaves would not be counted. Of course, both of these measures were roundly opposed by the Slave Power, and the secessionist delegates challenged them instantly. As if the convention did not already have enough on its plate, these resolutions just added to the chaos—Willey's actions were not helpful at this moment in time. For the remainder of the month, the taxation and apportionment issues would come up from time to time with heated debate the result. On March 19, Chairman Conrad reported that the Committee on Federal Relations had completed its work, a series of proposed amendments to the Constitution of the United States, and asked that they be printed and referred to the convention for debate and action.

Next up for the secessionist cause was the distinguished law professor from the University of Virginia, James Holcombe. Holcombe, from heavily enslaved Albemarle County in the Piedmont, was an articulate spokesman for the minority. A devout defender of slavery, his speech opened with the typical racist statement of the era as he noted the "the immense superiority of the white man over the black man." He outlined the advantages of Virginia joining the Southern Confederacy, but what he really did was outline the advantages for Virginia's Slave Power to join with the Slave Power of the Lower South. Holcombe had no interest in a border state conference because it would have little interest in preserving or protecting the Slave Power, which was losing ground rapidly throughout the borderland because of the rising Unionist tide. He ended with the mantra of the Slave Power: "Every material interest we possess would be destroyed by the subjugation of the Gulf States…I would rather see her [Virginia] fall in a glorious struggle for her own rights, and the rights of her sister States [Slave Power–dominated states], and leave to future history the memorable response in her behalf, 'dead upon the field of honor.'"[250] Within a few short months, "dead upon the field" would be known to all Virginians.

The next day, March 21, the unconditional Unionists countered Holcombe with their powerful spokesman, John B. Baldwin. Although some historians do not give him the highest marks, many Unionists in Virginia did. The *Richmond Whig* and his hometown newspaper, the *Staunton Spectator*, constantly referred to Baldwin as the ablest speaker for the "Union cause" in the state, even the nation. A letter to the editor of the *Richmond Whig*, dated March 21, captured the point: "Col. John B. Baldwin is making the ablest speech we ever listened to. He winged the 'game cock' of the University [referring to Holcombe] at the first fire, and stript him of his gayest feathers. He has laid a foundation broad and deep, and solid, upon which he is making a great, patriotic and statesmanlike speech. He will resume his argument tomorrow…come and see."[251] Lankford's view on Baldwin and his speech follows: "On March 21, John Brown Baldwin, one of the unionists floor leaders, confidently laid out the argument of the largest faction in the convention…He had blazed a brilliant path through the University of Virginia and, at only forty, had become an accomplished lawyer, the owner of ten slaves, and a captain in the Staunton militia…He was a man of blunt manners and eloquent speech. His address offered an important statement, the first but not the last or the most crucial instance in which he would play a part in the unfolding national drama."[252]

Baldwin hailed from a distinguished family of Virginia. He not only served on the Board of Visitors of the University of Virginia but was also a sought-after figure in business, commerce and law. His speech lasted for the best part of three days and was criticized (rightly) for being wordy and too long, but it was a magnificent defense of the Union and a repudiation of the extremists, both North and South. "I am strongly convinced that in the North and the South, the great masses of the people, leaving out the politicians and fanatics of both sections, have this day an earnest yearning for each other, and for peace." He ended with an impassioned call that produced a standing ovation: "I would rejoice to see the country, in all aspects, socially, industrially, politically united…I intend not to be driven back by frowns of opposition or threats of intimidation; but sustained by my own sense of right and my own conviction of patriotic duty, I shall march forward and leave the result to God."[253] Next, Mr. Carlile read the Peace Conference's proposed amendment into the record of the convention.

The Unionists in the convention remained in control, and that control was now driven by Seward's statements from Washington that Sumter would be evacuated soon. A number of days had passed since word of the evacuation had become public, and although some in the Republican Party had initially reacted in a hostile way, upon more sober reflection, the reaction was settling down and most were willing to accept it because of the "military necessity." This reaction was reported in the Northern press and in the Richmond press as well. Gideon Welles had recorded in his diary just a few days after the evacuation became public, "An impression has gone abroad that Sumter is to be evacuated and the shock caused by that announcement has done its work. The public mind is becoming tranquilized under it and will become

View of Richmond from Gambles Hill with the Virginia Manufactory of Arms in the foreground. Richmond factories could produce much fighting equipment for the war. *Courtesy of the Library of Virginia.*

fully reconciled to it when the causes which have led to that necessity shall have been made public and are rightly understood."[254]

As a result, most Virginians remained solidly opposed to secession despite huge sums of money being spent by the Slave Power to influence them otherwise. At this point, the only thing that could derail the "Unionist express" would be an outbreak of armed conflict with the new Confederacy. Summers relayed this message to Seward on numerous occasions in mid-March, and that drove Seward to redouble his efforts to evacuate Sumter so as to prevent any inadvertent military clash. Seward, and the military high command in Washington, were well aware of events in Charleston, as "from Fort Sumter itself, Major Anderson was reporting almost daily giving details of his own defensive plans and those of the Confederates virtually surrounding him."[255]

Again, Seward felt he had won the battle in Washington—and won the battle in Richmond as well. If Virginia stayed in, North Carolina, Tennessee and the Border South states of Maryland, Kentucky and Missouri would follow. His Southern Policy to conciliate the Upper South would have succeeded. And with its success, the new Confederacy would be in serious trouble, as only 10 percent of the nation's white population lived there, and a sizable minority of those whites, perhaps 30 percent, did not support the new Confederate government in March 1861. If the Confederate States of America wanted to start a fight, Seward would happily take them on with such odds.

In Washington, Abraham Lincoln was continuing to waffle. Seward became increasingly worried—and increasingly unhappy. Radical Republicans continued to badger Lincoln to resupply Fort Sumter, even if it meant starting a fight. To them, Sumter was a "political necessity," as the rabid secessionists in Charleston must be "taught a lesson." Journalist James E. Harvey (a close associate of Seward) of the *Philadelphia North American* had openly remarked that Sumter involved "nothing more than a point of honor."[256] Horace Greeley was at the White House on March 18 to push the Radical Republican agenda, no compromise with traitors. The next day, Gustavus Fox gave Lincoln another briefing on his "plan" to resupply Sumter before departing for Charleston. Fox wrote to his wife that evening, "Our Uncle Abe Lincoln has taken a high esteem for me and wishes me to take dispatches to Major Anderson at Fort Sumpter [*sic*] with regard to its final evacuation and to obtain a clear statement of his condition which his letters, probably guarded, do not fully exhibit. I have really great curiosity to see the famous Fort and several of my naval intimates are there in command."[257] Abraham Lincoln began to show signs of extreme fatigue. On March 20, he found out his sons had the measles. Mary Lincoln was "acting out."

Meanwhile, the Northern papers (at least most of them) were urging Lincoln to compromise and avoid war. "The *National Intelligencer* called peaceful separation 'wisdom and sound policy' while the *New York Times* reported 'growing sentiment throughout the North in favor of letting the gulf states go.'"[258] Of course, public opinion in the North was divided and even fickle, but a clear majority of Northerners rejected war in the spring of 1861. New York newspapers carried added weight because of the importance of the state and city in national life. "Though officially nonpartisan, the *Herald* [*New York Herald*] tended to take a Democratic slant…it took an outspoken pro-compromise position, consistently berating the Republican Party and the Lincoln administration for refusing to offer essential concessions. The *Herald* warned incessantly that the Upper South would soon follow the cotton states out of the Union unless the Crittenden Compromise were rapidly adopted."[259] Even Greeley's hard-line *Tribune* opined that the government was based "not on force but on reason; not on bayonets and battalions, but on good will and general consent."[260]

On March 21, Fox arrived in Charleston, followed a day or so later by Hurlbut and Lamon. Under the assumption that he was arranging for its evacuation, Fox was permitted to visit Fort Sumter, where he had a long and substantive discussion with Major Anderson and his officers. On Monday, March 25, Hurlbut and Lamon, now in Charleston as well, met with various political authorities and had interviews with Governor Pickens and General Beauregard. In Washington, the scene muddled along. Lincoln had made no public statement on Fort Sumter—or anything else, for that matter—and ominously for Seward and General Scott, he had not signed the order to evacuate the fort, which had been on his desk now for over a week. In New York, banking interest became concerned about the new higher tariff and its impact on revenues for running the government (tariff revenues were the main source of government funds in 1861), and the commercial magnates began to see the possibility of a real negative economic impact from secession. Seward parried these concerns by promising that new sources of revenues could be found much easier than managing war—here was the mark of a true statesman.

In Congress, Radical Republicans became more and more intransigent. "A caucus of Republican congressmen warned the President that failure to reinforce Sumter would bring disaster to the party." Lyman Trumbull, Illinois Senator and supposedly Lincoln's "voice" in that body, introduced a resolution regarding Sumter: "It is the duty of the President to use all means in his power to hold and protect the public property of the United States."[261] March 23 was another bad day for Abraham Lincoln, as he privately continued to struggle with the Fort Sumter question while Fort Chadbourne in Texas was abandoned by the army, again leading the country to believe Federal forts were not going to be held. He had yet another long cabinet meeting, where he raised more and more questions about Fort Sumter. It was reported that he looked "worn." The chaos at the White House had become so intolerable that the president finally restricted visitors to a few hours in the morning and a few more in the afternoon. His secretaries, Nicolay and Hay, were approaching total exhaustion, as they had not had a moment's rest in nearly three weeks.

Seward became increasingly concerned about Lincoln's lack of decisiveness on Fort Sumter, as he had promised virtually all of the key players in the country that the fort would be evacuated soon. Along with everyone else close to the president, he did not know him well enough at this point in time to fully understand him. Lincoln was "shut-mouthed" and simply did not let anyone know just how he truly felt about any given issue. Seward had sent Congressman Cochrane to see Lincoln after his visit to Richmond to relay the message from George Summers that the proposed evacuation of Fort Sumter had acted like a "charm" and strengthened the Unionist cause enormously. In addition, he had sent delegation after delegation to see Lincoln to urge that it be done. Time was fast approaching for action—it was time for William Henry Seward to produce on his promises.

———

In Richmond on Monday, March 25, the Unionists flexed their muscles regarding the report of the Committee on Federal Relations and pushed to bring the resolutions up for debate. The following day, Hugh Nelson, Unionist delegate from Clarke County in the Valley region, delivered a memorable speech. He spoke of the great gamble facing Virginia if it seceded, noting that it would become a border state with the North and would thus be without Fugitive Slave Laws. After losing the right to take slaves into any of the territories, war would most likely consume Virginia, bringing death to its young men. He asked, "When they are brought back to you in the cold embrace of death, will it assuage your grief to reflect you have urged them on to an unnecessary contest in a deadly civil war?" He challenged Virginians to work for compromise, for peace and for restoring the union of states: "Virginia, by the noble sacrifices and successful efforts she has from time to time made, for the formation and preservation of this Union, has well-earned for herself, the proud position of a great pacificator…I want Virginia to be that great central point in our political system, by her unfettered influences, to draw them all back, to resolve once more in harmony in their accustomed orbits."[262] At this same time, George Summers, concerned that no word had been received regarding movement at Fort Sumter, had written to Seward, "What delays the removal of Major Anderson?" He reiterated in no uncertain terms "the positive effect it would have on Virginians and the disastrous effect if it were not done."[263]

On Wednesday, March 27, debate began on the primary resolution of the Committee on Federal Relations, a proposed eight-part constitutional amendment. The key components included reestablishing the Missouri Compromise line, forbidding Congress from interfering with slavery where it already existed, renewed support for the Fugitive Slave Law, a permanent prohibition on the importation of slaves, compensation to slave owners for runaway slaves prevented from return by Northern mobs and prohibiting African Americans from having the right to vote or hold public office. While these issues might seem repulsive to the modern reader, it should be noted that these measures were generally supported throughout the nation.

In addition to the proposed amendment, the report also included a set of resolutions that were not part of the amendment but were to be voted on and submitted with the amendment. The resolutions addressed a wide range of issues, including jurisdiction over federal forts, the right to secede, coercion by the Federal government, conferring to the Federal government the powers to deal peaceably with a seceded state, a desire to meet with the Northern states for the purpose of redressing the sectional issues, opposing reinforcement of federal forts and calling for a conference of slaveholding states that had not seceded.

Chairman Conrad then addressed many of the objections that had been raised by secessionists to the majority report. He ended his presentation of the resolutions with a blistering attack on the immediate secessionists, stating, "It is proper that some efforts should be made on the part of the immediate representatives of Virginia here to settle and compose the existing difficulties of the country. With those gentlemen who will entertain no other than the proposition of an instantaneous withdrawal from the Union, and the instant disrupture of this great nation without further effort and further consideration, it is utterly impossible…that I can agree."[264] Conrad, speaking for the vast majority of Virginia Unionists, sincerely believed Virginians were "here to settle…the difficulties of the country." Virginians thought they had the answers.

What the Unionists of Virginia were essentially doing was outlining the position of political moderates throughout the nation: states had a right to secede, the seceded states should be permitted "to go in peace," no attempt should be made to coerce states to remain in the Union, Federal property should not be reinforced or recaptured by force of arms, a call for a conference of border states should be made forthwith and, of course, a call for a meeting with Northern states or a Constitutional Convention to redress Southern grievances should take place as soon as possible. William Henry Seward, in one way or another, had encouraged the Virginians on all of these efforts and was doing all that he could to promote the new Union Party—the coalition of Unionists that held the key to keeping Virginia, and thereby the Upper South, in the Union.

At the convention, the Unionists remained in full control during the last week of March. Various secessionist delegates continued to present resolutions from their respective counties calling for immediate secession. On Friday, March 29, debate continued on the resolutions of the Committee on Federal Relations. William Cabell Rives had been invited to speak at the convention and made a long and stirring speech against secession and for compromise proposals, such as the Peace Conference amendment. Although a lifelong opponent of slavery, Rives defended the institution at this time because Virginians—and, indeed, most of the thoughtful moderates in the nation—knew more time was needed to determine just how to end the institution peacefully.

Henry Wise, sometimes referred to as a "political opportunist," was having an increasingly bitter dispute with Governor Letcher regarding Virginia's preparedness for conflict. Wise now determined that the best course for Virginia would be to join the Southern Confederacy and prepare for armed conflict. Wise "was temperamentally suited and intellectually predisposed" to be an obstructionists, and he quickly became the leader of the minority forces trying to delay passage of any compromise proposal. "The limitations placed on debate during the last month before the firing on Fort Sumter meant that Wise, because of his parliamentary skills, usually acted as spokesman for the secessionist caucus and advanced its measures."[265] O.J. Wise, Henry's son, had become editor of the secessionist *Richmond Enquirer* newspaper and was even more radical than his father. He bent to the task of throwing sand in the Unionist machinery.

Even as Wise was holding forth in the convention—"no one else spoke as much, evoked as much laughter from the delegates or the galleries, or won as much attention"[266]—the Unionists were still enjoying widespread support throughout the state as anti-secession sentiment continued to increase. In late March, "a reporter for the *Washington Evening Star* rejected claims by the 'Richmond disunion newspapers' that a 'considerable change' of opinion had taken place since the election in early February." He vowed that "if anything, the reverse was true. Many who had been 'uncertain' about the policy of the Lincoln administration no longer feared that it would be 'aggressive.'" This was especially true in the Northwest, as "a large majority of our people are warm Union men. There has been no decline in that respect since you left [referring to a delegate who had left to attend the Virginia State Convention] but on the contrary an increase in Union feeling."[267] Indeed, the general feeling persisted that secessionism was "dead" in the Upper and Border South unless fighting broke out between the Federal government and the new Confederacy.

So March ended with the Unionist leadership still united but with rising concern about events transpiring in the nation's capital. George Summers had received no official word, but "it was rumored in Washington that Fort Sumter would be evacuated." Lack of word from Seward was causing tensions to rise among the Unionists. On March 31, Fort Bliss, in Texas, had been turned over to that state's authorities, again leading to the perception that Sumter would be next.[268] But unbeknownst to the Unionists in Richmond, in the nation's capital on Friday, March 29, Abraham Lincoln would finally make his decision—he would attempt to resupply Fort Sumter. Here is how it happened.

Monday, March 25, began the final, and as it turned out, fateful week in Washington. Henry Seward, still very confident that he had won the battle over abandonment of Fort Sumter, was now determined to see that it was done. He knew time was running out and it was time for Lincoln to sign the evacuation order.

Gustavus Fox had returned from Charleston and presented Lincoln with an extremely optimistic report regarding Fort Sumter. He stated that it could be resupplied—in fact, he stated it could be done with a minimum number of ships and men. Major Anderson, during his interview with Fox at the fort, expressed complete opposition to the plan at this late date. An eyewitness account of the encounter follows: "When they reached the parapet Major Anderson turned the conversation upon his position, and knowing that the author of the proposed scheme for his relief was before him, he at once earnestly condemned any proposal to send him reinforcements. He asserted that it was too late; he agreed with General Scott that an entrance by sea was impossible; and he impressed upon Captain Fox his belief that any reinforcements coming would at once precipitate a collision and inaugurate civil war."[269] Anderson had informed the military as early as March 9 that "any vessels coming in by the Morris Island channel would be under fire of the batteries from the time they crossed the bar until they reached this work."[270] But for some reason, Lincoln had taken a "liking" to Fox, and despite his marginal credentials in naval tactics or in planning such a movement, he would decide to endorse Fox's plan while rejecting the best judgment of his senior military advisors. It is difficult to understand just why Lincoln liked Fox, but Lincoln was certainly looking for a way to justify not abandoning Fort Sumter at this point. Fox might just have been the most expedient conduit.

On March 26, the cabinet met for another long session to discuss Fort Sumter. Seward's impatience was rising by the hour as he continually thought the decision had been made and the president ought to sign the evacuation order. Lincoln was still spending long hours interviewing prospective political appointees, as his limited staff was not able to sort out those who really needed to see the president from those who did not. On the twenty-seventh, Hurlbut and Lamon submitted their report on "public opinion" in Charleston. They found no allegiance to the Union there. But this would have surprised no one who had been in Washington during the Secession Winter. In fact, when Lamon had met with both Governor Pickens and General Beauregard, he had informed them that Fort Sumter would be evacuated—but on whose authority is a debate that continues to this very day.

David Potter concluded, "Lamon's dogmatic promises of evacuation, coupled with the general expectation in Washington, led to a widespread and unqualified belief that the question was settled…It is clearly evident that a general understanding existed that Major Anderson was to be withdrawn. It is also evident that Lincoln shared in this understanding."[271] Again, it is critically important to note that Henry Seward "shared in this understanding," too. Seward, ever the "Washington insider," now made another move. He either wrote or edited a note from General Scott to Lincoln stating that both Fort Sumter and Fort Pickens should be abandoned to "soothe and give confidence to the eight remaining slave-holding States, and render their cordial adherence to this Union perpetual."[272]

Scott and Seward were "working like hands in a glove" at this point, Scott having the highest regard for Seward and probably considering him as the premier. "Owing to the intimacy between Scott and Seward, it was assumed that Scott's recommendation was really Seward's, adroitly and tentatively made in this way in order to avoid hazarding the Secretary of State's influence within the administration."[273] Both Seward and Scott were longtime Washington power brokers, and neither thought the president was acting "presidential" at this point in time, so a gentle nudge was in order, thus the note. Additionally, Scott had had a conversation with Lamon when he returned from Charleston, and Lamon had led the general to believe Lincoln was ready to sign the evacuation order. So Scott felt very comfortable in delivering the note.

While many historians have roundly criticized Scott for sending "political advice"—that is, abandoning Fort Pickens to "soothe" Upper South Unionists (Donald called it "shocking")—he clearly thought he was on solid ground. But the note proved to be a huge mistake. The Lincolns had scheduled their first state dinner for the evening of the twenty-eighth. Mary was very tense, ordering servants to and fro, with the president desperately trying to control the White House scene. Lincoln had called Scott (who was to attend the dinner) to the White House for talks. "Scott went down Pennsylvania Avenue unconcerned. The President had apparently given in, albeit reluctantly, on the matter of evacuating Fort Sumter, and he had so far voiced no objection to evacuating Fort Pickens, in Pensacola Harbor… Scott entered the White House confidently, armed with a set of convincing arguments for evacuating both forts, and plans for doing so drawn up by his military assistant, Lieutenant Colonel E.D. Keyes. Scott expected authority to put the evacuation order into effect."[274] Seward had led Scott to believe that this was the case also.

But the scene turned ugly from the start. "Lincoln, truly worn out with his nerves near the breaking point, exploded in a rage at reading the message, lashing out at the old general and shouting that he would find someone else to lead the military if Scott would not follow orders. Scott, truly shaken by Lincoln's violent reaction, asked to be excused from the dinner party and left."[275] Lincoln managed to compose himself and get through the dinner, some even described him as "charming" with his usual bevy of jokes, but then the president asked his cabinet officers to stay for a brief meeting. "Then, in a voice choked with emotion, he told them of Scott's recommendations. Blair erupted that the general was not offering military advice but was 'playing politician.' Except Seward, whose views Scott was echoing, the others tended to agree. Lincoln gave notice that he would hold a formal council the next day. That night he slept not at all, aware that the time had come for decision."[276] Lincoln undoubtedly felt the general had abandoned his "Sumter Policy," a policy that called for reinforcement of Fort Pickens in the event Sumter was evacuated. Now Lincoln wondered whether he could even trust the general's judgment on Fort Sumter, and he questioned Anderson's views, as both were Southerners. Could they be giving him "political" advice rather than military?

Lincoln had a violent temper that was displayed from time to time, as General Scott witnessed. William H. Herndon, Lincoln's longtime law partner and one who had traveled with him regularly, asserted that Lincoln sometimes "got angry at the bar, and when he did get mad he was then ugly." One time he became "so angry that he looked like Lucifer in an uncontrollable rage." But as the unsuspecting General Scott found out, he had a "special venom…for those who abandoned party or principle. Lincoln feared abandonment, probably because in childhood he felt abandoned by his mother, who died when he was nine, and his father, who was emotionally distant. Lincoln seems to have displaced the repressed anger he felt for his parents onto political 'abandoners.'"[277] In addition to these possible psychological factors, the new president had become totally isolated. Surprisingly, his Illinois friends had recently left town resentful that they had not gotten enough recognition (and political appointments). David Davis was simply shocked that he did not get some kind of important post. Consequently, Lincoln had "no one around him he felt he could trust."[278]

March 29 would prove the decisive day. The cabinet meeting was inconclusive, as usual. Lincoln's "compound" cabinet, a cast of strong personalities who were bitterly divided politically, rarely gave him solid advice. At this, the first of many truly important meetings, the cabinet was hopelessly divided, and each member was as much concerned about enhancing his "standing" in the council as anything. Blair and Chase continued to favor resupply (we need to teach those secessionists a lesson, they preached), and Seward and Smith continued to urge abandonment (Sumter was untenable and not worth starting a war over, they retorted). Bates was undecided, and Cameron was absent. Welles, however, changed his mind and voted for resupply. Thus, the cabinet now stood at three in favor and two opposed. It is worth mentioning, though, that had Cameron been at the meeting, he would have voted with Seward, and the cabinet would then have stood at three in favor and three opposed. Seward, sensing Lincoln was moving toward reinforcing Sumter, next made a proposal to reinforce Fort Pickens, rather than Sumter.

But sometime during his sleepless night on the twenty-eighth, Lincoln had made up his mind. In spite of his inharmonious cabinet, he ordered the Fort Sumter resupply effort to move forward. The exact message to Secretary of War Cameron was: "I desire that an expedition, to move by sea, be got ready to sail as early as the 6th of April next."[279] He also ordered that Fort Pickens be reinforced with troops and supplies, as Seward had urged. Something had tipped the scales for Lincoln to move away from Seward's conciliatory policy. The hard-liners in Congress probably had an impact, the hard-liners in his cabinet probably had an impact and the hard-liners in the press probably had an impact. Horace Greeley, who hated Seward because of a long-standing personal feud, blasted Seward's Southern Policy throughout March, stating over and over it would "ruin the Republican party." Nicolay's statement that it was "the President's own inclination" to resupply might have come to the fore also. Whatever the cause or causes, Lincoln made the most momentous decision of his presidency alone and in a state of total physical and mental exhaustion.

Henry Seward was stunned—and bitterly disappointed that Lincoln had now sided with the hard-liners. But Seward was never at a loss for ideas and, in fact, was the most accomplished Washington manipulator on the scene. He now sought to make his Fort Pickens expedition the centerpiece of the president's plan, while at the same time developing a new plan to change Lincoln's mind on the Fort Sumter expedition. McClintock observed, "If the government's presence at Pensacola were secured, perhaps Lincoln could be persuaded even now to cast off the albatross in Charleston Harbor."[280] Seward immediately grabbed Montgomery Meigs, the handsome, young army engineer who was managing the construction of the new Capitol, and rushed him to the White House for an introduction to the president. After a brief conversation, Lincoln agreed with Seward that Meigs was their man. Seward then instructed Meigs to quickly draft a plan for the relief of Fort Pickens.

March 30 was a terrible day for Abraham Lincoln. Still not sleeping, and still feeling isolated and alone, he met with a delegation of California politicians and again lost his temper. "Frustrated at their leader's arrogance, Lincoln barked at him heatedly, then grabbed his speech, crumpled it, and threw it into the fire before angrily inviting the entire deputation to leave."[281] Abraham Lincoln had now lost control; he collapsed from a sick headache. "The strain under which Lincoln labored in arriving at this decision was immense. All the troubles and anxieties of his life, he told Browning, did not equal those he felt in these tense days. The pressure was so great that Mary Lincoln reported that he keeled over; and had to be put to bed with one of his rare migraine headaches."[282] Could a more experienced leader— one steeped in the affairs of Washington, one intimately connected to the leadership of the country and one closely tied to the nation's political moderates, both North and South—have made a different decision?

Virtually all the evidence suggests that William Henry Seward would have made a different decision. Seward continued with his plans to reinforce Pickens and somehow scuttle or delay the reinforcement of Sumter. On the morning of March 30, still in a state of shock over the president's decision to abandon his conciliatory policy, Seward laid out his next moves. He would confer with General Scott as soon as possible, he would consult with Thurlow Weed (his political "partner") and he would summon Henry Raymond, editor of the *New York Times*, to Washington for consultation. Boldly, he decided to manage the Pickens affair. Unbelievably, he decided not to inform the secretary of war, Simon Cameron, or the secretary of the navy, Gideon Welles, of the Pickens expedition or of his involvement. Seward, as secretary of state, began to manage a military operation—with the president's apparent approval.

March 31, Easter Sunday, was an exciting day for Henry Seward—and the most critical day so far for the peace of the nation. He had met with and convinced Scott that they should "manage" the reinforcement of Fort Pickens and let Welles, Blair and Fox (the navy men) "manage" the Fort Sumter affair. Welles made the *Powhatan*, the largest available navy warship, the "flagship" of the Sumter expedition and had sent Fox with such orders to New York Harbor to make final arrangements. But the arrangements were not going well. On the morning of March 31, Fox telegrammed Montgomery Blair, "I saw Mr. Aspinwall [the New York businessman who owned the tugs that Fox needed to lease for the expedition] yesterday and in the evening Capt. Marshall [the senior navy officer in New York who was to acquire supplies, men, etc]…they are now astonished at the idea of the Govt attempting it, declaring that the time has passed and that the people are reconciled to leaving this position and making the stand on Pickens. We argued the point till midnight." Throughout the day, Fox desperately tried to make arrangements so that the mission could proceed, but he was getting nowhere. In the evening, he sent another telegram to Blair indicating his frustration and despair: "I am writing this at Mr. Aspinwall's house. He has just had an interview with Capt. Marshall who declines to have anything to do with the matter. This is serious as he was expected to obtain all provisions… The arguments of opposition to this act of solemn duty are all political. Capt. Marshall has been in Washington for two weeks and wishes to know if Mr. Seward goes for it…I feel like abandoning my country, moving off somewhere. I am sick down to my heel."[283]

Seward, desperate to avoid a confrontation with the Confederacy, now pulled out all the stops. That he did not inform Wells and Cameron of the pending mission to Pickens was indicative of a broader scheme. And that scheme included Seward assuming the role of "premier." He next "launched a series of desperate moves to reverse Lincoln's decision to resupply Fort Sumter."[284] William Henry Seward was now certain the nation was headed toward civil war. Little did he know that such a war would start in a mere twelve days.

⸺⸺

So March ended in Richmond with the Unionists remaining in solid control of the Virginia State Convention—and with public support in the state solidly in their favor. Ominously for the peace of the nation,

March ended in the nation's capital with the president, his cabinet, the military high command and all their subordinates in a state of extreme turmoil and confusion. It was a scene from a tragic-comic opera, as the first days of April will attest.

CHAPTER 6

A STATE BETRAYED

Lincoln made a profound mistake with the particular wording [in the Proclamation of Insurrection]…*he asked Virginians to fight fellow Southerners.*
—*William W. Freehling, speech given in Old House Chamber, Richmond, Virginia, April 17, 2011*

April 1861 was the month when peace ended for the nation. Slavery had become the catalyst for the impending conflict, for sure, but the actions of misguided politicians (both North and South), a series of chance occurrences and even some bad luck contributed also. Historian Michael Holt captured the point: "Yet sectional differences over slavery had existed for decades without causing a shooting war…As even the most compelling modern critic of the revisionists recognizes, moreover, the Civil War resulted from a specific chain of events. And those events did not just happen; they were not just products of sectional differences. Rather, specific human actors—and, yes, specific political leaders—usually caused them to happen."[285]

In Virginia, as documented in this work, the fight would come down to one between the Slave Power, dominated by the aristocratic planters who owned large numbers of slaves, and the Unionists, the majority of whom did not own slaves. During the Secession Winter of 1860–61, the vast majority of Americans, again in both North and South, did not want to see the nation go to war with itself—over slavery, over saving the Union, over whatever. Americans, for the most part, had real confidence that their political leaders would find a workable solution to the crisis. In the end, peace-loving Americans, and especially peace-loving Virginians, were terribly disappointed in the "specific chain of events" caused by "specific political leaders." The remarkable events of the first seventeen days of April will be discussed below.

———

"Easter Monday, April 1, 1861, was not a good morning for Abraham Lincoln, Henry Seward, or the nation. The two principals in the new Administration were again at odds, and the risk of war for the nation had suddenly increased dramatically."[286] In fact, exactly two weeks from this very day, April 15, President Lincoln would stun the nation by issuing a Proclamation of Insurrection, the statement that started the Civil War. The proclamation will be discussed fully in the Epilogue.

During the previous evening, Thurlow Weed, who had been in Washington, had a long and substantive conversation with Henry Seward. Henry Raymond had been summoned from New York and arrived at Seward's house after midnight for talks. After these conferences, Seward somehow found time on April 1 to draft a message for the president, which he titled "Some Thoughts for the President's Consideration." It was a bold, rash attempt to grab the reins of power from Abraham Lincoln. It was Seward's supreme effort to become "premier," to turn around the decision to resupply Fort Sumter and to preserve the peace. Weed and Raymond were to publish "Thoughts" in their respective newspapers, along with the response from Lincoln, whom they all felt would endorse Seward's recommendations. "They hoped to create the necessary public support for Lincoln to abandon Fort Sumter and to adopt Seward's plans for cultivating Southern Union sentiment as the first step toward peaceful reunification."[287]

Historians, for the most part, have not given Seward's "Thoughts" high marks. Some have suggested they were a travesty, and one even called it an April Fools' joke. But in Seward's defense, he was in a political quagmire of the highest order on this spring day. Indeed, he had promised "the nation" that Sumter would be abandoned. Suddenly, and without telegraphing his motive, Lincoln had reversed that position. Seward, more than anyone in Lincoln's inner circle, knew that war would be the result.

Since Lincoln's first day in office, most contemporary observers did, in fact, feel that he had not been acting "presidential." Furthermore, he had collapsed from exhaustion or tension less than forty-eight hours before; thus,

Seward thought it was time for him to take charge. After all, he was Mr. Republican, the most recognized and experienced political leader on the scene that spring. He had become impatient with the president and was not about to give up on his Southern Policy—and peace—without a fight. Charles Francis Adams had recorded in his diary about this time, "The impression which I have received is that the course of the President is drifting the country into war…everywhere at this place is discouragement, not loud in words but in hopelessness of a favorable issue. For my part I see nothing but incompetency in the head. The man is not equal to the hour." If viewed in this light, Seward's "Thoughts" take on a different perspective.

Among other things, Seward's "Thoughts" stated that the administration did not have any policies, "either domestic or foreign," and it was time to adopt some and urged the president to "change the question before the public from one upon slavery, or about slavery for a question upon Union or Disunion" and to demand explanations from Spain and France for their interventions in the affairs of Santo Domingo and Haiti and declare war on either or both if their response was not satisfactory. Seward also stated that someone must energetically carry out the policies— "either the President must do it himself, and be all the while active in it; or devolve it on some member of his Cabinet."

However one wants to interpret it, Seward's "Thoughts" was the most extraordinary document ever sent to a sitting president by a member of his cabinet, with "devolve it on some member of his Cabinet" a thinly veiled attempt to seize control. Lincoln did not approve of the "Thoughts," but it is unclear how he responded to Seward. However, "when the President unexpectedly rejected Seward's proposals, the plans to publish the memorandum and Lincoln's reply collapsed."[288] The cabinet would have firmly resisted Seward as "premier"; needless to say, it did not happen.

Meanwhile, Seward continued his "maneuverings." He had a meeting with Lieutenant David Porter that morning about the mission to reinforce Fort Pickens. It is generally understood that Porter recommended using the warship *Powhatan* for the mission and also recommended it be kept secret from the Department of the Navy because so many "known secessionists" were still employed there who would leak news to the Confederacy. Seward agreed with Porter's assessment and then took him (and Captain Meigs) to the White House, where they briefed Lincoln on the plan. Lincoln approved the plan, including keeping it secret, and said he would "take care" of Welles when the time came. Lincoln then sent the following telegram to Commodore S.L. Breese, commandant of the Navy Yard in Brooklyn, New York: "Fit out the 'Powhatan' to go to sea at the earliest possible moment, under sealed orders. Orders by a confidential messenger go forward tomorrow."[289]

Gideon Welles, who had just assigned the *Powhatan* as flagship of the Fort Sumter expedition, also sent telegrams to Commodore Breese. The first one read, "The Department revokes its orders for the detachment of the officers of the 'Powhatan' and the transfer and discharge of her crew. Hold her in readiness for sea service." Later, he sent a second telegram: "Fit out the 'Powhatan' to go to sea at the earliest possible moment." The commodore telegrammed back, "The 'Powhatan' after landing her stores went out of commission at two o'clock. Crew on board the 'North Carolina,' officers mostly left with their leaves of absence. I shall agreeably to the last orders refit the 'Powhatan' for sea, with quickest dispatch. As there will be but few men left not wanted for the 'Powhatan,' I shall not send the men to Norfolk in the chartered steamer, but remain ready to send them in the 'Harriet Lane,' if so ordered."[290] The navy, unaware of the planned missions, was proceeding to do routine service on the *Powhatan* when the telegrams from Washington arrived.

Montgomery Blair also got into the act. After he received the distressing telegrams from Fox on the evening of March 31 indicating that "problems" in New York were delaying the mission, Blair wired Fox the following message: "I have yrs of yesterday. The President wishes you to come here to shape the orders. I will write to Gnl Cameron who is now in Harrisburg to return immediately. You will have time enough to organize the expedition by coming on tomorrow night and returning Wednesday or Thursday night." While Fox was returning to Washington for consultation with Blair and the president, Seward was sending Porter and Meigs to New York with a pile of cash ($10,000) to prepare the secret Fort Pickens expedition. Blair did not know of the Pickens expedition at this point in time either.

Chaos continued at the White House with hundreds of people standing in line to see the president, letters piling high to be answered by Lincoln's overwhelmed secretaries and important telegrams and dispatches arriving hourly. The latest communication from Major Anderson stated he had supplies to last a few more days. He pointedly asked when the order to evacuate the fort would be forthcoming. At Fort Sumter, Samuel Crawford, assistant surgeon on Anderson's staff, recorded his eyewitness account: "Every hour now tended to strengthen the belief that the garrison was to be withdrawn, and the preliminary steps to be taken were considered upon both sides. The public press as well as private advices from Washington all seemed to place the fact of withdrawal beyond doubt. The engineer officer had made his arrangements, and had reported to his chief his intentions, and had received from that official his instructions as to the disposition to be made of the property."[291] Thus, while the military officers "on the ground" at Sumter were moving ahead with preparations to evacuate, the politicians in Washington were playing a soon-to-be-deadly duplicitous game.

April 2 was a day of high tension for Lincoln and Seward. Most likely, Lincoln had informed Seward that he had received his "Thoughts" and stated his policies were outlined in his Inaugural Address and that he would see that they were carried out. Undeterred, Seward played yet another card—somehow he convinced Lincoln that they should try one more time to get Virginia to reject secession and disband the convention *sine die* (no future meeting date) in exchange for the abandonment of Fort Sumter, the "fort for a state" proposition that had been talked about for weeks. Lincoln acquiesced, but most likely only to mollify Seward. The secretary of state then asked one of his assistants, Robert Chew, to recommend someone who could be trusted to take a secret message to Richmond. Chew quickly chose Allan B. Magruder, an attorney in Washington who was a native Virginian and known to have close ties to the Unionist leadership at the convention.

Seward immediately summoned Magruder to his office, interviewed him and then took him to see the president. Lincoln asked Magruder if he would go to Richmond without delay and ask George Summers to come to see him quickly on a matter of the highest importance. "Tell Mr. Summers, I want to see him at once, for there is no time to be lost; what is to be done must be done quickly...If Mr. Summers cannot come himself, let him send some friend of his, some Union man in whom he has confidence."[292] Magruder, totally overwhelmed by the interviews with the president and secretary of state, dashed to the train station and took the very next train to Richmond, arriving in that city in the evening. Despite rejection of his "Thoughts," Seward still appeared to be in charge. Potter noted, "It is significant that, when Lincoln decided to communicate with the Virginia Unionists, Seward made all the arrangements."[293] No other cabinet officer was consulted or brought into the discussion—this was a two-man show, with Seward apparently in the lead.

Throughout the morning of April 3, Lincoln had been huddled with his cabinet discussing the plans to relieve Fort Sumter. While the Sumter mission was being actively planned, incredibly, neither Lincoln nor Seward told the cabinet about the secret mission to Fort Pickens or the secret message sent to Summers. Seward's team of army and navy officers had arrived at the Navy Yard in Brooklyn and immediately began preparing the *Powhatan* for the Pickens mission. Meanwhile, Gustavus Fox had returned to Washington to meet with Lincoln, Blair and Welles. Fox, still dismayed by the lack of progress, wrote to his friend Dr. Lowery on the afternoon of the third, "My expedition is ordered to be got ready, but I doubt if we shall get off. Delay, indecision, obstacles…Shall leave here tomorrow afternoon."[294]

Thursday morning, April 4, found the White House, the War Department and the Department of the Navy firing telegrams and messages to the Navy Yard in New York. Meigs, an army officer, showed his secret orders to A.H. Foote, acting for the commodore of the Navy Yard, and Foote sent a telegram to Welles: "Captain Meigs has called on me with a letter showing his authority from the government to have certain preparations made and things placed on board of vessels soon to go to sea, about which you are familiar; but as the orders do not come direct I make this report, but as no time is to be lost I am preparing what is called for and report my action." Welles now was perplexed, for he had chosen Captain Samuel Mercer of the navy to command the *Powhatan* and lead the Sumter expedition with Fox in overall command, and he did not quite know what to think about Meigs.

Meanwhile, John B. Baldwin, responding to Lincoln's urgent summons, had taken the evening train from Richmond to Washington. According to the train schedule of the Richmond, Fredericksburg and Potomac Railroad (RF&P), Baldwin left Richmond on the evening train the night of April 3, arrived at Aquia Creek (where the train tracks ended) before midnight and then took the steamboat to Washington, arriving sometime around dawn.[295] Exhausted from his sleepless night on the train and steamer, Baldwin arrived at Seward's office midmorning "running on adrenalin." Seward explained to Baldwin that the president had a vitally important message for him and took him to the White House, arriving just before 11:00 a.m.

Seward had assumed Lincoln was going to offer the "fort for a state" proposal to the Virginia Unionist. Lincoln took Baldwin to a bedroom for a very private discussion. Unfortunately, no staff member was present to record the discussion or follow up with any decisions made. It is unclear whether the absence of staff was deliberate on Lincoln's part, for he did not offer, in writing, a proposal (or anything) to Baldwin. Thus, it is impossible to determine what actually happened. Given his overnight train ride from Richmond to Washington on such short notice—a truly supreme effort—Baldwin left the meeting greatly disappointed, even wondering why he had been summoned. He said he received nothing of substance. After the meeting, he went back to see Seward at the State Department, where Seward continued to assure him the administration would opt for peace. Seward, surprised that Baldwin did

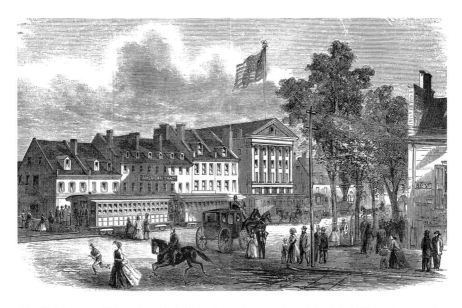

John Baldwin would have boarded this train on the evening of April 3, 1861, as it stopped in downtown Richmond. He would be in President Lincoln's office at eleven o'clock the following morning. *Courtesy of the Library of Virginia.*

not mention the "fort for a state" proposal, now realized that Lincoln was not about to back down on the Fort Sumter mission. For Baldwin's part, upon his return to Richmond the next day, he reported to the Unionist leadership (in a secret meeting) his extreme disappointment in the interview with the president, stating that Lincoln had opened the meeting saying he had come too late. The Unionist leaders were dumbstruck—what did this mean?

After the war, Baldwin appeared before the Committee on Reconstruction (the joint committee of the Congress controlled by the Radical Republicans and the one that attempted to impeach President Andrew Johnson) and stated that at no time during the interview did Lincoln offer the "fort for a state" proposal. His exact words are noteworthy: "I am as clear to my recollection as it is possible under the circumstances that he made no such suggestion, as I understood it, and said nothing from which I could infer it, for I was so excited—the matter involving what I thought would give promise of settlement to the country—that I am sure no opening of that sort, no overture of any sort could have escaped me."[296] Later, Baldwin would remark that the meeting with Lincoln was "the most significant event of my life." No doubt most Americans even to this very day would say the same about a one-on-one interview with a sitting president.

The "Powhatan Affair" came to a head on April 5. On the afternoon of the fourth, as Baldwin was leaving the White House, both Simon Cameron and Winfield Scott gave orders to Fox to proceed to Charleston with supplies and troops to relieve the garrison at Fort Sumter. Cameron ordered Fox "to use his entire force to open a passage...and place both the troops and supplies in Fort Sumter." Fox had returned to New York on the fifth and found preparations moving forward, but he still did not know of the secret mission to Fort Pickens. Welles, who still did not know of the Pickens mission either, had sent a telegram to Captain Mercer, his commander of the *Powhatan*, stating, "You will leave New York with the 'Powhatan' in time to be off Charleston bar, ten miles distant from and due east of the lighthouse, on the morning of the 11th inst., there to await the arrival of the transport or transports with troops and stores."[297] Mercer showed this order to Lieutenant Porter and Captain Meigs, who were busily preparing the *Powhatan* to head to Florida and Fort Pickens. Meigs then wired Seward that Mercer had orders to take the *Powhatan* to Charleston. Welles had continued to send orders to the commanders of the other ships in the flotilla to head for Charleston forthwith. When Seward received the conflicting telegrams indicating that two missions were in preparation involving the *Powhatan*, one headed by Porter to Pensacola and one headed by Mercer to Charleston, he (with his son Frederick) went to see Welles at his suite in the Willard Hotel late in the evening. Seward then told Welles of the secret mission to Fort Pickens with the *Powhatan*, commanded by Porter, as the lead ship.

The tragic-comic opera began anew at this point. Welles exploded in a fit of rage, insisting that the *Powhatan* was scheduled to lead the Fort Sumter expedition. Seward could not calm him. Welles then insisted they go to the White House to consult the president. It was almost midnight by this time, and Seward pleaded to wait until morning, but Welles would have none of it. They woke Commodore Silas Stringham, and the foursome headed to the White House. Lincoln, in his bedclothes, was heading to bed but received his cabinet officers. The president was truly shaken by the "mad scene." He had not realized that the *Powhatan* was assigned to two missions and, in spite of Seward's strenuous objections, sided with Welles, ordering Seward to have the *Powhatan* returned to the Fort Sumter mission. Seward, before retiring for the night, telegrammed Porter to return the *Powhatan* to New York Harbor to be made part of the Fort Sumter expedition. He signed it "Seward." Porter was under way when overtaken by a fast boat, under the direction of Lieutenant R.A. Roe, bearing Seward's new order. Porter reviewed Seward's order against his original order signed by the president and concluded an order signed by the president superseded one signed by the secretary of state. He continued on to Fort Pickens and wired Seward the following: "I received my orders from the President and shall proceed and execute them."[298] Whether Seward deliberately "set up" this scenario will never be known, but there can be no question he was trying to delay the Fort Sumter expedition. Incredibly, Seward did not inform Fox that the flagship of his mission to Fort Sumter would not be available.

By the morning of April 6, news of warship preparations in New York Harbor had been confirmed and wired south—to Washington, to Richmond and to Charleston. Lincoln and Seward had been discussing whether to inform the South Carolinians of the resupply mission as a way to position it in the "right" light. They wanted it seen as a humanitarian effort to send food only—"an attempt will be made to supply Fort Sumter with provisions only" was the key part of Lincoln's message, although it was contrary to Cameron's message to Fox. If the Confederates fired on such a mission, they would be seen as the aggressors, or so they hoped. Seward had notified the Confederate commissioners in Washington that Fort Sumter would be evacuated and was now being pressed to reaffirm that message. Given the rumors circulating wildly at this point, Lincoln and Seward decided to notify South Carolina governor Pickens (yes, the same spelling as the fort) that the resupply mission was on the way. The same State Department clerk mentioned earlier, Robert Chew, was dispatched to Charleston with the message of the relief expedition.

Also on April 6, a little-known dispatch was received at the War Department from Major Anderson in Fort Sumter of an event that occurred in Charleston Harbor on April 3. "I have the honor to send herewith a report of the circumstances attending a firing yesterday afternoon by the batteries on Morris Island [Confederate] at a schooner bearing our flag, bound from Boston to Savannah, which, erroneously mistaking the lighthouse off this harbor for that of Tybee [Savannah harbor light], and having failed to get a pilot, was entering the harbor."[299] The schooner was not damaged and soon after discovering its error turned out to sea. But the significance of the dispatch was unmistakable—any expedition of a ship or ships flying the United States flag would be fired on when attempting to enter Charleston Harbor. Anderson had consistently informed the War Department of his scant supplies, lack of ammunition and even the Confederates "practicing" with mortars to determine the exact range to the fort—now he informed them that no ship would be allowed to reach the fort. In a terse message to the War Department later that day, Anderson pleaded, "The truth is that the sooner we are out of this harbor the better. Our flag runs an hourly risk of being insulted, and my hands are tied by my orders, and if that was not the case I have not the power to protect it."[300] The White House was informed immediately that a ship carrying the United States flag had been fired on while attempting to enter the harbor at Charleston.

Sunday, April 7, was a day of heightened activity—Chew was on his way to Charleston; Porter, commanding the *Powhatan*, was on his way to Pensacola and Fort Pickens; and Gustavus Fox had left New York Harbor on the *Baltic*. The latter wrote to his wife that evening, "We have come to anchor just inside of Sandy Hook, being too late for the evening tide. We shall go over the bar in the morning…I am afraid we are too late, from no fault of mine, but I pray earnestly that I may be permitted to do something for a country dear to me above all others…We have three officers and 200 men, I have instructions to them and the Capt of the ship and shall not deliver them until the pilot leaves us, so no one has the least idea of the voyage though I think it will be in tomorrow's papers."[301] After meeting with Seward in the morning, John Minor Botts had a one-on-one interview with Lincoln after dinner. Botts pleaded with Lincoln to maintain a conciliatory policy and urged him to abandon both Fort Sumter and Fort Pickens. Lincoln replied that it was too late. This is the interview in which, after the war, Botts claimed Lincoln told him he had offered the "fort for a state" proposal to Baldwin on the fourth and that Baldwin had rejected it.

In Richmond, April 1 was a day of rising concern for the Unionists. No word had been received from Washington about the evacuation of Fort Sumter. George Summers had received a telegram from Henry Seward asking him to come to Washington immediately. Summers at first did not think it was authentic, but he eventually responded that he could not come at this critical time, as the resolutions from the Committee on Federal Relations were to be voted on and he needed to be present to manage the debate. Secessionists, unaware of the summons, nevertheless seized on the "silence" regarding Sumter to demand that it was now time for Virginia to withdraw from the Union.

James Barbour, from Culpeper County in the black belt of the eastern Piedmont, was the youngest delegate at the convention and, along with many other delegates, a member of a distinguished Virginia family. He was the first Unionist delegate to break and "go over" to the secessionist ranks.

His speech on this date was a bitter denunciation of the Unionist argument. He read a statement from Alexander Stephens, new vice president of the Confederacy, in which Stephens argued that the huge land mass, wealth and sustainability of the new government was doable. Barbour, echoing Stephens, then spoke of the economic benefits of Virginia joining the Confederacy and challenged the idea of a Border State Convention, stating that it would not protect slavery.

Barbour asked his secessionist colleague from neighboring Orange County (also in the black belt of the Piedmont) to relieve him, and Jeremiah Morton continued with the Slave Power argument. Morton presented data that showed the seven seceded states nearly evenly split between whites and slaves (2,656,481 whites to 2,311,210 slaves) versus the eight slaveholding states that had not seceded, where whites outnumbered slaves by more than 4 to 1 (5,624,009 whites to 1,638,277 slaves). He then presented data to support his argument that the slave states must stay united. "The institution of slavery is assailed every where—all the world is making war upon it…If the greatest Abolitionist in America would apply himself to the task of devising a plan to injure the institution of slavery, he could have hit upon no better plan than that of entering a wedge between the Border States and the seceded States, such as must be the effect of the plan which the Committee on Federal Relations proposes. Divide and conquer—that is the great maxim of an enemy."[302]

Morton had, indeed, hit upon Seward's ultimate plan—to divide the South. And Virginians were very much aware of the "divide the South" issue because of their intrastate division. Of the 149 counties in Virginia in 1860, only 28 had more than 50 percent enslaved, and those counties were all concentrated in the eastern Piedmont and the Tidewater regions, the infamous black belts. In the Valley region, only two small counties had over 30 percent enslaved. In the Southwest and Northwest regions, there were no counties with a high percentage of slaves. To repeat for emphasis, the Slave Power, represented by Holcombe, Randolph, Wise and others, had nowhere else to go—they had to unite with Slave Power aristocrats in the seceded states if they were going to ensure the ultimate safety of black belt slavery.

The secessionist onslaught continued on April 3 and 4 as word on Sumter did not arrive. George Richardson, from heavily enslaved Hanover County in the Tidewater region, espoused the "wounded honor" theme of the Slave Power. With a thunderous message that belied his standing in the Slave Power (he owned few slaves), he spoke the obvious—it was the heavily enslaved counties of the state that had the most to lose by staying in the Union. He chastised the North for causing the trouble, defended the right to secede ("this great country was formed by the compact of independent sovereignties") and pleaded with the delegates to accept the benevolent, patriarchal society created by (and for) the Slave Power. He spoke of Virginia's heroes of the past and asked that Virginians return to a bygone era.[303] Such was the message of the Slave Power, the tiny minority of Southerners (less than 10 percent) who owned enough slaves to be called "planter."

Despite the rising secession momentum as a result of the lack of news on Fort Sumter, the Unionists held their coalition together largely because of the constant urging of Summers, Sandy Stuart, John Baldwin and a few others to stay the course. Debate on the resolutions presented by the Committee on Federal Relations proceeded at a steady pace. Then, during the evening of the third, the previously mentioned Allan Magruder arrived at the convention and quickly summoned George Summers. Summers, somewhat irritated by the interruption, nevertheless met with Magruder to see "what was up." Summers was stunned with Magruder's message that the president needed to see him "immediately" on a matter of the "highest importance." Magruder had no particulars to offer about "a matter of the highest importance" but was so insistent that Summers quickly called a secret meeting of the Unionist leadership. Magruder, still enthralled by his meeting with the president and the secretary of state, pleaded with the Unionists to respond. The Unionists, truly bewildered, kept pressing Magruder for specifics for which the poor messenger just did not have answers. Why was the president calling for a secret meeting with Summers? Did it have something to do with the lack of word about Fort Sumter? Finally, after some debate, it was determined that Summers had to stay and manage the Unionist effort on the resolutions, so the leadership decided to send Baldwin, their rising young star, to meet with the president.

For the Unionists of Virginia, April 4 turned out to be a day they would remember for the rest of their lives. After the first five resolutions proposed by the Committee on Federal Relations were approved, largely because the Unionist majority held together, the key sixth resolution came up for vote. "The 6th Resolution read in part, 'we indulge in the hope that an adjustment may be reached by which the Union may be preserved in its integrity, and peace, prosperity and fraternal feelings restored throughout the land.'"[304] The sixth resolution was the centerpiece of the Unionist campaign—to reject secession and work for an "adjustment" to solve the national crisis. The secessionist leadership met and determined that it was time to strike at the heart of the Unionist campaign and defeat this proposal for a national adjustment. They claimed that Fort Sumter was not going to be evacuated and that the rumored warship preparations meant war was at hand. Indeed, the Unionists seemed increasingly vulnerable. So Lewis Harvie took the floor to propose an Ordinance of Secession be substituted for the sixth resolution, demanding that it be put to a vote. Harvie's motion electrified the convention. Debate intensified throughout the day, with leaders of both factions making persuasive arguments pro and con. The first real test of the division within the convention was at hand—and it was a test that had enormous implications for Virginia and the nation.

John Baldwin's absence was noted by the secessionists, and rumors swirled that he had been seen at the railroad. Spirited debate continued, but finally the question was called and the vote took place. In a stunning victory for the Unionists, Harvie's Ordinance of Secession was defeated by a vote of ninety to forty-five.[305] Of the forty-five votes for the Ordinance of Secession, 70 percent came from the black belt counties of the Piedmont and Tidewater regions of the state (representing the Slave Power), a handful came from heavily enslaved pockets in the Southwest region and, as previously noted, three votes came from the Northwest region, where those three delegates were clearly not representing the wishes of their constituents. Secessionists Leonard Hall of Wetzel County (where 99 percent voted against the Slave Power) and Sam Woods from Barbour County (where 90 percent voted against the Slave Power) were the two most notable examples.

So despite the lack of word on Fort Sumter and the swirling rumors of war preparation in the North, the Unionist coalition remarkably stayed intact, soundly defeating the secessionists. It must be emphasized that the Unionist vote was driven by William Henry Seward's assurances that the administration was going to pursue a conciliatory policy toward the South; in its most basic form, this meant the administration was not going to ask Southerners to fight Southerners, at least not yet. An "adjustment" of some kind would be forthcoming, the Unionist were assured, as the vast majority of Northerners did not want war. Fort Sumter, the flash point, would be evacuated so as not to start a fight with the new Confederacy. What the new Union Party needed was time to consolidate its newfound political strength. Again, had the Upper and Border South states remained in the Union, the seven seceded states, containing only 10 percent of the nation's white population, would have been hard-pressed to sustain themselves if some future fight were to occur. It was an enormous victory for Seward and his plan to divide the South. It should have been an enormous victory for Abraham Lincoln as well. Indeed, the Virginians at their convention in Richmond had delivered "the state."

April 4 could very well have become, sometime in the future, a "Grand Day of Peace" celebrated throughout the nation as the day that the Unionists of Virginia prevented civil war. Many Northern newspapers trumpeted the vote as "the death of secession"—and it should have been just that.

On April 5, Chapman Stuart from the Northwest region, representing Tyler and Doddridge Counties, where over 98 percent of the citizens voted for the referendum, challenged the secessionist argument that slavery could be protected only by joining the Confederacy. He presciently proclaimed, "Then I hold that secession or revolution is no remedy for the evils complained of, but will tend as an aggravation of them, and will, if persisted in, lead to the extermination of slavery." Waitman Willey's "equal taxation" of slaves proposal was still front and center during this time of rising tension, and Chapman, representing counties where there were virtually no slaves, could not help but bring up the taxation issue in his speech. "Unless you remove the state's constitutional ban on full taxation of your slaves, Stuart warned eastern slaveholders, 'you might as well undertake to remove the Alleghany Mountains from their base, as to induce the people of the Northwest, for present causes, to secede from the union.'"[306] As previously noted, Willey's equal taxation initiative divided the delegates in different ways, and it turned out to be truly unhelpful during the secession debate.

On April 5, an exhausted John Baldwin returned from Washington and took his seat in the convention late that morning. Summers had called the Unionist leadership together for a secret meeting after the convention adjourned for the day. Key delegates present were John Janney, president of the convention; Sandy Stuart, Baldwin's mentor from Augusta County and one of the convention's most highly respected members; Robert Scott, the dynamic Unionist leader from evenly divided Fauquier County; and Samuel Price from heavily Unionist Greenbrier County in the Southwest region, a county that would become a part of West Virginia. Baldwin then briefed them on his visit with the president.

Baldwin was dismayed. He said that the meeting had been inconclusive and also that he was somewhat perplexed about the urgent summons. He said that Lincoln commented "you have come too late" and later during a particularly difficult part of the exchange had burst out, "I wish you had come sooner." Summers and Janney cross-examined Baldwin at some length, with the others pressing him repeatedly on the Fort Sumter issue. Baldwin emphatically stated that Lincoln had made no offer to withdraw the troops from the fort. In fact, Lincoln had made no remark that would even strengthen the Unionist position in Virginia. Sam Price later recalled his feelings about Lincoln's "I wish you had come sooner" statement, saying "it chilled the very blood in my veins…and I inferred from this remark…that he had taken a step which he could not retrace…and which would result in war and bloodshed."[307]

Summers was truly shaken by the report also. He had been the point of contact for Seward and had been assured on many, many different occasions that Fort Sumter would be abandoned and that the administration would follow a conciliatory policy toward the South in general and support Virginia Unionists in particular. Now there seemed to be a change in course. Bewildered and baffled, Summers returned to his hotel to "sleep on" the message. Little did he know that Robert Chew was on his way to Charleston to inform Governor Pickens that an attempt to resupply Sumter was at sea and would arrive off Charleston shortly.

Summers returned to the convention on the morning of April 6 determined to hold the Unionist coalition together and to continue the vote on the resolutions of the Committee on Federal Relations. Resolution 9 was adopted by a substantial Unionist majority, and Resolution 8 was adopted with consent from both Unionists and secessionists. But on this Saturday afternoon, all was not going according to plan for the Unionists. "The convention had been in session for forty-five days, and while unaware of Baldwin's unsuccessful mission, they had begun to receive telegraphic reports of military activities at the Port of New York. The convention had also learned that the Lincoln administration had negotiated a multi-million dollar loan for unknown purposes but which many delegates feared would be used to finance military operations against the seceded states."[308] Many Unionists demanded answers to these rumors; Summers had none.

William Ballard Preston, a leader of the conditional Unionists from heavily Unionist Montgomery County in the Southwest region and a politician of considerable stature (he had served in the Virginia legislature, in the U.S. Congress and as secretary of the navy), proposed that a three-person delegation be appointed immediately to go to Washington to meet with Lincoln to determine what the policy of his administration was toward the seceded states—and toward Virginia. With war preparation rumors increasingly prevalent, Preston (and most other delegates) were increasingly frustrated by the lack of word on Fort Sumter. He stated, "This long silence is operating most injuriously upon every interest in the land…Is it an intrusion to ask him [Lincoln] what his policy is to be?"[309] The Unionists, whether unconditional or conditional, needed to know just what was going on.

Preston asked John Baldwin to review his proposal, but Baldwin, exhausted and with little time, instead drafted a preamble to the motion, which Preston accepted. The convention then became embroiled by harsh debate between the unconditional Unionists and the secessionists over the purpose of the Preston delegation's trip to Washington. Baldwin cautioned both sides to tone down the rhetoric, but to no avail. Then, President Janney, outraged at the harsh words and ungentlemanly conduct of some delegates (and urged by Baldwin and James Dorman), declared that the debate would resume on Monday morning, after Sunday's day of rest. The war preparation rumors strengthened the secessionists considerably, and they now became more and more aggressive. Before departing the floor, secessionist delegates Wood Bouldin (Charlotte County) and John Randolph Chambliss (Greensville County) demanded immediate secession. Unionist delegates left the convention in a state of great unease. Sunday, April 7, would be a day of deep prayer for the Unionists of Virginia.

In Washington, Monday, April 8, began the last week of peace—it would prove to be one of the most fateful weeks in the nation's storied history.

On this Monday in New York Harbor, the *Harriet Lane* departed the docks loaded with supplies for Fort Sumter. Many "Southern eyes" were present to witness the event—telegrams flashed southward. Robert Chew arrived in Charleston and was immediately received by Governor Pickens. Chew then read the governor the message from President Lincoln that Sumter would be resupplied but not reinforced unless attacked. Next, Pickens read the message to General Beauregard, who instantly placed all of his military forces on full alert. "Man your stations" was the order of the day. In addition, more troops were called to service, some five thousand contingent militia. Alerting the South Carolinians in advance had precisely the wrong effect, especially for Major Anderson and his troops at Fort Sumter. The Confederate commissioners in Washington sent their emissary, Justice Campbell, to contact Seward to confirm or deny the rumors of war preparation. Seward replied with his soon-to-be-famous message (which was misleading at best), "Faith as to Sumter fully kept; wait and see."[310]

General Beauregard next informed Major Anderson that no more mail would be forwarded to the fort. The previous day, Anderson had been informed that no more supplies of any kind would be allowed. Of critical importance to Anderson and his men, on the morning of the eighth, a house was torn down on Sullivan's Island (very near Fort Sumter), exposing "a battery of four heavy guns, well constructed, with sod revetments." The guns could not only reach the fort easily but would also "enfilade" the work and command the only anchorage near the fort. "The discovery of this battery produced a marked and depressing effect upon Major Anderson."[311] The Confederate authorities had intercepted Anderson's dispatches to the War Department and now knew everything about the situation in the fort. Anderson had made it clear to the War Department that he did not approve of Fox's plan to reinforce the fort, stating quite emphatically that it would not work under present circumstances.

The tragic-comic opera continued. The Department of the Navy did not have enough warships or transports available for both the Sumter and Pickens expeditions. So they rented ships as needed. On Tuesday morning, April 9, the rented steamer *Baltic* left New York Harbor with "commander" Gustavus Vasa Fox on board, headed for Charleston. Fox, determined to be a national hero, did not care if his ship was rented or not. He still did not know that the *Powhatan*, the lead warship for his expedition, would not meet up with him off the coast of Charleston. In Charleston, the Confederates were busily manning their guns, securing additional ammunition and placing riflemen in key positions to oppose a landing. At Fort Sumter, the situation was becoming more precarious by the hour. Crawford recorded that "the garrison of Fort Sumter numbered at this point ten officers and sixty-five enlisted men…The rations were fast diminishing; there was but little bread and rice, but by putting the command on half rations, he [Anderson] thought that he could make his bread ration last until the 13th…For their greater protection the whole command was now moved into the gun-casements by Major Anderson's orders."[312] No further communication was received at the fort. The command was now totally isolated, thanks mostly to the bungling politicians in Washington.

In the nation's capital, tension was mounting by the hour. Rumors of "war to begin" were everywhere. Abraham Lincoln had decided to continue business as usual at the White House. He spent most of the day interviewing folks for minor offices and received various messages about the Fort Sumter and Fort Pickens missions. Correspondents for the nation's newspapers were madly dashing to and fro as they tried, with little success, to track down rumors from A to Z. Many of the nation's leading papers had suddenly begun to urge caution. "To what good end shall we inaugurate a civil war?" asked the *Daily Chicago Times*. "Evil, and evil alone, can come to us by civil war."[313] Seward kept up a "fair face" but was disheartened by the unfolding events that he now knew surely meant war.

Wednesday, April 10, was not a good day for the Fort Sumter mission. A terrific storm had dumped so much rain on central Virginia that it had washed out some rail service. The storm was now off Cape Hatteras and began to engulf the ships of the Sumter mission as they steamed south. Ships became separated, supplies were lost overboard and men got seasick. From Hampton Roads, a real Navy warship, the *Pawnee*, sailed into the storm, bound for Charleston. Crawford recorded a riveting scene at the fort on the morning of the tenth: "[I] saw Major Anderson alone, walking slowly backward and forward among his guns. He was greatly depressed; he seemed to realize that upon himself rested mainly the great responsibility. He had endeavored to avert the crisis upon him by every means in his power; he had failed, and the struggle was unavoidable and imminent. His sense of duty now overcame every other consideration, and he prepared to meet the worst."[314] Indeed, Anderson was alone, cut off from receiving new orders, cut off from knowing anything that was happening or about to happen.

That morning, General Beauregard received this terse telegram from Confederate secretary of war LeRoy Walker. Assuming Fort Sumter was to be resupplied, "you will at once demand its evacuation, and if this is refused proceed, in such manner as you may determine, to reduce it."[315] Jefferson Davis had responded to Lincoln's resupply mission. Beauregard ordered the newly constructed floating battery be moved into position near Sullivan's Island, its guns aimed at Fort Sumter. In Pensacola, Lieutenant Worden had arrived "with his message from President Lincoln to land troops to reinforce Fort Pickens. He obtained permission from Gen. Bragg to visit the fort."[316] Bragg was commander of the Confederate forces in the area, and in the days before war began, no one quite knew what to do. After war began, there would be no "permission" granted for visitations. In fact, Worden would be arrested by Confederate authorities on his way back to Washington.

In Washington, the president was busily maneuvering to "manipulate" the Northern press to cast the Fort Sumter mission in the right light. "Lincoln issued orders barring newsmen from all government departments while at the same time permitting the leak of information about the peaceful provisioning of Sumter."[317] The *New York Tribune* and *New York Times*, Republican papers, did cast it in the right light: "If rebels fire at an unarmed supply ship, and make a perfectly proper act the pretext for shedding blood of loyal citizens, on their heads be the responsibility."[318] The "supply ships," of course, were accompanied by warships with troops on board, and they had orders to "open" an entrance way to the fort. The Democratic press, fully aware of the military nature of the expedition, did not cast the mission in the right light. The *New York Herald*, the hugely influential paper of Gordon Bennett, blasted Lincoln in its editorial of April 10, stating, "Our only hope now against civil war of an indefinite duration seems to lie in the over-throw of the demoralizing, disorganizing, and destructive Republican sectional party, of which 'Honest Abe Lincoln' is the pliant instrument."[319] It was, indeed, a stern rebuke from the opposition press.

Thursday, April 11, would be the last day of peace. From Fort Sumter, Anderson and his men saw nothing but activity. Again, Crawford's riveting observation: "From the early hours of the morning the waters were covered with the white sails of the shipping putting hastily to sea. The guard-boats were busily plying the harbor and the bar, incessantly signaling. Constant communication was kept up between the batteries and forts, and town. Steamers conveying men and material left to the last moment, passed under the guns of the fort, while small boats with officers bearing special and final instructions crossed and recrossed the waters of the harbor at all hours."[320] His bread ration exhausted, and with limited ammunition, with "the enemy" making preparations to destroy his fort at will and being cut off from communications with his government (not that that would have made a difference), Anderson was sure he would star in the final act of the tragic-comic opera *How Not to Start a Civil War*.

But war was to commence. About four o'clock in the afternoon, a small boat bearing a white flag was seen approaching the fort. Anderson sent a couple officers to meet it, and they docked the boat and brought three men to see the major: Colonel James Chestnut, the recently resigned U.S. Senator from South Carolina; Captain Stephen D. Lee, West Point graduate recently resigned from the U.S. Army; and Lieutenant Colonel A.R. Chisolm, representing Governor Pickens. They delivered a message from General Beauregard that ended, "I am ordered by the Government of the Confederate States to demand the evacuation of Fort Sumter." Anderson consulted his officers and refused. As the three were departing, Anderson remarked that he would be "starved out" in a few days.

Chestnut, Lee and Chisolm returned to Charleston and reported to General Beauregard Anderson's refusal, as well as his statement about being starved out. Beauregard decided to wire Secretary Walker for further instructions, not wanting to open fire on the fort after having received the starvation news. Walker responded that if Anderson would give a time for evacuation in the immediate future, Beauregard was authorized to accept the terms and assist Anderson in leaving the fort. So at eleven o'clock that same night, the three Confederates returned to the fort under another flag of truce to ask Anderson when he would evacuate the fort. Anderson's reply to General Beauregard was: "I have the honor to acknowledge the receipt by Colonel Chestnut of your second communication of the 11th instant, and to state in reply that, cordially uniting with you in the desire to avoid the useless effusion of blood, I will, if provided with the proper and necessary means of transportation, evacuate Fort Sumter by noon on the 15th instant, and that I will not in the meantime open my fires upon your forces unless compelled to do so." Anderson overplayed his hand with Beauregard, for he knew that his food would run out before the fifteenth, and he knew he had no hope of winning the military contest. It was now after 3:00 a.m., and the Confederates knew the resupply mission was to arrive off Charleston within the next few hours—a delay of four days was clearly unacceptable. Chestnut and Lee stated the delay in evacuation was not soon enough and handed Anderson the following note, marked 3:30 a.m.: "By authority of Brigadier General Beauregard, commanding the provisional forces of the Confederate States, we have the honor to notify you that he will open the fire of his batteries on Fort Sumter in one hour from this time." They then left the fort on their small boat and returned to Charleston. At 4:30 a.m., a signal gun was fired over the harbor. Within minutes, Fort Sumter was under bombardment.[321]

Anderson did not return fire until daylight, about 7:00 a.m., and a lively exchange occurred throughout the day. Fire slackened considerably as night fell, with only occasional mortar fire from the Confederates breaking the night's silence. Early on the morning of the thirteenth, the firing was renewed by both sides. The fort was heavily damaged at this point, and fires had consumed much of the quarters. Ammunition was nearly exhausted, as was the food supply. Fox's "fleet" was in sight but "had made no movement" toward the fort. Anderson had received no communication from anyone since the firing had begun. He decided to surrender. "The formal and final terms agreed to by the general commanding, were presented to Anderson by some messengers from General Beauregard at 7 o'clock P.M., in regard to which Anderson expressed his gratification; and it was arranged that he should leave in the morning [the fourteenth], after communicating with the fleet."[322] Unbelievably, after thirty-four hours of almost continuous bombardment, where something on the order of four thousand shells had been fired, not one man in Anderson's command had been killed, although a few had been slightly wounded.

But what happened to Fox and his resupply (or rescue) mission? While there are many accounts of the mission, some official, some not, the account of Sam Crawford will be presented here. Not only was he there, but he also had a message to deliver.

Following is the paraphrased version of Crawford's account, written after the war. In the early morning of the twelfth, the scattered fleet began to arrive off the Charleston bar in heavy seas. First to arrive was the *Harriet Lane*; the tugs *Uncle Ben* and *Yankee* had been driven off course by the storm. The rented transport *Baltic* with "commander" Fox on board was next to arrive, followed by the small warship *Pawnee*, commanded by an active duty navy officer, Commander Rowan. Fox immediately boarded the *Pawnee* and ordered Rowan to head for Charleston Harbor forthwith. Rowan, not about to take orders from a retired officer, refused, stating he was ordered to wait for the warship *Powhatan*. Fox still did not know the *Powhatan* was not coming. The *Baltic* then headed toward Charleston, followed by the *Harriet Lane*. The *Pawnee*, not wanting to be left out, decided to follow the others. As they approached the land, the firing of the guns at Sumter was heard, and the smoke and shells of the batteries were distinctly visible.

But in the haste to depart New York, nobody had thought to have a pilot on board who knew the entrance so as to guide the ships safely into the harbor; the tragic-comic opera resumed when the *Baltic* ran aground. When finally free, it went back to sea and anchored several miles from the other ships. As night fell, Fox was back on board the *Baltic*, and he continued to signal for the *Powhatan* all night. Another small warship, the *Pocahontas*, was the last ship to arrive, on the afternoon of the thirteenth. The tugs, the only boats with drafts shallow enough to approach the fort, were nowhere to be seen. Several other commercial ships were anchored near the fleet. Then Fox, in a classic "grasping at straws" moment, decided to "seize" a shallow-draft schooner, loaded with ice, to make an attempt to reach the fort. Preparations began immediately to prepare the schooner for its heroic mission. Late in the afternoon, Fox finally received word that the *Powhatan* would not arrive— he was totally stunned. The shallow-draft tugs would never arrive either— the *Uncle Ben* ended up in Wilmington, North Carolina, and was seized by the Confederates, while the *Yankee* ended up off the entrance to Savannah, never to connect with Fox's so-called fleet. The plan put forward by Fox and company was hair-brained, according to the military high command.

Anderson himself thought the plan could never work and told Fox as much. As it turned out, the execution of the plan was hopelessly flawed.

Years after the war, and after careful reflection, Crawford had the following reaction to the Fox mission. It was telling.

> *Thus almost every element that was essential to the success of the expedition was wanting. As it failed, it is impossible to estimate what might have otherwise been the result…it was all too late—too late in conception, too late in execution; mainly due to the political exigency that existed…Had the* Powhatan *remained with the fleet, her usefulness, even if she had arrived in time, is questionable. She could not pass the bar, drawing as she did twenty-one feet, and her boats, so much relied upon, were worthless for service, and swamped when put in the water…The storm dispersed the tugs when the conditions for their use were most urgent, and the Pocahontas arrived only in time to witness the surrender.*[323]

Beauregard, in his report of the battle to the Confederate government, praised Anderson and his men:

> *The barracks in Fort Sumter were in a blaze, and the interior of the work appeared untenable from the heat and from the fire of our batteries… whenever the guns of Fort Sumter would fire upon Fort Moultrie the men occupying Cummings Point batteries…at each shot would cheer Anderson for his gallantry, although themselves still firing upon him; and when on the 15th instant he left the harbor on the steamer* Isabel *the soldiers of the batteries of Cummings Point lined the beach, silent, and with heads uncovered, while Anderson and his command passed before them, and expressions of scorn at the apparent cowardice of the fleet in not even attempting to rescue so gallant an officer and his command were upon the lips of all.*[324]

In Washington, the thirteenth brought a few telegraphic reports that "action" was occurring at Fort Sumter. Lincoln received reports from the War Department throughout the day, and tensions were on the rise everywhere in the nation's capital. Henry Seward was distraught. He had received a truly sincere letter from John Gilmer that touched a nerve: "I am so deeply distressed that my heart seems to melt within me…I cannot but still believe that the course I suggested would have been wise, and the results, had it been pursued, most beneficial…If what I hear is true that

Advertisement of the Richmond, Fredericksburg and Potomac Railroad (RF&P) promoting its line as the fastest route to Washington, D.C. *Courtesy of the Library of Virginia.*

we are to have fighting at Sumter or Pickens, it is what the disunionists have most courted, and I seriously apprehend that it will instantly drive the whole South into secession."[325]

The Preston delegation from the Virginia State Convention had been delayed because of the severe rainstorm that had struck central Virginia—it had washed out railroad bridges that connected Richmond to Washington. They had taken a boat to Baltimore and then the B&O train to Washington. When they finally arrived late on the twelfth, Seward arranged for them to see Lincoln, but he could not see them until the morning of the thirteenth. With the reports of action at Fort Sumter now coming in, Lincoln took a decidedly tough stance. After a brief interview, he read them his message: "If, as now appears to be true…an unprovoked assault has been made upon Fort Sumter, I shall hold myself at liberty to repossess, if I can, any and all federal forts that the Confederacy seized, before or after [my] Inaugural."[326] Sandy Stuart, the unconditional Unionist on the delegation, was terribly disheartened; George Randolph, the secessionist delegate, was elated. This was very good news for the secessionists of Virginia, for they now had their "coercion bullet" to fire at the Unionists. Randolph noted with true glee that Abraham Lincoln had played into the hands of Virginia's secessionists at last.

In Charleston Harbor, Sunday morning, April 14, found Major Anderson conducting the formal surrender ceremony at Fort Sumter. He had arranged for a one-hundred-gun salute as the U.S. flag was lowered. Hundreds of Charlestonians had come in large and small boats to watch the proceedings. Unfortunately for all, a pile of cartridges next to one of the cannons accidentally exploded as the firing began. One solider was killed outright, while a second would die the next day. A telegraph message reached Washington in the morning notifying the government that Anderson had surrendered Fort Sumter. Lincoln called his cabinet into emergency session. Gustavus Fox and his rescue fleet headed north.

In Montgomery, Alabama, temporary capital of the Confederacy, Jefferson Davis was informed that Fort Sumter was "in their hands." Incredibly, not a single soldier was killed on the Confederate side either, although one Confederate horse died (probably from fright). Davis expressed gratitude that no blood had been shed and intriguingly stated that "separation was not yet final."

Henry Seward had written to his friend Anson Burlingame, soon to be ambassador to China, "It will be deeply regretted if the energy of this great

Government is to have its first serious trial in a civil war instead of one against a foreign foe."[327] But the Unionists of Virginia would not give up, even after news reached Richmond that Fort Sumter had fallen. Here is the story of their last days in power.

———

In Richmond, April 8 brought more consternation to the Unionist majority at the Virginia State Convention. On this Monday, telegraphic news from New York stated that warships had left the harbor and headed out to sea on some "secret mission." Debate regarding the Preston motion resumed and now included a preamble drafted by John Baldwin, who had become the undisputed leader of the compromisers. But Baldwin remained concerned about the delegation. Would they challenge Lincoln or merely present the convention's desire for a "pacific policy"? Debate continued for some hours until finally the vote was taken. Ominously for the Unionists, their ranks "broke" for the first time. In one of the closest votes during the entire convention, the motion passed sixty-three to fifty-seven. "Preston, Robert Y. Conrad and Robert E Scott were among those who favored the plan; Janney, Baldwin, Baylor, Dorman, Early, Moore, Price and A.H.H. Stuart were among the Unionists voting no."[328] As previously mentioned, President Janney then named Preston, Stuart and Randolph as the three commissioners to see the president.

On April 9, the Preston delegation departed Richmond for Washington amidst a torrential rainstorm. At the convention, debate began on the tenth resolution, a resolution to confer constitutional authority to the Federal government to deal with the Confederate government. Baldwin led the Unionist charge, stating, "Let us confine our duty to the mere declaration that, if the Government had the power, we want it, in God's name, to exercise all it has in favor of peace. If it has not the power, we are ready to give them all the power necessary to maintain the peace."[329] The Unionists pushed for peace at every moment. To repeat for emphasis, they were able to maintain the upper hand as long as there was no fighting between the Federal government and the Confederate government. The convention continued to debate and vote on the resolutions, one by one.

Amid the resolution debates, the final confrontation between westerners and easterners on the fair taxation of property concluded when Henry Wise rose to challenge Willey's proposal to establish a committee to resolve the taxation question. Wise correctly pointed out that it was "unjust to the people of Virginia, either East or West, to seize upon a moment like this…to divide us upon our own internal questions." He went on to hammer the westerners on the central question of the day: "Before giving to these gentlemen [westerners] additional power to tax slave property, [I need] to be well satisfied that they are willing to unite with me to defend the rights of slave property." Cyrus Hall from the Northwest region answered Wise: "If you fail to equalize the taxes in Virginia, you would do more to divide the people of Virginia by that act, than any other course you could pursue."[330] Because the unconditional Unionists were so emboldened by their huge win in the February elections, they sought to finally win the decades-long struggle with the Slave Power over taxation of slave property. The next day, the Unionist coalition held together and passed Willey's committee proposal, sixty-three to twenty-six.

The final resolution, the fourteenth, turned out to be very important. It called for a convention of the eight slave states that had not seceded to meet in Frankfort, Kentucky, in late May to develop measures to protect their interests (slavery) in the Union. Robert Scott offered an important amendment that would call for a full Congress to convene in the event the Frankford measures were not accepted. The Congress would include all states and would be instructed to draft a new constitution to protect the interest of all states. The secessionists had strongly opposed the Frankford Convention from the outset, preferring that Virginia act on its own and not delay a vote on secession. They opposed anything that would cause secession to be put off, knowing that time would erode what little momentum they had in Virginia. After various amendments were proposed, debated and voted on, on the morning of April 12, John Baldwin offered a final amendment requiring any new constitution be submitted to the voters for approval. Baldwin blasted the new Confederacy for failing to abide by democratic procedures, stating, "I need not refer to the Confederate States, in their secession, and in the formation and ratification of their Constitution, up to the present time, to show how utterly the principle of ratification by vote of the people, has been disregarded and despised in all their movements."[331] Baldwin stung the Slave Power yet one more time by calling attention to the fact that they were the aristocrats, those who did not favor democracy but rather rule by the elites.

The fourteenth resolution with Baldwin's amendment finally passed, seventy-six to forty-two. "What had begun as a resolution with a limited objective now became the most important Resolution to be considered by the convention, a limited reconstruction of the Union, where slavery would be recognized in the areas where it existed."[332] On Saturday morning, April 13, the convention took up the proposed eight-part constitutional amendment. Early in the afternoon, Governor Letcher sent a message to President Janney stating that Governor Pickens of South Carolina had telegraphed him "the war is commenced" and then asked Letcher what Virginia intended to do. "Letcher responded that 'the Convention now in session will determine what Virginia will do.'" The news halted debate. The secessionists, now sensing victory at hand, demanded the convention vote on an Ordinance of Secession. "Henry Wise, ecstatic that combat had begun, insisted that the delegates must now act rather than talk."[333]

To the utter astonishment of the secessionists, who were now in a heated lather, the Unionists answered the news with questions: Was the report authentic? Did the rash South Carolinians start it? Next, staunch Unionist Jubal Early expressed his heartfelt sorrow about the news from Charleston and spoke sympathetically about the plight of his friend Major Anderson. He pointedly poked the secessionists, stating that Virginians would never permit an army of the Confederacy to march across its soil to invade the nation's capital. Thomas Goode, an outspoken leader of the secessionists, jumped to his feet to answer Early, stating that Early "misconceives the sentiment of the people of Virginia" and that Virginians would answer the call to fight with the South, even if they had to fight the Unionists in the state first. Early then challenged Goode's loyalty to Virginia. Goode took it as an insult, stating, "I shall press the question…whether he designed to cast any imputation or reflection upon me?" A duel with pistols was avoided only when Early backed off: "I hope every gentleman will understand that what I said was intended to reach a political aspect of the case, and not to apply to the gentleman personally."[334]

John Baldwin then moved that the convention adjourn until Monday morning to allow the news to be verified (and to allow tempers to cool). He was trying with all his political skill to avoid any vote at this moment of extreme passion. Baldwin's motioned carried, and the delegates left the Hall of the House of Delegates (the convention had moved back to the Capital) in a state of extreme anxiety.

Sunday, April 14, was a day of "shock and awe" for the citizens of the country. War was apparently at hand. Newspapers in Washington and across the nation carried headlines about the surrender of Fort Sumter. The people in the North were electrified. "It was not that Fort Sumter itself was so valuable; strategically, Fort Pickens was far more significant. But the city of Charleston had become equated in the public mind with rebellion, and the very act of firing on the American flag aroused the nation much as it would be aroused again, eighty years later, by the Japanese attack on Pearl Harbor."[335] Lincoln called his cabinet into emergency session with General Scott present. It would become a very long session that lasted into the night. The time had come for action.

During the week, Lincoln had met with several governors of Northern states to alert them that their militias might be needed. He had held a secret meeting with Pennsylvania governor Andrew Curtin and wired him the following on April 8: "I think the necessity of being ready increases. Look to it."[336] Some suggested calling up 50,000 men. Seward suggested 100,000, and they finally settled on 75,000. Next, the cabinet discussed calling a special session of Congress to approve both the administration's calling up troops and authorizing funds for a war effort, as well as to address other wartime measures. After considerable debate regarding when to call the Congress, the cabinet followed Seward's suggestion and decided to call the Congress into session on the Fourth of July.

On Monday morning, April 15, 1861, President Lincoln stunned the nation, both North and South, by issuing a Proclamation of Insurrection that called for seventy-five thousand troops to put down the rebellion. His exact language follows:

> *Now, therefore, I, Abraham Lincoln, President of the United States, in virtue of the power in me vested by the Constitution, and the laws, have thought fit to call forth, and hereby call forth, the militia of the several States of the Union, to the aggregate number of seventy-five thousand, in order to suppress said combinations, and to cause the laws to be duly executed. The details, for this object, will be immediately communicated to the State authorities through the War Department.*

The War Department had set a quota for each state and then sent a telegram to each governor calling for the appropriate number of militia from the respective state.

In the North, the firing on the flag and the surrender of the fort galvanized the populace to support the president. Governors of Northern states responded to the call enthusiastically. Governor Morton of Indiana responded, "I tender to you for the defense of the nation and to uphold the authority of the Government 10,000 men." Ohio's Governor Dennison wired, "Your dispatch calling...for thirteen regiments...will be promptly responded to by this State." From Illinois, "The Governor's call was published on yesterday and he has already received the tender of forty companies...Our people burn with patriotism and all parties show the same alacrity to stand by the Government and the laws of the country." And from Massachusetts, "Two of our regiments will start this afternoon—one for Washington, and the other for Fort Monroe; a third will be dispatched tomorrow, and the fourth before the end of the week."[337] Although many of the troops had fancy uniforms, virtually none were trained for combat, and many did not even have guns or tents or eating utensils.

In the states of the Upper and Border South, the response to Lincoln's call for state militia was just the opposite. Virginia was called on to provide three regiments of state militia, but Governor Letcher flatly refused to furnish any troops "for any such purpose as they have in view." North Carolina governor Ellis stated, "I can be no party to this wicked violation of the laws of the country and to this war upon the liberties of a free people. You can get no troops from North Carolina." From Tennessee, Governor Harris replied, "In such an unholy crusade no gallant son of Tennessee will ever draw his sword." Kentucky's Governor Magoffin barked, "I say emphatically Kentucky will furnish no troops for the wicked purpose of subduing her sister Southern States." And from Maryland, Governor Hicks wired, "I think it prudent to decline responding affirmatively to the requisition made by President Lincoln for four regiments of infantry."[338] Many Southerners considered Lincoln's call for troops a declaration of war on the South, and they responded accordingly.

Abraham Lincoln, whether intentionally or not, had risked war by his decision to resupply Fort Sumter. Historian Richard Current summarized persuasively, "The evidence on the whole makes it hard to believe that Lincoln could have counted on a peaceful provisioning of Fort Sumter. He knew well what had happened to Buchanan's attempt to send supplies in a lone, unarmed merchant steamer, *Star of the West*. He had little reason to expect a more friendly welcome for his own much larger expedition, which included warships."[339] As documented above, Major Anderson, the senior Federal military commander on the ground, had repeatedly pleaded with Washington (through his normal chain of command) to abandon the fort. Any attempt, argued Anderson, to resupply the fort would be met with overwhelming resistance by the Confederates and could never succeed. Anderson had been told numerous times during the preceding weeks that the fort would be abandoned, and he asked time and time again for orders to do so.

Much debate has ensued about whether Lincoln, in fact, induced the Confederates to fire on the fort so as to awaken a warlike spirit in the North. On May 1, the president wrote to Gustavus Fox, "I sincerely regret that the failure of the late attempt to provision Fort Sumter should be a source of any annoyance to you…You and I both anticipated that the cause of the country would be advanced by making the attempt to provision Fort Sumter, even if it should fail; and it is no small consolation now to feel that our anticipation is justified by the result."[340] Lincoln would reward Fox by appointing him assistant secretary of the navy.

Without question, the firing on the fort did galvanize the North and the South to a great extent, at least initially. Within a few months, however, the war spirit had hit its apex. The downhill spiral would then begin and continue to war's end in both sections of the country. Americans became truly disheartened by the war, as most considered the destruction and the loss of life unacceptable.

Abraham Lincoln—ignoring the advice of his military high command, ignoring the advice of delegation after delegation of Southerners and Northerners advising him to seek compromise, ignoring the calls in the press to seek peace, ignoring the will of the vast majority of Americans of that time and ignoring the advice of his most senior political advisor, Mr. Republican—had made the decision to risk war by attempting to resupply Fort Sumter. He now made the decision to start war by issuing a proclamation calling for troops to fight the South, rather than a call for troops to protect the nation's capital.

In Richmond, Sunday, April 14, was a day like none other. Groups of young men marched around the city with Confederate flags flying, demanding that Virginia secede. "Jubal Early, the future Confederate general, insisted that Virginia's 'masses' still opposed secession, Richmond mobs notwithstanding."[341] Governor Letcher was under mounting pressure to use Virginia militia to seize Federal installations in the state. Unionists were frantically sending wires to Washington to ascertain just what was going on. "The same train that brought the commissioners back from Washington on Sunday evening also brought unverified reports of an even more ominous development—Lincoln planned to raise an army to fight the Confederacy."[342]

Nevertheless, the Unionists of Virginia stood firm, although they realized the news of Fort Sumter had seriously weakened their position. William Rives called for "Virginia and the other border slave states to maintain their mediatorial position" so they could bring the warring factions together after the Frankford Convention, still scheduled for late May. Some Unionists, however, began to sense that the voters of Virginia needed to be offered a choice—a popular referendum to choose between the border state conference or immediate secession. Convention delegates would not be going to church for vespers on this Sunday evening; the time had come to choose a course for the Commonwealth.

The convention assembled at its normal time, 10:00 a.m., on Monday morning, April 15. The early editions of Richmond newspapers carried Lincoln's Proclamation of Insurrection calling for the states to provide 75,000 troops. Simon Cameron had sent Governor Letcher the following wire: "Call made on you by to-night's mail for three regiments of militia for immediate service [2,340 officers and men]."[343] Governor Letcher, a staunch Unionist, now knew the game was about over.

Unionists could not believe the proclamation was real. Sandy Stuart, who had had a long and fruitful conversation with Henry Seward less than two days before, read the document at breakfast and "did not for a moment believe that it was authentic." He thought Lincoln could not be "guilty of such duplicity." He immediately telegraphed Seward to ask if it was a "fabrication."[344] At the convention, Unionist Robert Scott took the floor and "hinted at the Unionists' fallback position if the news of Lincoln's proclamation was verified...he would propose calling on the people (instead of the convention) to decide between secession and a border state conference."[345]

Amid tension just shy of having delegates engage in physical combat, Preston and the other commissioners delivered the report of their meeting with Lincoln, including the president's written response. Preston quoted Lincoln's response: "As now appears to be true, in pursuit of a purpose to drive the United States authority from these places, an unprovoked assault has been made upon Fort Sumter, I shall hold myself at liberty to repossess, if I can, like places which had been seized before the Government was devolved upon me. And, in any event, I shall, to the best of my ability, repel force by force."[346] Sandy Stuart called Lincoln's response "in the highest degree unsatisfactory." Secessionist James Holcombe then moved that the convention suspend its rules and go into secret session. Scott, Baldwin and

Early immediately opposed a secret session; Henry Wise pleaded for secrecy because the "welfare of the people must be the supreme law" in a military crisis. After more highly contentious debate, Holcombe's motion was approved in a circuitous "test" vote, eighty to forty-five, "with the Unionist leadership now divided, Janney, R.Y. Conrad and R.E. Scott voting in favor, Baldwin, Price, A.H.H. Stuart and Summers voting against."[347]

Baldwin sensed the momentum shift and, in an attempt to buy time, called for the proclamation to be verified. He stated, "I think that all of us have a right to ask of our associates in this body, that we shall not be pressed into any extraordinary course of proceeding upon half gathered information."[348] Many others agreed, and Henry Gillespie, from heavily Unionist Raleigh County in the Southwest region, proposed adjournment until the following morning. Although the motion carried sixty-three to forty-four, and the convention adjourned just before 1:00 p.m., the wheels were beginning to come off the Unionist wagon.

Tuesday, April 16, was the beginning of the end for the Unionists of Virginia. The Virginia State Convention went into secret session shortly after 10:00 a.m. The galleries were cleared, with the exception of one reporter. Lincoln's proclamation had now been verified, and the secessionists demanded action. A committee was dispatched to see the governor to ask him to relay all information received from Washington to the convention. Governor Letcher, in spite of his Unionist proclivities, had tersely responded to Cameron's call for troops, stating that "the militia of Virginia will not be furnished to the powers at Washington for any such purpose as they have in view. Your object is to subjugate the Southern States, and the requisition made upon me for such an object…will not be complied with. You have chosen to inaugurate civil war, and having done so we will meet you, in a spirit as determined, as the Administration has exhibited towards the South."[349] Letcher now prepared himself to lead his state out of the Union.

The Preston commissioners had the floor as a result of their report on the fifteenth. George Randolph, the secessionist on the commission, now assumed a secession ordinance would pass and laid out the secessionist position, echoing Henry Wise's speech of the previous day. Randolph claimed that "military necessity…required not only instant secession but also immediate seizure of federal military treasure, in the name of the people and before they ratified the convention's secession ordinance." This was very strong stuff for the Unionists to handle, even at this moment of declining strength.

Sandy Stuart, who had taken a back seat to his fellow Augustan John Baldwin for most of the convention, now urged that Virginia look to a border state conference rather than immediate secession. He stated forcefully that the state must not seize Federal property of any kind. He still did not favor joining the Confederacy. Stuart, one of the convention's most distinguished members, presciently declared, "In my opinion, secession is not only war, but it is emancipation; it is bankruptcy; it is repudiation; it is wide-spread ruin to our people."[350] Four years later, in April 1865, his words would ring true with a thundering finality—Virginia saw the most military engagements of any state, 2,154. But revolution was in the air. Unionist William Ballard Preston then introduced an Ordinance of Secession.

The Unionists were now scrambling to hold their coalition together in the face of serious defections from their ranks caused by Lincoln's proclamation. Robert Scott then offered the last hope for the Unionist cause—he proposed a substitute to the Ordinance of Secession that called for the people to vote on whether to participate in a border state convention or move to immediate secession, stating that "secession now on the part of Virginia is instant war."[351] John Baldwin then gave

an impassioned speech in support of Scott's proposed substitute, expressing total opposition to Preston's secession ordinance. He spoke of his disappointment that Union men (Preston and others) had deserted the cause without proper deliberation and pleaded with delegates to think of what war would mean for the state: "I think [it] promises nothing but calamity and mischief." He concluded soulfully, "I regard this as an exceedingly dark hour in the history of this State...I cannot concur in the act which is about to be done."[352] Baldwin was a Union man, through and through, and his speech kept enough Union men in the fold to pass a motion to adjourn, but just barely, seventy-six to sixty-six.

After Baldwin's emotional plea, and despite strenuous

John Brown Baldwin fought against the secessionists and their leader, Henry Wise, to the bitter end. He would vote against the Ordinance of Secession on April 17, 1861. *Courtesy of the Library of Virginia.*

objections from rabid secessionists, the convention did adjourn for the night. Several delegates had stated they needed time to consider how they would vote—a vote that would be the most momentous decision of their lives. "Many delegates returned to their lodgings with deep sadness, heavy hearts and misgivings over the situation with which they would be confronted on the following day."[353] Henry Wise and his radical secessionist friends were exasperated. What would come next?

Perhaps the most intriguing, but rarely mentioned, episode to occur in Richmond during this highly volatile time was the People's Spontaneous Convention, a meeting, as fate would have it, scheduled to convene in Metropolitan Hall, some two blocks from the Capital, on Tuesday, April 16. This was by invitation only, and the invites had been sent to the most radical secessionists in the state—the group paid by and wholly committed to the Slave Power. Prior to the scheduled meeting, organizers had concurred in a radical plan of action. If the Unionists in the state convention would not vote for secession, "this clique of strident southern rights men plotted to overthrow the state government and, in the words of a delegate, 'break up the Convention by violence.'"[354] There was no secret about this planned meeting, as it had been mentioned in the local press for weeks—what was secret was their planned *coup d'etat*. They intended to arrest Governor Letcher and most of the Unionist leadership in the convention and then install a secessionist government headed by the enigmatic Henry Wise. The aristocrats had had enough of debate, of rule by law, of democracy. They intended to seize power and, if required, kill any who resisted.

The Spontaneous Convention "delegates" had been gathering all during the week, and by the morning of the sixteenth, nearly two hundred had arrived, including John D. Imboden, Oliver Funsten, John and Alfred Barbour, Richard and Turner Ashby and John A. Harman.[355] They elected David Chambers of Halifax as the "president" and prepared to implement the planned coup. Throughout March and April, these rabid secessionists had threatened and sometimes physically attacked Unionists throughout the state. By mid-April, they were thoroughly frustrated by the Unionist majority in the convention. Sometime after the convention adjourned on the sixteenth, Henry Wise had the "delegates" notified of Preston's secession ordinance and his view that it would pass the next day. So the delegates decided to hold off implementing their coup until the vote on the secession ordinance was taken. The special correspondent for the *New York Times* in Richmond reported to New York, "They [the Southern Rights Convention] are waiting, it is avowed, for the [Virginia State Convention] to act. It is supposed that the latter body will pass an ordinance of secession. If so, the Southern Rights Convention will have nothing to do but ratify and go home. If not, then—to quote an ancient Virginia editor—*nous verrons*. We shall see what we shall see. Prepare yourself to hear stirring news from old Virginia."[356]

After the Ordinance of Secession passed on the seventeenth, even though the vote was supposed to be kept secret, Lieutenant Governor Montague rushed from the convention to Metropolitan Hall to tell the crowd the good news. "A few minutes later, Henry Wise arrived in triumph at Metropolitan Hall to prolonged applause and shouts of exultation…he 'electrified the assembly by a burst of eloquence, perhaps never surpassed by mortal orator'…Tears filled the eyes of many. What Wise desired had come to pass."[357] Many of those assembled, including the handsome, young Turner Ashby, would not survive the next four years.

After the war, John Minor Botts claimed that Lincoln's proclamation came just in the nick of time to avert this revolutionary movement. He stated that had it not, Lincoln "might have received a call from the executive of this state for the aid of the general government to sustain the lawful authorities of Virginia." Botts went on to speculate that had that occurred, nothing could have "driven Virginia or other border states into a participation with the Cotton States."[358]

Daniel Crofts hypothesized:

> *If the administration had decided against trying to hold Sumter—or if it had even held back or delayed the proclamation for seventy-five thousand troops—Wise and his friends would have been put to a far more severe test…What the conspirators would have done under such circumstances is impossible to judge, but they might have overplayed their hand…Had Southern Rights conspirators in Virginia actually tried to maintain control over a federal installation, or to move forcibly against the governor or the convention while calling for Confederate aid, that would have produced a grave crisis.*[359]

If Governor Letcher and the Unionist leadership at the convention had been "captured" by the Southern Rights conspirators, would Robert E. Lee have been dispatched to Richmond to "put down" the Southern Rights conspiracy as he had been dispatched to Harpers Ferry to "put down" John Brown's raid? Often in the course of the nation's history, events have been driven by chance, by the eccentricities of individuals or, as in this case, by an incredible stroke of timing.

Before returning to the narrative, a final episode of outrageously inappropriate (and illegal) behavior must be noted, and that is Henry Wise and "his" orders to several units of the Virginia state militia to seize Federal property. By this time, Wise and Governor Letcher were at loggerheads. Wise, in fact, considered Letcher a traitor to the South. Late on the afternoon of the sixteenth, "Wise and his friends badgered [Letcher] to take action as though a state of war existed between Virginia and the national government. He should call out the militia and seize the navy yard near Norfolk and the federal arsenal at Harpers Ferry."[360] Letcher would have none of it, though, as the convention had not passed an ordinance of secession or ordered any such use of state militia. Wise, following the *modus operandi* of the Slave Power in the seceded states, now decided to take matters into his own hands.

He encountered Captain John D. Imboden of Staunton, who commanded a secessionist-leaning militia unit in Augusta County. Imboden had been soundly defeated by the citizens of Augusta as a delegate to the convention because he had been viewed as secessionist-leaning in the Unionist-dominated county. Wise, in an unbelievable usurpation of authority, wrote Imboden an order to take his militia unit from Staunton to Harpers Ferry by train and capture the arsenal. Without any constitutional or legal or authorized right, Imboden decided to obey the "order" from Wise, a former governor. In an even more outrageous move, Wise telegraphed South Carolina governor Pickens and asked him to send troops to Virginia. Pickens, of course, refused, stating that any such request must come from Governor Letcher. Next, Wise received a telegram from one of his secessionist associates in Norfolk stating that the navy was evacuating the Gosport Navy Yard and asking if the local militia should seize the yard; again, Wise gave the order to do it.

While many historians have reviewed these actions and drawn conclusions ranging from dismissive to grave, it is historian Nelson Lankford who captured the essence of the scene. He wrote, "If the governor and the convention would not bend to their will, they [Wise and his radical secessionists] intended to commit a private act of war against the United States government in order to stampede their fellow Virginians and rally them to the banner of secession."[361] The Slave Power was taking control.

Wednesday, April 17, would see the end of Virginia's great effort at national reconciliation. The first order of business was the reading of Governor Letcher's message to Simon Cameron rejecting his call for Virginia troops. Then speeches by westerners began opposing Preston's Ordinance of Secession and supporting Scott's substitute motion to let Virginia voters decide the issue. Alpheus Haymond from Marion County in the Northwest region, where 95 percent voted for the referendum, pleaded with the delegates not to pass an ordinance of secession, as it would isolate his county, the people would not accept it and dissolution of Virginia would result. Next, John Hughes, who would be the only delegate from the Northwest region to desert the Unionists and go over to the secessionists, stated that Lincoln's proclamation was a declaration of war on the South and must be resisted. Chapman Stuart responded to the reports that Virginia militia were about to seize Federal military installations in the state: "Our mission here… was to deliberate and consult together…and to submit our action to the people for their adoption or rejection…let me warn you, that your unwanted usurpation of power will arouse a spirit of resistance in [western] Virginia, that you are not now prepared to realize."[362]

Following Stuart's dramatic speech—in which he implied western Virginians would oppose secession, by force if necessary—the vote was taken on Scott's substitute motion. The Unionist coalition fractured. The motion was defeated seventy-seven to sixty-four. Just thirteen days before, on April 4, the Unionist coalition had garnered ninety votes when it defeated Harvie's Ordinance of Secession. But now, 26 Unionist delegates deserted the ranks and voted with the secessionists to defeat Scott's motion. A total of 6 more delegates voted on this motion than on April 4 (141 versus 135), but had only 19 Unionists switched sides instead of the 26 (just seven votes), the coalition would have upheld Scott's proposal and defeated the second ordinance of secession. The vote on Preston's Ordinance of Secession was taken after Scott's motion failed; it passed eighty-eight to fifty-five. How close they came.

In the evening session of the convention, one of the most extraordinary moments in Virginia's history unfolded. "Shortly after this rather close Unionist defeat, Henry Wise ascended to the podium. He placed his huge horse pistol before him. He waved his large pocket watch at the delayers. Then he announced that at this hour Virginia troops were marching toward the two key federal military installations in Virginia, Harpers Ferry Arsenal and Norfolk's Gosport Navy Yard."[363] Wise presented the convention with the *fait accompli* that Virginia had declared war on the Federal government. The "delegates" from the Spontaneous People's Convention had moved to the Capitol and paraded outside the convention doors, threatening to hang anyone who resisted Wise and his extralegal measures. The Slave Power, indeed, had carried out their "coup."

John Baldwin, not at all intimidated by the hotheads, immediately sprang to his feet and denounced Wise in the strongest possible terms. He stated he would advise troops not to follow orders that Wise, or any other non-elected official, issued. He insisted that the people of Virginia had directed the matter be settled at the polls (the vote for a referendum) and accused Wise (and the Slave Power) of degrading Virginians by taking this step without their consent. In spite of the vote on Preston's Ordinance of Secession, in which the secessionists prevailed, Baldwin would not cede.

Later that evening, Wise and Baldwin engaged in an exchange for the ages. "The ensuing convention debate would have been anticlimactic except for its oratorical brilliance, its relevance to western Virginia's still unmade critical decision, and its illumination of a timeless democratic puzzle…when Henry Wise and John Baldwin explored the dilemma of military necessity versus constitutional necessities, their confrontation elevated the convention's verbal clashes to a historic importance."[364] Baldwin, a constitutionalist of the first rank, would not and could not tolerate Wise's unauthorized, revolutionary actions.

Wise denounced Baldwin, stating that *salus populi*, protecting the welfare of the people, was the supreme law and took precedent over constitutional authority. "The safety of the people for every law, moral, divine, political or popular, justifies the overriding for a time at least of acts and statutes and even the constitution itself." Baldwin responded that that was nonsense. "I deny that we have any higher law under our system of government than the Constitution," he said. He ended his magnificent rebuttal of Wise's illegal orders by stating, "In the name of my constituency; in the name of constitutional law; in the name of constitutional liberty; in the name of representative responsibility, I protest against this act."[365] In a few short weeks, arguments of this very nature would be hurled at Abraham Lincoln by Democrats in the North.

For John Baldwin and the Unionists of Virginia, time had run out on the afternoon of April 17. Extralegal events in Washington and Richmond had combined to destroy their coalition. Lincoln's Proclamation of Insurrection, hastily conceived and disastrously worded, was viewed as a declaration of war on the South by many Virginians, as it was asking them to fight fellow

Southerners. The Slave Power in the state, led by Henry Wise and others, illegally ordered secessionist militia units to seize Federal property (and thus confront the national government) before an ordinance of secession was voted on by the convention or, for that matter, before the citizens had a chance to confirm or reject any of the convention's actions.

In hindsight, it is easy to see the reasoning of many Virginians in relation to their Unionism. In mid-April 1861, looking forward, and not knowing that war would soon envelope them, these men were loyal, patriotic Americans who believed the leadership of the country would not desert them. In the end, the heroic Unionists of Virginia were betrayed by the politicians in Washington—and by the aristocrats in their very own state.

The final comment belongs to award-winning historians James G. Randall and David Donald. Here is their compelling summary of the events of April 1861.

> *Throughout the whole situation one sees the unfortunate effect of Lincoln's April policy. Feeling that Lincoln should have given conciliation a better trial, that he should above all have avoided a crisis at Sumter, conservative Southerners were deeply outraged at what they deemed both a stroke of bad policy and a breaking of administrative promises. As for his call for troops, it served in one flash to alienate that whole mass of Union sentiment, which, while not pro-Lincoln, was nevertheless antisecessionist and constituted Lincoln's best chance of saving the Union without war.*[366]

Abraham Lincoln, faced with a country in peril like no other president had faced before, made two momentous decisions in the first six weeks of his presidency: the decision to resupply Fort Sumter, which would risk war, and the decision to issue a Proclamation of Insurrection that would start war. The reactions of Virginians to these two events—and what could have happened had they not been made—will be discussed in the Epilogue.

EPILOGUE

The war was greeted in its first few weeks almost as a festival. Everybody seemed relieved. People went out and celebrated, both in the North and in the South. There were parades, bands playing, flags flying; people seemed almost happy. Large numbers of troops were enlisted; as a matter of fact, again in both North and South, more men offered themselves than could be handled...the grim awakening would come later.
—*Bruce Catton,* Reflections on the Civil War

Thursday, April 18, 1861, was an unbelievable day in Richmond. The "delegates" to the People's Spontaneous Convention had been up most of the night firing cannons, drinking and singing around bon fires and parading through the streets. Unionist delegates, especially those from the western part of the state, were busily making preparations to leave (or flee) the city, as ugly words and threats of violence were being hurled at them by the young rowdies. John Brown Baldwin, George Summers, Sandy Stuart and their hard-core Unionist colleagues who had voted against the Ordinance of Secession were disconsolate. What next, they pondered, for their dear home state?

As previously documented, at the convention, the "what next" was happening. Henry Wise was leading the charge to arm the state, to call up the militia, to seize the Federal installations at Harpers Ferry and Norfolk and to begin preparations for placing Virginia in the Confederate States of America. Governor John Letcher was now committed, reluctantly, to

Crowds similar to this one gathered at the Virginia State Capitol throughout the week before the Ordinance of Secession passed on April 17, 1861. *Courtesy of the Library of Virginia.*

Virginia's new course. Many delegates, led by those from western Virginia, were furious with Wise for employing extralegal tactics. What about the referendum scheduled for May 23, they exclaimed. These actions are pre-empting the vote of white Virginians to decide their fate, this is a democracy they declared. To these men, "in the Republic where the consent of white equals lent republicanism its legitimacy, unequal government, especially without the consent of the governed, chillingly resembled enslavement."[367] At the end of the secession debate, they simply would have none of Wise and the slavocracy. On April 22 in Clarksburg, over one thousand white Virginians, men of the west, gathered to begin the process of seceding from the government at Richmond. They had had enough of the Slave Power. As war commenced, "it is likely that class-based resentments—directed against their own increasingly wealthy, powerful, and self-conscious local elites—aided in keeping the mountain people of central western Virginia neutral or inclined, if pressured, to repudiate the Confederacy."[368]

John Brown Baldwin, feeling betrayed by the powers in Washington, had run out of answers. His debate with Wise the previous evening had left him dismayed. He entered the convention on the morning of the eighteenth determined to promote lawful actions: "I still entertain, that it would be wiser and better for us to confine ourselves strictly within the limits of power under the Constitution of Virginia." He told the body that he would not be a "factious opponent" and would consider in good faith "every measure that comes before this body." He ended with his last moment of protest, stating, "I still believe the Convention would better serve the Commonwealth by another course." He then joined with those favoring secession and helped prepare the state for war.[369] When he returned to his home in Staunton, he found his staunch Unionist friends and neighbors, to a man, now in favor of secession. The citizens of Staunton ratified the Ordinance of Secession 556 to 0. What happened?

———

For the Unionists of Virginia, their grand plan to find a workable solution to the sectional crisis began to unravel on Thursday, April 11, 1861, in Charleston Harbor. A rarely cited but exceedingly important fact is that both secretaries of state in their respective governments were totally opposed to starting a war over Fort Sumter.

Former U.S. senator (and governor) from New York and now secretary of state in the Lincoln cabinet, William Henry Seward, had done everything humanly possible to ensure the evacuation of Fort Sumter and then to prevent the Fox expedition from sailing to Charleston. He went so far to delay the Fox expedition, in fact, that he came close to committing treason.

In the government of the Confederate States of America, former U.S. senator Robert Toombs of Georgia had been appointed secretary of state in the Davis cabinet. Toombs, a Washington insider of the first rank, argued incessantly to avoid attacking Fort Sumter. He preached to everyone who would listen, "You will wantonly strike a hornet's nest...Legions, now quiet, will swarm out and sting us to death. It is unnecessary; it puts us in the wrong; it is fatal."[370] His prescient words would, indeed, begin to come true in just a few short days.

After the bombardment, nowhere was there greater consternation than in Virginia. When Friday morning, April 12, brought reports of fighting in Charleston Harbor, newspapers ran special editions throughout the day, and the news spread "on the wings of lightning to the most remote corners of the land."[371] The new, and rapidly expanding, telegraph system in the nation was permitting many citizens to be informed of events with a rapidity that astounded. The Unionists of Virginia were stunned but not ready to "fold their tent."

On Saturday afternoon, the telegraph pounded out the news that Anderson had surrendered the fort. How would the government at Washington respond? The Unionists of Virginia spent most of the day trying to determine just who started the fight, as they were ready to blame either side. Most felt that Lincoln had provoked the fight by sending the Fox expedition to Charleston, and most also felt that Davis was dead wrong in ordering an attack on the fort. Now the Unionists sensed that they, and only the political moderates of the great border, could save the nation from plunging into total war. As the secessionists celebrated the news of fighting and demanded an immediate vote on secession, some Unionists felt that the voters in the state should be given the opportunity to decide whether to secede now or attend the border state conference planned for May. It is noteworthy that the Unionists still were in control of the convention on the thirteenth. And they were still in control of public opinion because leading statesmen, such as distinguished moderate Whig William Cabell Rives, were still preaching restraint.

On Sunday, April 14, once again, the train that brought the Preston delegation home from the nation's capital also brought reports (really rumors at this point in time) that President Lincoln intended to raise an army. When Monday morning, April 15, brought the shattering news of Lincoln's Proclamation of Insurrection, the Unionists were, indeed, shattered. As the delegates gathered for their usual 10:00 a.m. opening of the convention, Unionist Jubal Early proclaimed that Seward was a true "statesman" and certainly could not be "guilty of the blunders which appear in that proclamation."[372] Throughout the day, the Unionists clung, perhaps unrealistically, to the notion that the proclamation was a fabrication produced by the secessionists. But on Tuesday morning, April 16, the proclamation was authenticated, and the Unionist "gig was up."

———

Abraham Lincoln, under extreme stress and tension from the news about Fort Sumter, called his cabinet into special session on Sunday, April 14. They debated just how to respond to the surrender. Lincoln pushed for a call-up of state militia as he had been meeting for several days with Northern state governors, alerting them to be ready for such a call. A proclamation was drafted that stated the "laws of the United States…now are opposed…

by combinations too powerful to be suppressed." It called for seventy-five thousand militia from the states (Lincoln had no army to summon) "in order to suppress said combinations" and stated that they would "re-possess the forts, places and property which have been seized from the Union." The proclamation called for "the persons composing the combinations aforesaid to disperse." Lincoln essentially said a rebellion was in progress and that the militia would put it down.[373]

William Freehling remarked that "Lincoln made a profound mistake by putting it this way." He could have called up the militia to protect the nation's capital from a possible invasion from the Lower South—and that would have been supported by a majority of Virginia Unionists. Shortly after the proclamation was issued, in fact, two Virginians on different occasions asked Lincoln why he did not issue a call for militia for a more narrow purpose, such as to protect the nation's capital, rather than launching a general war on the seceded states. Lincoln reportedly replied, "Oh sure, that's what I meant." By calling for militia to be engaged in an effort to "suppress said combinations," it clearly meant to wage war. It meant the Federal or central government was intent on coercing or forcing the seceded states to return to the Union.[374] Seward had repeatedly told the leaders of Virginia's Unionists that that would never happen.

Many Unionists, indeed, felt that Lincoln, through his emissary Seward, had misled them—the administration in Washington was raising an army to fight the South. And now Virginians were being asked to join that army and fight fellow Southerners. This most Virginians simply would not do. By calling for Southern Unionists to fight fellow Southerners, John Gilmer, the leader of North Carolina's Unionists, told Seward that he had done "the very thing which the disunionists most desired." He had played right into the hands of the secessionists and lost the chance to save the Upper and Border South for the Union. "All hope is now extinguished," he told Seward, as he joined the secessionists with the greatest trepidation.[375]

Could Lincoln have worded the proclamation differently so as to keep Unionism alive in the Upper South? Many of his contemporaries surely thought so. John Bell, the Constitutional Unionist Party candidate for president in the November election, stated that when he first heard of the proclamation, he concluded that the militia was being called forth "mainly for the protection of the Capitol and other points threatened, and that no invasion of the South was then meditated." So he "waited with eager hope and expectation" for news that the army would be used only for defensive purposes. When word came that Lincoln intended to invade the South, Bell with great sadness endorsed Tennessee's move toward secession.[376]

Throughout the Upper and Border South, most of the leaders of the Unionist movement reacted to the proclamation in the same way. Typical reaction from Unionist leaders in Tennessee, North Carolina and Virginia are cited below at some length because their words are so graphic, so searching and so profound.

Congressman Horace Maynard from East Tennessee, an area of the state that would furnish more soldiers to the Union army than the Confederate, made this heartfelt observation:

> *The President's extraordinary proclamation had unleashed a tornado of excitement that seems likely to sweep us all away. Men who had heretofore been cool, firm and Union loving had become perfectly wild….Never was published a more unfortunate state-paper. It has done more, and I think I speak considerably, to promote disunion than any and all other causes combined.*[377]

Charismatic Raleigh, North Carolina editor William Holden, who had deserted the Southern Rights Democrats to take up the Unionist cause, remarked bitterly:

> *If Mr. Lincoln had only insisted on holding the federal property, and had called in good faith for troops to defend Washington city, the Union men of the border states could have sustained him…but he "crossed the Rubicon" when he called for troops to subdue the Confederate States. This was a proclamation of war, and as such will be resisted.*[378]

The Unionist leader of the North Carolina state legislature, Jonathan Worth, who would become state treasurer during the war and reconstruction governor after the war, stated with utter sadness:

> *A large majority up to the time of issuing Lincoln's proclamation were firm for the Union. But then Lincoln prostrated us. He could have devised no scheme more effectual than the one he has pursued, to overthrow the friends of the Union here.*[379]

The Virginia Unionist leadership reacted in similar fashion, none more bitter and perplexed than unconditional Unionist John Minor Botts. "The Bison" lamented the issuance of the proclamation because it had such a devastating impact on Unionism in Virginia. He claimed it played into the hands of "demagogues with which the land was filled" and became "in many respects the most unfortunate state paper that was ever issued from any executive since the establishment of the government."[380]

But the real devastation to Unionism caused by the proclamation was the impact it had on the great American middle, those non-slaveholders who had opposed the Slave Power so vigorously. It can best be seen in this report from Rockbridge County in the Valley region of the state. Rockbridge was overwhelmingly Unionist, voting 91 percent for the referendum, with both of its delegates to the convention strong Unionists. From Lexington, the home of Washington College, came this dramatic report describing the turnaround:

> [On Saturday, April 13] *when news of the fall of Sumter arrived, Secessionists raised a Confederate flag in front of the courthouse, but the "more numerous Unionists"—who included many "working men"—built a higher "union pole" with an "eagle on it," to fly the American flag. When a few secessionist cadets from the Virginia Military Institute objected, a scuffle ensued and "the Unionists handled them roughly." But on Tuesday, April 16, after news of the proclamation reached Lexington, the same men who had raised the Union pole cut it down. A month later, Rockbridge County voted 1,728 to 1 for secession.*[381]

Most of the Unionists of Virginia, feeling betrayed and abandoned by the government in Washington, decided they would not join Mr. Lincoln's army to shoot fellow Southerners.

Robert E. Lee, a Virginian of the first rank and hailing from a decidedly pro-Union family, was in a terrible quandary in mid-April 1861. He had had long connections with the nation, even dating back to its founding fathers. His father, "Light Horse" Harry Lee, had given a part of the eulogy at the funeral of General Washington, coining the memorable phrase "First in war, first in peace, first in the hearts of his countrymen."[382] Now a colonel, Robert had spent the better part of his life serving in the Unites States Army. A Mexican War hero of the first order, General Scott had called him "the very best soldier I ever saw in the field."[383] He had been the superintendent of West Point in the early 1850s and was widely regarded as the most popular senior officer in the force. He knew virtually all the young officers

Robert E. Lee in the spring of 1861 was handsome beyond description. This is how he would have appeared on April 18 as he met with Francis Blair Sr. and General Winfield Scott. *Courtesy of the Library of Virginia.*

in the corps, and they looked at him in true awe. His reputation within the military was known throughout the nation.

As a result, Lee was much more than just another colonel in the army. His stance on the secession issue—his decision on whether to support Lincoln—would have a profound impact on the Unionists of his home state. If Lee chose to side with Lincoln, thousands, perhaps a majority, of Virginia's Unionists would have followed his lead. Had he rebuked a decision on the part of Virginia to secede, it would have had a dramatic impact on the state—at the very least it would have weakened secession substantially. As the secession crisis intensified, so did Lee's dilemma. Writing to his family, he spoke of his anguish: "Secession is nothing but revolution…Still a Union that can only be maintained by swords and bayonets…has no charm for me."[384]

Lee had read Lincoln's proclamation on the fifteenth and found it unacceptable. The statements "to suppress said combinations" and "to re-possess the forts, places and property seized from the Union" were clearly a call to wage war on the South. Still, he was hoping against hope that Virginia would not secede. He became increasingly dejected as it became increasingly clear the proclamation destroyed any option to find a peaceable solution. And he realized his personnel options were becoming increasingly narrow, too. "Mary remembered her father as sad and deliberate at the time, rather than passionate."[385] He now knew that the officer corps of the United States Army—his army—would be summoned to lead the suppressing and repossessing mentioned in Lincoln's proclamation.

As the Virginia State Convention was adopting an Ordinance of Secession on the seventeenth (Lee would not find out about it until April 19), he received a message from General Scott summoning him to his office. In the same envelope was a letter from his cousin John Lee asking him to see Francis P. Blair on his visit to Washington. The next day, Lee rode across the bridge that linked Arlington to the nation's capital and tied up his horse at the home of Montgomery Blair. "Waiting for him was the balding seventy-year-old Francis Preston Blair. There is no exact record of the words, but we know that Blair, after the usual courtesies, grew solemn and told Lee that he had been authorized by President Lincoln to offer him command of the northern army that would assemble when the 75,000 volunteers reached Washington."[386]

Lee, in the gravest of moods, turned down Blair's offer, stating he could not take part in an invasion of the Southern states as directed by the proclamation. Blair tried for over an hour to persuade Lee to change his mind, but Lee would not yield. Next, the colonel went to see General Scott, who told him of his secret plan to have Lee head a large army so the South would be intimidated enough to talk peace. Lee was unmoved, stating he could not lead an army in an invasion of Virginia and felt he should sit out the conflict at Arlington. Scott then said that any officer who would not accept an assignment should resign at once. Lee, devastated by Scott's command, returned to Arlington and, for the better part of the next two days, struggled with whether to resign his commission.[387]

After Lee's death in October 1870, his eldest daughter, Mary Custis Lee, wrote an account of those tense days of April 1861 that has been recently discovered. Following are some of her thoughts, first-person remembrances written some nine years after the fact.

Mary said her father was "worn and harassed" when he returned from his meetings in Washington on April 18. On the nineteenth, he received word that Virginia had seceded and then, in the early morning hours of the twentieth, drafted his letter of resignation. He then "called us into his private room" and read them his letter to General Scott. Mary pointed out that it was not the secession of Virginia that caused Lee to resign, but the meetings with Blair and General Scott. Lee had written, "I am liable at any time to be ordered on duty which I could not conscientiously perform. To save me from such a position, & to prevent the necessity of resigning under orders, I had to act at once." In a visit to Arlington that same afternoon by their cousin Orton Williams, who was on General Scott's staff, Mary mentioned Orton's comments about "how heavily the blow had fallen upon the poor old General." She quoted her cousin as saying that the general, "lying upon a sofa, had refused to see every one, & mourned as for the loss of a son." And even more significantly, Orton commented, "Now that 'Cousin Robert' had resigned every one seemed to be doing so."

Perhaps the most astonishing information revealed by the letter is the news that Robert E. Lee's decisions were made despite the Unionist sentiments of his immediate family. His wife, Mary, had written just about this time, "For my part, I would rather endure the ills we know, than rush madly into greater evils & what could be than the Division of our glorious republic into petty states, each seeking its private interests & unmindful of the whole." For Lee, it was an intensely personal decision, and one that troubled him greatly—the key seemed to be Lincoln's call to wage war on the South. Lee's daughter's closing comment was that her father left Arlington "as if there were a death in the house."[388]

Many Virginia Unionists struggled in the same way as Lee. While most in the heavily Unionist Northwest region would not support secession because of their abiding hatred of the Slave Power centered in eastern Virginia, most in the heavily Unionist Valley region (just east of the mountains) did swing to support secession. They became the reluctant Confederates. A typical example of the thinking of many delegates from the Valley can be found in this public letter from Unionist delegate Logan Osburn from Jefferson County. Jefferson County had been a strong Unionist county, voting 78 percent in favor of the referendum. Osburn addressed a letter to his constituents, dated June 13, 1861, after the Ordinance of Secession was overwhelmingly approved. Osburn's letter is presented almost in its entirety because it so centrally captures the feelings of so many Unionists.

> *When I was a candidate for a seat in the Convention, I denied...the constitutional right of a State to secede from the Union; and regarded a resort to secession as a dangerous exercise of a very doubtful power, that could only be justified after every constitutional means had been exhausted, and failed...I voted against its ratification by the people. I regarded it as mischievous in its tendency, and destructive in its consequences, to all our best interests, socially, politically and commercially...But my opinions have been overruled by a large majority of the freemen of my State. I therefore bow (from a sense of patriotic and public duty) in humble submission to their will, and acquiesce in their decision. My lot has been cast. I am a son of Virginia, and her destiny shall be mine.*[389]

Despite Osburn's heartfelt letter, Jefferson County would become one of only six counties in the Valley region to become a part of the new state of West Virginia in 1863.

———

Could the Unionists of Virginia have prevented the Civil War in the spring of 1861?

Speculative history is just that—and there is no research methodology to support the "what-could-have-beens." What does seem axiomatic, though, based on data presented in this work, is that Virginia was the key state to "have and to hold." Had Lincoln followed Seward's plan to divide the South by appeasing the Upper and Border South moderates—and had Jefferson Davis followed Toombs's advice and not ordered an attack on Fort Sumter—Virginia would not have seceded. The Unionists had the votes, as demonstrated so decisively on April 4, 1861. Had Virginia not seceded, it is quite likely that North Carolina and Tennessee would have followed suit—Unionists in those states had the votes, too. The Border South, even more Unionist than the Upper South, would have not only stayed firm to the Union but would also have furnished even fewer troops to just a Lower South Confederacy.

And what about Robert E. Lee? While it is impossible to state with total authenticity, given his struggle to resign his commission, caused primarily by the wording of Lincoln's proclamation, and given the decidedly pro-Union feelings of his wife, sons and daughters, had Lincoln not issued the Proclamation of Insurrection (Virginia then remains in the Union), it is probable that Lee would have accepted command of the United States Army in the spring of 1861, as General Scott had so fervently desired.

With Lee in command of the Union army, and with the Upper and Border South states committed to staying in the Union, it is speculative but quite reasonable to argue that the seven states of the Lower South could not have won a military conflict if one would have occurred at a future date. Nearly 70 percent of Southerners lived in the Upper and Border South, leaving just 10 percent of white Americans living in the Lower South. Wealth, manufacturing capability and the accoutrements for waging war (horses, mules, wagons) were even more heavily concentrated in the Upper and Border South.

Seward's plan to isolate the Slave Power in the Upper and Border South states by creating a new Union Party not only had real merit in preventing civil war, but it also could have realigned the political parties so as to isolate the radical Northern politicians. To repeat for emphasis, James Barbour, the highly regarded Virginia Unionist, speaking for many like-minded moderates, wrote to Seward, "You may lose a portion of your own party North. But you place yourself and the new administration at the head of a national conservative party which will domineer over all other party organizations North and South yet many years to come."[390] The great American center stood poised to rally behind Seward's plan.

A Union Party of Southern and Northern moderates held great hope for the Unionists of Virginia. They were clearly headed for a major victory in the scheduled May elections that would have placed Unionists in key positions in Washington and Richmond. Furthermore, isolating the radical, uncompromising Northern politicians and abolitionists could very well have prevented an outbreak of war. These radicals were constantly badgering and vilifying Lincoln for not going after the secessionists with armed force. Henry Ward Beecher, William Lloyd Garrison and Wendell Phillips were the most notorious abolitionists—one called Lincoln a "slave hound." The Radical Republicans were led by Thaddeus Stevens, Ben Wade and Zachariah Chandler, all of whom felt Lincoln was not up to the task at hand. Lincoln had come to truly hate Phillips, even exclaiming, "I don't see how God lets him live." Boston's Oliver Wendell Holmes Jr., who was severely wounded twice in the war and would become the most celebrated associate justice of the Supreme Court after the war, bitterly denounced the abolitionists for "getting us into the war." "Communists show in the most extreme form what I came to loathe in the abolitionists—the conviction that anyone who did not agree with them was either a knave or a fool."[391]

The Unionists of Virginia defeated secession handily on April 4, 1861, and had they been able to sustain it, quite likely war would have been prevented that spring.

———⟡———

What impact could a victory by the Unionists of Virginia have had on the institution of slavery and on total war?

Again, we are in the speculative arena, but some observations are worth noting. Although social historians have demonstrated that slavery was still very profitable in Virginia (and the Deep South) as war approached, the institution had been eliminated in the Northern states peacefully during the early part of the nineteenth century, and it was dying in the Border South states by mid-century. Maryland had as many free blacks as slaves in 1860. Increasing numbers of slaves escaping across the Mason-Dixon line and the Ohio River made owning slaves more and more precarious in Maryland, Virginia and Kentucky. While excess slaves could be (and were) hired out, changing agricultural methods and changing crops decreased the need for large "slave gangs." Modernization, specifically the advent of mechanized farming equipment, would increasingly have an impact on the need for slave gangs as well. And of course, the emerging enlightenment that was sweeping the Western world posed a moral dilemma for slave owners. Virginians were not blind to these developments, as the comments by secessionists in the Virginia State Convention so aptly illustrated.

Brazil, with only slightly fewer slaves than the United States, eliminated the institution over several decades by gradual emancipation, manumission and government purchase of slaves. In the United States, it is possible the same could have occurred. Manumission was occurring in the Upper and Border South, and various political leaders (including Lincoln and Seward) had spoken of government purchase of slaves. Runaways hastened the demise of slavery in Brazil and were doing so in this country, too. "Slavery could not last if the slaves had freedom within arm's length," noted historian Jeffrey Hummel. Harriet Tubman was proving the point monthly. Toward the end of the war, "Civil War runaways so weakened the peculiar institution that the Confederacy itself turned toward emancipating and arming blacks."[392]

Unlike Brazil, in the United States, it was violence that ended slavery, but not that "revolutionary violence wielded by bondsmen themselves from the bottom up, a violence that at least had the potential to be pinpointed against the South's minority of guilty slave owners," those 15 to 20 percent of white men who owned slaves. Astonishingly for the men and women in the South who did not own slaves, slavery was ended by a civil war that "involved indiscriminate State violence directed from the top down."[393] And the indiscriminate violence impacted all in its path. When Lincoln unleashed Grant, Sherman and other Union generals to wage "total war," they did just that. The Virginians who owned slaves (and their sons) were killed, but non-slaveholders and their families and many, many slaves were killed, too.

Not only non-slaveholders but also slaveholding Union loyalists were caught in the path of total war. In 1864, when Grant ordered Sherman to turn the Shenandoah Valley into "a barren waste," everyone living in the valley was impacted. Confederate supporters had their farms ransacked and burned (as they should have, some would argue), but staunch Unionists suffered the same fate. Harrisonburg's die-hard Unionist Isaac Bowman watched as "his Union soldiers" destroyed his farm. No family in Virginia was more well known for their unyielding Unionism than the Lewis family of Rockingham County. John F. Lewis, the only Virginia State Convention delegate east of the mountains who refused to sign the Ordinance of Secession, watched hopelessly as his business, Mount Vernon Furnace, was burned and his family's farms and homes stripped of everything of value. The furnace was destroyed by the Ninth New York Infantry, and the unit's regimental history seems almost apologetic about it: "The 9th N.Y. unfortunately burned the iron works in Brown's Gap belonging to a Mr. Lewis, who was a non-combatant and had refused to join the secessionists."[394]

Towns and cities and farms and crops were burned (in many areas that were pro-Union before the war), causing hundreds of innocent civilians (mostly women, children and slaves) to die of disease and even starvation. Libraries and courthouses were indiscriminately destroyed, along with their invaluable contents and records. Out-of-control soldiers, and the ragged thugs who followed the armies, engaged in countless crimes ranging from petty theft to grand larceny and worse. Total war had a lasting impact on those who survived it. The brutal siege of Vicksburg, Mississippi, where the citizens ended up eating rats when not dying of starvation, resulted in the residents refusing to celebrate Independence Day until July 1944, some eighty-one years after its surrender. When the concept of total war was implemented, Union general George McClellan protested to General-in-Chief Henry Halleck about departing from "civilized warfare." "Halleck responded that he could not revoke the orders as he understood they had been seen and approved by the president."[395] Total war, engaged in by both sides, but primarily by the North, was brutal in the extreme. And the cost of the war was outlandish, about $6.6 billion (roughly $100 billion in today's dollars) for both North and South, which was enough to purchase all the slaves and give them "forty acres and a mule."[396]

The imponderable question is whether the loss of one million lives was necessary to free four million slaves. The Unionists of Virginia felt there was a better way than that of total war.

While the war began with young men on both sides clamoring to enlist so they could witness the excitement of battle and demonstrate their "manly courage," the grim awakening soon materialized. New research puts the total war dead at 750,000 rather than the oft-cited 620,000. The total number of battle deaths and related deaths, soldier and civilian, will likely never be known, but surely it approaches one million. How many future great men and women, white and black, whether physicians or scientists or artists or musicians or farmers or managers or "whatevers" were killed is an enigma of the highest order? How many slaves were left unprotected to be slaughtered by Confederate troops or roving bands of malcontents? How many slaves were left to die of starvation or disease by the Grand Army of the Republic? Whatever the number, it was a staggering loss for the nation, and one that can never be fully evaluated or understood. Nearly an entire generation of young people were killed, maimed or emotionally destroyed.

Drew Faust, in her widely praised book *This Republic of Suffering*, chronicles the enormous scope of death and dying during the Civil War. The governments of both North and South were utterly unprepared for the war that evolved. Americans of all political persuasions were

Virginians who survived the slaughter of war are seen taking the oath of allegiance in the Virginia State Capitol after Appomattox. *Courtesy of the Library of Virginia.*

dumbfounded by the magnitude of the destruction and the unbelievable number of deaths (mostly from disease). Faust notes hauntingly, "As war continued inexorably onward and as death tolls mounted ever higher, soldiers on both sides reported how difficult it became to believe that the slaughter was purposeful and that their sacrifice had meaning."[397] Soldiers on both sides had had enough.

Even more hauntingly, Gettysburg's Gabor Boritt ponders Abraham Lincoln's reaction to the ever-growing loss of life: "Had Lincoln admitted to himself that a colossal war would be the price of freedom, he might have been paralyzed. Could he have squarely faced…a future that would require, in the calculations of David Potter, 'the life of one soldier, either Rebel or Yank, for every six slaves who were freed?'"[398] Most likely he could not.

The Unionists of Virginia had pleaded for a chance to prevent war.

This work is dedicated to the Pulitzer Prize–winning twentieth-century Civil War historian David M. Potter. Potter coined the phrase that challenged the meaning of the secession crisis for a generation of historians: "Lincoln was far more fit to become than to be president."[399]

Again, could the Unionists of Virginia have prevented the Civil War? They certainly had some of the right attributes. Politically moderate, cosmopolitan and modern, they were the forward-looking men of the state—the men who believed in democracy and its essential ingredient: compromise. And they may just have been the men who could have responded to the moral imperative of ending slavery over time. Had they been given a chance to demonstrate their political judgment when in firm control of the state government, they could have become the unsung heroes of the Civil War era.

"Wait for Virginia. See what she does" was not only the clarion call of the Upper and Border South; it was the call of political moderates throughout the land—those who opposed total war. And the war seems to never end, as this letter from President Jerry Ford to the governor of Virginia, 110 years after Appomattox, so aptly demonstrates.

THE WHITE HOUSE

WASHINGTON

November 18, 1975

Dear Mills:

As you are aware, I recently signed into law the legislation which restored the citizenship of General Robert E. Lee.

This was legislation that properly recognized a great American. I was honored that I could participate in remedying this historical oversight.

I requested a limited number of copies of this legislation be reproduced, and I have signed for you a copy of the original bill. I am sending it to you as a reminder of the signing ceremony at the Custis-Lee Mansion.

With kindest personal regards,

Jerry Ford

The Honorable Mills Godwin
Governor of Virginia
Richmond, Virginia 23219

President Ford notified Governor Goodwin that the citizenship of Robert E. Lee has been restored by legislation—110 years after Appomattox. *Courtesy of the Library of Virginia.*

NOTES

Preface

1. In his recent book *The Madness of Mary Lincoln* (Southern Illinois University Press, 2007), Jason Emerson documents the travails of Mrs. Lincoln during her confinement.
2. Catton, *Reflections on the Civil War*.

Chapter 1

3. The works of many secession crisis experts will be cited throughout this book, especially works by the leaders of this movement, Daniel W. Crofts and William W. Freehling. A lesser-known source, but one of particular note, is the doctoral dissertation of Patricia E. Hickin, "Antislavery in Virginia, 1831–1861," presented in June 1968 to the graduate faculty of the University of Virginia. Although modern social historians have downplayed her work, the 832-page, two-volume study is still the most detailed reference on the subject and should not be dismissed.
4. Crofts, *Reluctant Confederates*, 104–05.
5. Ibid., 105–06.
6. Ibid., "Late Antebellum Virginia Reconsidered," 254.
7. Ibid., *Reluctant Confederates*, 106.

8. Tarter, *Grandees of Government*, 69. Tarter's book is a must read for any reader seriously interested in the long political life of Virginia's aristocrats.
9. Freehling, *Reintegration of American History*, 149.
10. Hickin, "Antislavery in Virginia," 13–14.
11. Crofts, *Old Southampton*, 98.
12. Ibid., 94–95.
13. Hickin, "Antislavery in Virginia," 573.
14. Craven, *Coming of the Civil War*, 11.
15. Tarter, *Grandees of Government*, 164.
16. Freehling, *South vs. South*, 34.
17. Faust, *Mothers of Invention*, 246–47.
18. Randall and Donald, *Civil War and Reconstruction*, 62.
19. Wolf, *Race and Liberty*, 201.
20. Hickin, "Antislavery in Virginia," 145.
21. Crofts, *Old Southampton*, 109.
22. Freehling, *Reintegration of American History*, 154.
23. Ibid., 191.
24. Ibid., *South vs. South*, 34.
25. Appleton, *Slavery and the Union*, 4.
26. Freehling, *Reintegration of American History*, 156.
27. Hickin, "Antislavery in Virginia," 175.
28. Crofts, *Old Southampton*, 118.
29. *Richmond Whig*, July 24, 1835, as cited in Crofts, *Old Southampton*, 119.
30. Hickin, "Antislavery in Virginia," 19–20.
31. Ibid., 17.
32. Ibid., 185.
33. Fisher, *No Cause for Offense*, 10.
34. Zaborney, *Slaves for Hire*, 162–64.
35. Freehling, *Reintegration of American History*, 190.
36. Shanks, *Secession Movement in Virginia*, 13.
37. Deyle, *Carry Me Back*, 5.
38. Hickin, "Antislavery in Virginia," 622.
39. Ibid., 637.
40. Ibid., 665.
41. Crofts, *Late Antebellum Virginia Reconsidered*, 265.
42. Holt, *Political Crisis*, 217.
43. Tarter traces the origins of this domination to the very founding of the colony in the 1600s.
44. Gaines, "Virginia Constitutional Convention."

45. Wolf, *Race and Liberty*, 226.

46. Ibid.

47. Gaines, *Virginia Constitutional Convention*, 140.

48. Deyle, *Carry Me Back*, 5-6.

49. Stealey, *West Virginia's Civil War–Era Constitution*, 25.

50. Gaines, *Virginia Constitutional Convention*, iv.

51. Ibid., 141.

52. Freehling, *Road to Disunion*, vol. II, 506.

53. Ibid., *Reintegration of American History*, 192.

54. Craven, *Coming of the Civil War*, 11.

55. Tarter, *Grandees of Government*, 192–93.

56. Shade, *Democratizing the Old Dominion*, 264–65.

57. Shanks, *Secession Movement in Virginia*, 85.

58. Toomey, *War Came by Train*, 5.

59. Shanks, *Secession Movement in Virginia*, 86.

60. Ibid., 87–88.

61. Crofts, *Late Antebellum Virginia Reconsidered*, 270.

62. Hickin, "Antislavery in Virginia," 222–23.

63. Hitchcock, "Limits of Southern Unionism," 57–72.

64. Crofts, *Old Southampton*, 134.

65. Ibid., 180.

66. Hickin, "Antislavery in Virginia," 220–24.

67. Ibid., 228–40.

68. Crofts, *Old Southampton*, 17–18.

69. Ayers, In the Presence of Mine Enemies, 20.

70. Hickin, "Antislavery in Virginia," 68–69.

71. Bowman, "Conditional Unionism and Slavery in Virginia," 38.

72. Freehling, *South vs. South*, 141–42.

73. Holland, "War Graph, Southern Unionists," 18.

74. Crofts, *Old Southampton*, 206.

75. Anderson, *Fighting by Southern Federals*, 10–13.

76. Varon, *Disunion*, 14.

77. Hickin, "Antislavery in Virginia," 242.

78. Inscoe and Kenzer, *Enemies of the Country*, 2.

79. Johnson, *Toward a Patriarchal Republic*, xx.

80. Egnal, "Rethinking the Secession of the Lower South," 261–90.

81. Freehling, *South vs. South*, xiii.

82. Dew, *Apostles of Disunion*, 59.

83. The reader interested in Seward's effort to prevent the war is referred to Denton, *William Henry Seward and the Secession Crisis*.

CHAPTER 2

84. Denton, *William Henry Seward and the Secession Crisis*, 37.
85. Bancroft, *Life of William H. Seward*, vol. 1, 525.
86. An analysis of Lincoln's incredible good fortune can be found in Denton, *William Henry Seward and the Secession Crisis*, Chapter 1, "Luck of the Draw."
87. Freehling, *Road to Disunion*, vol. II, 229–30.
88. Hickin, "Antislavery in Virginia," 721–39.
89. Link, *Roots of Secession*, 204.
90. Ibid., 205.
91. Ayers, *In the Presence of Mine Enemies*, 60.
92. Halstead, *Caucuses of 1860*, 111. Halstead is cited as a primary source. He attended all of the conventions that spring and thus had a somewhat unique perspective.
93. Halstead, *Caucuses of 1860*, 109.
94. Ibid., 106.
95. Ibid., 119.
96. Crofts, *Late Antebellum Virginia*, 271.
97. Link, *Roots of Secession*, 175.
98. *Staunton Spectator*, March 6, 1860.
99. Lankford, *Cry Havoc!*, 2–3.
100. Simpson, *A Good Southerner*, 214–18. Simpson offers a thorough review of the John Brown raid and its consequences in Chapter 11.
101. Crofts, *Late Antebellum Virginia*, 271–72.
102. *Wellsburg (VA) Herald*, June 17, 1859, as cited in Link, *Roots of Secession*, 174.
103. *Maryland Union*, November 1, 1860.
104. Thomas J. Pretlow to Thaddeus Stevens, December 27, 1865, Thaddeus Stevens Papers, LC, as found in *Crofts*, Old Southampton, 174.
105. *Staunton Spectator*, October 30, 1860.
106. Crofts, *Old Southampton*, 174–75.
107. John Underwood in *Delaware Republican*, October 17, 1859, as cited in Freehling, *Road to Disunion*, vol. II, 330.
108. J. Henley Smith to Alexander Stephens, May 7, 1860, Stephens Papers, LC, as found in Freehling, *Road to Disunion*, vol. II, 330.

109. Ayres, *In the Presence of Mine Enemies*, 60.
110. Dumond, *Secession Movement*, 96.
111. *Congressional Globe*, 36th Cong., 2d sess., A77, 580–83, A170, as cited in Crofts, *Reluctant Confederates*, 124–25.
112. Dumond, *Secession Movement*, 2–3.
113. Crofts, *Reluctant Confederates*, 76.
114. Ayres, *In the Presence of Mine Enemies*, 68.
115. Hildebrand, *Life and Times of John Brown Baldwin*, 71–72.
116. Ibid., 72–73.
117. Freehling, *Road to Disunion*, vol. II, 324.
118. *New York Times*, "Special Dispatch—The Campaign in Virginia," October 2, 1860.
119. Ayres, *In the Presence of Mine Enemies*, 62.
120. Link, *Roots of Secession*, 207.
121. Shanks, *Secession Movement in Virginia*, 118.
122. Freehling, *Reintegration of American History*, 226.
123. John M. Smith to John Letcher, September 23, 1860, as cited in Tarter, *Grandees of Government*, 200.
124. Crofts, *Reluctant Confederates*, 82–86.
125. Freehling, *Reintegration of American History*, 226.
126. Crofts, *Reluctant Confederates*, 47.
127. Ibid., 44–46.
128. Ibid., 47.
129. Shade, *Democratizing the Old Dominion*, 291.
130. Link, *Roots of Secession*, 209.
131. Ayres, *In the Presence of Mine Enemies*, 83.

Chapter 3

132. Donald, *Lincoln*, 256.
133. Long, *Civil War Day by Day*, 3.
134. Freehling, *South vs. South*, 39.
135. Long, *Civil War Day by Day*, 5.
136. Ibid., 11.
137. McPherson, *Battle Cry of Freedom*, 235.
138. Long, *Civil War Day by Day*, 13.
139. Reynolds, *Editors Make War*, 163.
140. Link, *Roots of Secession*, 216.

141. Long, *Civil War Day by Day*, 10.

142. Link, Roots of Secession, 222–23.

143. Ibid., 221.

144. Boney, *John Letcher of Virginia*, Preface.

145. Alexander H.H. Stuart to John B. Baldwin, January 8, 1861, in Baldwin's pardon application file, Virginia, RG 94, microfilm series M1003, NA, as cited in Crofts, *Reluctant Confederates*, 137.

146. Ayers, *In the Presence of Mine Enemies*, 104.

147. Hildebrand, *Life and Times of John Brown Baldwin*, 81.

148. Crofts, *Reluctant Confederates*, 139–140.

149. *Staunton Spectator*, February 12, 1861.

150. Denton, *William Henry Seward and the Secession Crisis*, 79.

151. Hochfield, *Great Secession Winter*, 23.

152. Link, *Roots of Secession*, 225.

153. Crofts, *Reluctant Confederates*, 138.

154. Hitchcock, "Southern Moderates and Secession," 871–84.

155. Davidson and Greenawalt, "Unionists in Rockbridge County," 78–102.

156. Crofts, *Old Southampton*, 177.

157. Crofts, *Reluctant Confederates*, 131–32.

158. Tarter, *Grandees of Government*, 203.

159. Link, *Roots of Secession*, 226.

160. In this analysis, Unionists are defined as those who voted against the Ordinance of Secession on April 4, 1861, the vote before Sumter and before Lincoln's call for troops. Conversely, secessionists are defined as those who voted for the Ordinance on April 4, 1861. Data was obtained from Gaines, *Biographical Register*. A total of 3 delegates are missing from this data, as the final number of delegates was 152, but those 3 do not alter the percentages cited here.

161. Summaries of the backgrounds of the delegates cited can be found in Gaines, *Biographical Register*.

162. Ayres, *In the Presence of Mine Enemies*, 107.

163. Potter, *Impending Crisis*, 507.

164. Ayres, *In the Presence of Mine Enemies*, 107.

165. Documents of the Convention of 1861, Appendix D, 792–96.

166. Shanks, *Secession Movement in Virginia*, 207.

167. Ibid., 154.

168. Ibid.

169. Denton, *William Henry Seward and the Secession Crisis*, 89.

170. Data from sources previously identified.

171. There are slight differences in the numbers cited from different sources, but they do not change the outcome or conclusions drawn.

172. Crofts, *Reluctant Confederates*, 364.

173. Link, *Roots of Secession*, 221.

174. Crofts, *Reluctant Confederates*, 363.

175. Shanks, *Secession Movement in Virginia*, 154.

176. Potter, *Impending Crisis*, 508.

177. Ayres, *In the Presence of Mine Enemies*, 108.

178. *Abingdon Democrat*, February 8, 1861, as cited in Tarter, *Grandees of Government*, 197.

179. Boritt, *Why the Civil War Came*, 6.

Chapter 4

180. Chittenden, *Report of the Debates and Proceedings*, 5.

181. Gunderson, "William C. Rives and the Old Gentlemen's Convention," 467.

182. Ibid.

183. Ibid., 468.

184. Denton, *William Henry Seward and the Secession Crisis*, 91.

185. Bancroft, *Life of William H. Seward*, vol. 2, 536.

186. McClintock, *Lincoln and the Decision for War*, 174.

187. Adams, *Letters of Henry Adams*, 87.

188. Soule, "Trials of a Virginia Unionist," 15.

189. Chittenden, *A Report of the Debates and Proceedings*, 225–26.

190. Gunderson, *Old Gentlemen's Convention*, 14.

191. Ibid., 100–01.

192. Crofts, *Reluctant Confederates*, 193.

193. A more complete analysis of Seward's Southern Strategy can be found in Chapter 4 of Denton, *William Henry Seward and the Secession Crisis*.

194. Donald, *Lincoln*, 281.

195. Gunderson, *Old Gentlemen's Convention*, 96.

196. McClintock, *Lincoln and the Decision for War*, 96.

197. Gunderson, *Old Gentlemen's Convention*, 94.

198. Ibid., "Letters from the Washington Peace Conference," 387.

199. Ibid., *Old Gentlemen's Convention*, 95.

200. Chittenden, *Report of the Debates and Proceedings*, 255.

201. Gunderson, *Old Gentlemen's Convention*, 95.

202. Ibid., 96.
203. Kirwan, *John J. Crittenden*, 400–01.
204. Most historians agree that the delegates should be divided into the three camps cited above. However, the number of delegates in each camp is subject to debate. While some delegates moved from one camp to another, I have used the division cited by Shanks in *Secession Movement in Virginia* because I feel they are closest to the real thing.
205. Boney, *John Letcher of Virginia*, 107.
206. Freehling, *Road to Disunion*, vol. II, 507.
207. *Staunton Spectator*, October 2, 1860.
208. Congressional Globe, 36th Cong., 2nd sess., A77, 580–83, A170, as cited in Crofts, *Reluctant Confederates*, 124–25.
209. Sandburg, *Abraham Lincoln*, 46–48.
210. Bancroft, *Life of William H. Seward*, vol. 2, 536.
211. Shanks, *Secession Movement in Virginia*, 165.
212. Freehling and Simpson, *Showdown in Virginia*, 4.
213. Donald, *Lincoln*, 257.
214. Soule, "Trials of a Virginia Unionist," 15.
215. This dialogue was recorded shortly after the meeting by Governor Morehead, who revealed it in a speech in Liverpool, England, on October 9, 1862. It is reprinted by Barbee and Bonham in "Fort Sumter Again," *Mississippi Valley Historical Review* XXVIII, 65-73, as found in Soule, "Trials of a Virginia Unionist," 18.
216. Long, *Civil War Day by Day*, 42–43.
217. *New York Times*, February 12, 1861, as cited in Crofts, *Reluctant Confederates*, 240.
218. McClintock, *Lincoln and the Decision for War*, 164.

CHAPTER 5

219. Crofts, *Reluctant Confederates*, 316.
220. Soule, "Trials of a Virginia Unionist," 18.
221. Freehling and Simpson, *Showdown in Virginia*, 20–21.
222. Denton, *William Henry Seward and the Secession Crisis*, 112.
223. Donald, *Lincoln*, 282.
224. Barringer, *A House Dividing*, 322–23.
225. Denton, *William Henry Seward and the Secession Crisis*, 115.
226. *Baltimore Exchange* in *Wheeling Daily Intelligencer*, March 1, 1861, as cited in Crofts, *Reluctant Confederates*, 254.

227. Donald, *Lincoln*, 285.
228. Freehling and Simpson, *Showdown in Virginia*, 27–30.
229. Gilmer to Seward, March 9, 1861, Lincoln Papers, as cited in Crofts, *Reluctant Confederates*, 258.
230. Denton, *William Henry Seward and the Secession Crisis*, 125.
231. The Abraham Lincoln Papers at the Library of Congress, Series 1, General Correspondence. William H. Seward to Abraham Lincoln, Saturday, March 9, 1861.
232. Thompson, *Confidential Correspondence of Gustavus Vasa Fox*, 8–9.
233. Crawford, *Genesis of the Civil War*, 281. Crawford was the assistant surgeon assigned to Major Anderson's staff in September 1860 and was present throughout the Fort Sumter crisis. His book, although published years after the war, is nevertheless considered one of the best first-person accounts of the events at the fort during the spring of 1861.
234. Long, *Civil War Day by Day*, 49.
235. Nicolay and Hay, *Abraham Lincoln*, vol. 3, 385.
236. Donald, *Lincoln*, 287.
237. Denton, *William Henry Seward and the Secession Crisis*, 128.
238. Freehling and Simpson, *Showdown in Virginia*, 47–48.
239. *Richmond Whig*, March 12, 1861.
240. Crofts, *Secession Crisis Enigma*, 90. Crofts's work uncovers, for the first time, that the famous diarist was William Henry Hurlbert, who wrote "The Diary of a Public Man." The diarist had long been thought of as the ultimate Washington insider during the secession crisis and as such has been quoted extensively by Civil War historians over the past century and a half.
241. Lankford, *Cry Havoc!*, 46.
242. Freehling and Simpson, *Showdown in Virginia*, 61.
243. Crofts, *Reluctant Confederates*, 275.
244. John G. Nicolay to O.M. Hatch, March 6, 1861, as cited in Donald, *Lincoln*, 285.
245. Donald, *Lincoln*, 285.
246. Charles Francis Adams, diary, March 10, 1861, Massachusetts Historical Society, as cited in Donald, *Lincoln*, 285.
247. Denton, *William Henry Seward and the Secession Crisis*, 36.
248. Jason Emerson, *Madness of Mary Lincoln*, 5.
249. Burlingame, *Inner World of Abraham Lincoln*, 280–301.
250. Freehling and Simpson, *Showdown in Virginia*, 62–74.
251. *Richmond Whig*, March 22, 1861.

252. Lankford, *Cry Havoc!*, 53.

253. Freehling and Simpson, *Showdown in Virginia*, 75–88.

254. Beale and Brownsword, *Diary of Gideon Wells*, vol. 1, 4–5, as cited in McClintock, *Lincoln and the Decision for War*, 203.

255. Long, *Civil War Day by Day*, 50.

256. Crofts, *Secession Crisis Enigma*, 91.

257. Thompson, *Confidential Correspondence of Gustavus Fox*, 9-10.

258. *National Intelligencer*, March 21, 1861, and *New York Times*, March 21, 1861, both cited in Crofts, *Reluctant Confederates*, 286.

259. Crofts, *Reluctant Confederates*, 292.

260. Potter, Lincoln and His Party, 329–31.

261. Donald, *Lincoln*, 288.

262. Freehling and Simpson, *Showdown in Virginia*, 89–93.

263. George W. Summers to James C. Welling, March 19, 1861, as cited in Crofts, *Reluctant Confederates*, 289.

264. Reese, *Proceedings of the Virginia State Convention*, vol. III, 705.

265. Simpson, *A Good Southerner*, 245.

266. Langford, *Cry Havoc!*, 50.

267. Crofts, *Reluctant Confederates*, 277–78.

268. Long, *Civil War Day by Day*, 52.

269. Crawford, *Genesis of the Civil War*, 371.

270. Ibid., 300.

271. Potter, *Lincoln and His Party*, 341–42.

272. Donald, *Lincoln*, 288.

273. Crofts, *Reluctant Confederates*, 297.

274. Eisenhower, *Agent of Destiny*, 360.

275. Denton, *William Henry Seward and the Secession Crisis*, 135; McClintock, *Lincoln and the Decision for War*, 229-231.

276. Donald, *Lincoln*, 288.

277. Burlingame, *Inner World of Abraham Lincoln*, 155.

278. McClintock, *Lincoln and the Decision for War*, 234.

279. Long, *Civil War Day by Day*, 51.

280. McClintock, *Lincoln and the Decision for War*, 234.

281. Ibid., 233.

282. Donald, *Lincoln*, 289.

283. Thompson, *Confidential Correspondence of Gustavus Vasa Fox*, 13–14.

284. Denton, *William Henry Seward and the Secession Crisis*, 139.

CHAPTER 6

285. Holt, *Rise and Fall of the Whig Party*, 982.
286. Denton, *William Henry Seward and the Secession Crisis*, 140.
287. Patrick Sowle, "A Reappraisal of Seward's Memorandum," 235.
288. Ibid., 239.
289. Thompson, *Confidential Correspondence of Gustavus Vasa Fox*, 15.
290. Ibid., 14–17.
291. Crawford, *Genesis of the Civil War*, 373.
292. Magruder, "A Piece of Secret History," 438–45.
293. Potter, *Lincoln and His Party*, 356.
294. Thompson, *Confidential Correspondence of Gustavus Vasa Fox*, 19.
295. RF&P schedule provided by Nick Fry, curator, John W. Barriger III National Railroad Library, University of Missouri–St. Louis.
296. Interview Between President Lincoln and Col. John B. Baldwin, April 4th, 1861: Statements & Evidence, (*Staunton Spectator*) Job Office –D.E. Strasburg, Printer, 1866), 10–15. This publication contains the full testimony of Baldwin and John Minor Botts (who had challenged Baldwin's testimony) before the committee, as well as pertinent letters from participants supporting Baldwin's claims.
297. Thompson, *Confidential Correspondence of Gustavus Vasa Fox*, 20–25.
298. Current, *Lincoln and the First Shot*, 106.
299. Crawford, *Genesis of the Civil War*, 378.
300. Ibid., 381.
301. Thompson, *Confidential Correspondence of Gustavus Vasa Fox*, 26–27.
302. Reese, *Proceedings of the Virginia State Convention*, vol. II, 697–98.
303. Freehling and Simpson, *Showdown in Virginia*, 122–29.
304. Hildebrand, *Life and Times of John Brown Baldwin*, 110.
305. Tarter, *Grandees of Government*, 420, note 33: "The twentieth-century edition of the *Proceedings* took its text from the debates as reported in the semiweekly *Richmond Enquirer*, which on 8 Apr. 1861 got the numbers wrong…The report of the 4 Apr. 1861 vote printed in the *Richmond Daily Whig* on 5 Apr. 1861 got the numbers and names correct."
306. Freehling and Simpson, *Showdown in Virginia*, 132–33.
307. Letter of ex-lieutenant governor Samuel Price as cited in Hildebrand, *Life and times of John Brown Baldwin*, 111.
308. Hildebrand, *Life and Times of John Brown Baldwin*, 113.
309. Freehling and Simpson, *Showdown in Virginia*, 156.
310. Current, *Lincoln and the First Shot*, 115.
311. Crawford, *Genesis of the Civil War*, 382–83.

312. Ibid., 398.

313. Langford, *Cry Havoc!*, 69.

314. Crawford, *Genesis of the Civil War*, 398.

315. Long, *Civil War Day by Day*, 55.

316. Ibid.

317. Denton, *William Henry Seward and the Secession Crisis*, 156.

318. Current, *Lincoln and the First Shot*, 120–21.

319. Sandburg, *Abraham Lincoln*, 200–01.

320. Crawford, *Genesis of the Civil War*, 398–99.

321. Ibid., 425–26.

322. Ibid., 442.

323. Ibid., 416–19.

324. Ibid., 447.

325. Gilmer to Seward, April 12, 1861, as cited in Crofts, *Reluctant Confederates*, 311.

326. Freehling and Simpson, *Showdown in Virginia*, 160.

327. Glyndon G. Van Deusen, *William Henry Seward*, 286.

328. Hildebrand, *Life and Times of John Brown Baldwin*, 114.

329. Ibid., 115.

330. Freehling and Simpson, *Showdown in Virginia*, 148–50.

331. Reese, *Proceedings of the Virginia State Convention*, vol. III, 633.

332. Hildebrand, *Life and Times of John Brown Baldwin*, 117.

333. Freehling and Simpson, *Showdown in Virginia*, 161.

334. Ibid., 161–64.

335. Eisenhower, *Agent of Destiny*, 368.

336. Current, *Lincoln and the First Shot*, 114.

337. Angle and Miers, *The Tragic Years*, 64–65.

338. *War of the Rebellion*, ser. 1, 2: 581.

339. Current, *The Lincoln Nobody Knows*, 123.

340. Crawford, *Genesis of the Civil War*, 420.

341. Crofts, *Reluctant Confederates*, 312.

342. Ibid., 313.

343. Reese, *Proceedings of the Virginia State Convention*, vol. IV, 21.

344. Alexander H.H. Stuart to Seward, April 15, 1861 (telegram), Seward Papers, as cited in Crofts, *Reluctant Confederates*, 313.

345. Freehling and Simpson, *Showdown in Virginia*, 165.

346. Reese, *Proceedings of the Virginia State Convention*, vol. III, 735.

347. Hildebrand, *Life and Times of John Brown Baldwin*, 121.

348. Reese, *Proceedings of the Virginia State Convention*, vol. III, 762.

349. Boney, *John Letcher of Virginia*, 112.
350. Freehling and Simpson, *Showdown in Virginia*, 174.
351. Reese, *Proceedings of the Virginia State Convention*, vol. IV, 42.
352. Ibid., 70-71.
353. Hildebrand, *Life and Times of John Brown Baldwin*, 125.
354. Langford, *Cry Havoc!*, 127.
355. Boney, *John Letcher of Virginia*, 112.
356. *New York Times*, "The Position of Virginia; Movements in Virginia Efforts for a Central Confederacy Prospects of the State, Richmond, Va, Tuesday P.M.," April 16, 1861.
357. Lankford, *Cry Havoc!*, 125.
358. Botts, *The Great Rebellion*, 206.
359. Crofts, *Reluctant Confederates*, 322.
360. Lankford, *Cry Havoc!*, 127.
361. Ibid., 128.
362. Freehling and Simpson, *Showdown in Virginia*, 192–93.
363. Ibid., 193.
364. Ibid., 196.
365. Ibid., 196–201.
366. Randall and Donald, *Civil War and Reconstruction*, 188–89.

Epilogue

367. Freehling and Simpson, *Showdown in Virginia*, xviii.
368. Simpson, *A Good Southerner*, 253.
369. Hildebrand, *Life and Times of John Brown Baldwin*, 131–32.
370. Sandburg, *Abraham Lincoln*, vol. 1, 206.
371. *Philadelphia Press*, April 16, 1861, as cited in Langford, *Cry Havoc!*, 90.
372. Crofts, *Reluctant Confederates*, 313.
373. www.angelfire.com/my/abrahamlincoln/Militia.
374. William W. Freehling, speech at Virginia State Capital, April 17, 2011.
375. John A. Gilmer to William H. Seward, April 21, 1861, as cited in Crofts, *Reluctant Confederates*, 340.
376. John Bell, speech of April 23, 1861, in *Nashville Republican Banner*, May 10, 1861, as cited in Crofts, *Reluctant Confederates*, 334–25.
377. Horace Maynard to Edward Bates, April 18, 1861, General Records of the Department of Justice, Record Group 60, National Archives, as cited in Crofts, *Reluctant Confederates*, 334.

378. *North Carolina Semi-Weekly Standard*, April 20, 1861, as cited in Crofts, *Reluctant Confederates*, 335.

379. Jonathan Worth to Springs Oak Co., May 13, 1861, as cited in Crofts, *Reluctant Confederates*, 336.

380. Botts, *The Great Rebellion*, 205–06.

381. Davidson and Greenawalt, *Unionists in Rockbridge County*, 100–01.

382. Wikipedia, "George Washington," http://en.wikipedia.org/wiki/George_Washington.

383. www.encyclopediavirginia.org/lee_robert_edward_1807-1870.

384. *Civil War Daily Gazette*, Robert E. Lee's Letter Against Secession, January 23, 1861.

385. Pryor, "Thou Knowest Not the Time of Thy Visitation," 5.

386. Fleming, Disease of the Public Mind, 268–69.

387. Ibid., 270–71.

388. Pryor, "Thou Knowest Not the Time of Thy Visitation," 1–18.

389. Logan Osburn, letter to the *Free Press*, June 13, 1861, from the family collection of Thomas H. Reynolds Jr., a good friend and neighbor in Oxford, Maryland. Osburn is Reynolds's maternal great-grandfather.

390. Bancroft, *Life of William Henry Seward*, vol. II, 536.

391. Fleming, *Disease in the Public Mind*, 304.

392. Hummel, *Emancipating Slaves*, 355.

393. Ibid., 354–55.

394. Fisher, *No Cause of Offense*, 50–52.

395. Eric Foner, *Fiery Trial*, 220.

396. Hummel, *Emancipating Slaves*, 355.

397. Faust, *This Republic of Suffering*, 30.

398. Boritt, *Why the Civil War Came*, 20.

399. Potter, *Lincoln and His Party*, 315.

SELECTED BIBLIOGRAPHY

Anderson, Charles. *Fighting by Southern Federals*. New York: Neale Publishing Co., 1912.

Angle, Paul M., and Earl Schenck Miers. *The Tragic Years, 1860–1865*. 2 vols. New York: Simon and Schuster, 1960.

Appleton, Nathan. *Slavery and the Union*. Boston: J.H. Kastburn's Press, 1860.

Ayers, Edward L. *In the Presence of Mine Enemies*. New York: W.W. Norton and Co., 2003.

Bancroft, Frederick. *The Life of William H. Seward*. 2 vols. New York: Harper and Brothers, 1900.

Barringer, William. *A House Dividing: Lincoln as President-Elect*. Springfield, IL: Abraham Lincoln Association, 1945.

Beale, Howard K., and A.W. Brownsword, eds. *Diary of Gideon Wells*. 3 vols. New York: Norton, 1960.

Boney, F.N. *John Letcher of Virginia*. Tuscaloosa: University of Alabama Press, 1966.

Boritt, Gabor S. *Why the Civil War Came*. New York: Oxford University Press, 1996.

Botts, John Minor. *The Great Rebellion: Its Secret History, Rise, Progress, and Disastrous Failure*. New York: Harper and Brothers, 1866.

Burlingame, Michael. *The Inner World of Abraham Lincoln*. Urbana: University of Illinois Press, 1994.

Chittenden, Lucius E. *A Report of the Debates and Proceedings in the Secret Sessions of the Conference Convention for Proposing Amendments to the Constitution of the United States, Held at Washington D.C. in February, A.D. 1861*. Project Guttenberg: Ebook #24561.

Craven, Avery. *The Coming of the Civil War*. Chicago: University of Chicago Press, 1957.

Crawford, Samuel Wylie. *The Genesis of the Civil War*. New York: Charles L. Webster and Co., 1887.

Crofts, Daniel W. "Late Antebellum Virginia Reconsidered." *Virginia Magazine of History and Biography* 107 (Summer 1999).

———. *Old Southampton: Politics and Society in a Virginia County, 1834–1869*. Charlottesville: University of Virginia Press, 1992.

———. *Reluctant Confederates*. Chapel Hill: University of North Carolina Press, 1989.

———. *Secession Crisis Enigma*. Baton Rouge: Louisiana State University Press, 2010.

Current, Richard N. *Lincoln and the First Shot*. Prospect Heights, IL: Waveland Press Inc., 1990.

Davidson, James Dorman, and Bruce S. Greenawalt. "Unionists in Rockbridge County: The Correspondence of James Dorman Davidson Concerning the Virginia Secession Convention of 1861." *Virginia Magazine of History and Biography* 73 (January 1965).

Denton, Lawrence M. *William Henry Seward and the Secession Crisis*. Jefferson, NC: McFarland & Company, 2009.

Dew, Charles B. *Apostles of Disunion*. Charlottesville: University of Virginia Press, 2001.

Deyle, Steven. *Carry Me Back*. Oxford, UK: Oxford University Press, 2005.

Donald, David. *Lincoln*. New York: Simon and Schuster, 1995.

Dumond, Dwight L. *The Secession Movement in the Middle Atlantic States*. New York: Macmillan Co., 1931.

Egnal, Marc. "Rethinking the Secession of the Lower South." *Civil War History* 50, no. 3 (2004).

Eisenhower, John S.D. *Agent of Destiny*. New York: Free Press, 1997.

Emerson, Jason. *The Madness of Mary Lincoln*. Carbondale: Southern Illinois University Press, 2007.

Faust, Drew Gilpin. *Mothers of Invention*. Chapel Hill: University of North Carolina Press, 1996.

———. *This Republic of Suffering*. New York: Alfred A. Knopf, 2008.

Fisher, Lewis F. *No Cause for Offence*. San Antonio, TX: Maverick Publishing Co., 2012.

Fleming, Thomas. *A Disease of the Public Mind*. New York: Da Capo Press, 2013.

Foner, Eric. *The Fiery Trial*. New York: W.W. Norton and Co., 2010.

Ford, Worthington C., ed. *Letters of Henry Adams*. Boston: Houghton Mifflin, 1930–38.

Freehling, William W. *The Reintegration of American History*. New York: Oxford University Press, 1994.

———. *The Road to Disunion*. Vol. II. Oxford, UK: Oxford University Press, 2007.

———. *The South vs. The South: How Anti-Confederate Southerners Shaped the Course of the Civil War*. Oxford, UK: Oxford University Press, 2001.

Freehling, William W., and Craig M. Simpson, eds. *Showdown in Virginia*. Charlottesville: University of Virginia Press, 2010.

Gaines, Francis Pendleton, Jr. "The Virginia Constitutional Convention of 1850–51: A Study in Sectionalism." Doctoral dissertation, University of Virginia, 1950.

Gaines, William H., Jr. *Biographical Register of Members Virginia State Convention of 1861*. Richmond: Virginia State Library, 1969.

Gara, Larry. *The Liberty Line*. Lexington: University Press of Kentucky, 1996.

Goodwin, Doris Kearns. *Team of Rivals*. New York: Simon and Schuster, 2005.

Gunderson, Robert G. "Letters from the Washington Peace Conference of 1861." *Journal of Southern History* 17 (August 1951).

———. *Old Gentlemen's Convention: The Washington Peace Conference of 1861*. Madison: University of Wisconsin Press, 1961.

———. "William C. Rives and the Old Gentleman's Convention." *Journal of Southern History* 22 (November 1956).

Halstead, Murat. *Caucuses of 1860: A History of the National Political Conventions of the Current Presidential Campaign*. Columbus, OH: Follett, Foster and Co., 1860.

Hickin, Patricia E. "Antislavery in Virginia, 1831–1861." Doctoral dissertation, University of Virginia, 1968.

Hildebrand, John R. *The Life and Times of John Brown Baldwin*. Staunton, VA: Lot's Wife Publishing, 2008.

Hitchcock, William S. "The Limits of Southern Unionism: Virginia Conservatives and the Gubernatorial Election of 1859." *Journal of Southern History* 47 (February 1981).

———. "Southern Moderates and Secession: Senator Robert M.T. Hunter's Call for Union." *Journal of American History* 59 (March 1993).

Hochfield, George. *The Great Secession Winter of 1860–61*. New York: Sagamore Press Inc., 1958.

Holland, Kevin. "War Graph, Southern Unionists." *Civil War Today* (December 2009).

Holt, Michael. *Political Crisis of the 1850s*. Charlottesville: University of Virginia Press, 1978.

Hummel, Jeffrey Rogers. *Emancipating Slaves, Enslaving Free Men*. Chicago: Open Court, 1996.

Inscoe, John, and Robert C. Kenzer, eds. *Enemies of the Country*. Athens: University of Georgia Press, 2001.

Johnson, Michael P. *Toward a Patriarchal Republic*. Baton Rouge: Louisiana State University Press, 1977.

Kirwan, Albert D. *John J. Crittenden: The Struggle for the Union*. Lexington: University of Kentucky Press, 1962.

Lankford, Nelson D. *Cry Havoc*. New York: Viking, 2007.

Link, William A. *Roots of Secession*. Chapel Hill: University of North Carolina Press, 2003.

Long, E.B. *The Civil War Day by Day*. New York: Da Capo Press, 1971.

Magruder, Allan B. "A Piece of Secret History: President Lincoln and the Virginia State Convention of 1861." *Atlantic Monthly* 35 (1875).

McClintock, Russell. *Lincoln and the Decision for War*. Chapel Hill: University of North Carolina Press, 2008.

McPherson, James M. *Battle Cry of Freedom*. New York: Oxford University Press, 1988.

Nicolay, John G., and John Hay. *Abraham Lincoln: A History*. New York: Century Co., 1917.

Potter, David M. *The Impending Crisis*. New York: Harper Perennial, 2011.

———. *Lincoln and His Party in the Secession Crisis*. Baton Rouge: Louisiana State University Press, 1995.

Pryor, Elizabeth Brown. "Thou Knowest Not the Time of Thy Visitation." *Virginia Magazine of History and Biography* 119 (2011).

Randall, J.G., and David Donald. *The Civil War and Reconstruction*. Boston: D.C. Heath and Co., 1961.

Reynolds, Donald E. *Editors Make War: Southern Newspapers and the Secession Crisis*. Nashville, TN: Vanderbilt University Press, 1966.

Sandburg, Carl. *Abraham Lincoln: The War Years*. New York: Harcourt, Brace and Co., 1939.

Shade, William G. *Democratizing the Old Dominion: Virginia and the Second Party System, 1824–1861*. Charlottesville: University of Virginia Press, 1996.

Shanks, Henry T. *The Secession Movement in Virginia, 1847–1861*. New York: Da Capo Press, 1970.

Shearer, Davis Bowman. "Conditional Unionism and Slavery in Virginia, 1860–1861." *Virginia Magazine of History and Biography* 96 (January 1988).

Simpson, Craig M. *A Good Southerner: The Life of Henry A. Wise*. Chapel Hill: University of North Carolina Press, 1985.

Soule, Patrick. "A Reappraisal of Seward's Memorandum of April 1, 1861, to Lincoln." *Journal of Southern History* 33 (May 1967).

———. "The Trials of a Virginia Unionist: William Cabell Rives and the Secession Crisis, 1860–1861." *Virginia Magazine of History and Biography* 80 (January 1972).

Stealey, John E., III. *West Virginia's Civil War–Era Constitution*. Kent, OH: Kent State University Press, 2013.

Tarter, Brent. *The Grandees of Government*. Charlottesville: University of Virginia Press, 2013.

Thompson, Robert M. *Confidential Correspondence of Gustavus Vasa Fox, Assistant Secretary of the Navy, 1861–1865*. New York: Devine Press, 1920.

Toomey, Daniel Carroll. *The War Came by Train*. Baltimore, MD: B&O Railroad Museum, 2013.

Van Deusen, Glyndon G. *William Henry Seward*. New York: Oxford University Press, 1967.

Varon, Elizabeth R. *Disunion*. Chapel Hill: University of North Carolina Press, 2008.

War of the Rebellion: Official Records of the Union and Confederate Armies. Washington, D.C.: Government Printing Office, 1881–90.

Wolf, Eva. *Race and Liberty in the New Nation*. Baton Rouge: Louisiana State University Press, 2006.

Wright, William C. *The Secession Movement in the Middle Atlantic States*. Rutherford, NJ: Fairleigh Dickinson University Press, 1973.

Zaborney, John J. *Slaves for Hire*. Baton Rouge: Louisiana State University Press, 2012.

INDEX

ABOUT THE AUTHOR

Larry Denton, an authority on the secession crisis, is a descendant of several Maryland families who predate the Revolutionary War. He holds a master's degree, with honors, from Johns Hopkins University, where he began his career as assistant to the dean. He held several academic administrative posts at the university from 1968 to 1978. In 1978, he accepted an appointment to serve as special assistant to the associate administrator of NOAA, a presidential appointee. He ended his career representing The Weather Channel in Washington, where he played an instrumental role in the production of its highly acclaimed TV series *Forecast Earth*.

The author with his longtime research assistant, Jennifer Potts, a history major graduate of Washington College in Chestertown, Maryland. *Author's collection.*

Denton is the author of *A Southern Star for Maryland: Maryland and the Secession Crisis* and *William Henry Seward and the Secession Crisis: The Effort to Prevent Civil War*. He lectures widely throughout the mid-Atlantic. Now retired, he lives with his wife, Susan, near Oxford on the Eastern Shore of Maryland.